Planting Tomorrow's Churches Today

MARTIN ROBINSON AND
STUART CHRISTINE

Centre for
Faith and Spirituality
Loughborough University

MONARCH
Tunbridge Wells

First published 1992
Reprinted 1992

Unless otherwise indicated, biblical quotations are from the
New International Version © 1973, 1978, 1984 by the
International Bible Society.

Front cover design by Vic Mitchell

ISBN 1 85424 162 1 (Monarch)
0 948704 20 9 (BCGA)

The BCGA acknowledges the
financial assistance received from the
Drummond Trust, 3 Pitt Terrace, Stirling,
in the co-publication of this book.

Printed in Great Britain for
MONARCH PUBLICATIONS
Owl Lodge, Langton Road, Speldhurst, Kent TN3 0NP by
Clays Ltd, St. Ives plc.
Typeset by J&L Composition Ltd, Filey, North Yorkshire

CONTENTS

6 CONTENTS

FOREWORD

'The key to revival is prayer'. However quotable and challenging this statement, in the final analysis it's an over simplification. Biblically it's something rather short of the whole truth. Though the call to prayer runs throughout Scripture, a closer examination reveals a number of other important principles which God's people, in every generation and culture, are called to recognise and consistently apply.

At a local level many churches in Great Britain are slowly coming to grips with the fact that prayer alone is not enough. That God is a strategist is the unmistakable conclusion of any serious reader of the Old or New Testament. This means that, contrary to the belief of some, when a local church carefully plans and develops its strategy, it is reflecting God's character, rather than denying his power. It seems strange then that on a national level this vital local lesson is often forgotten or ignored. All too easily we can find ourselves almost wanting to be seduced by the loud but shallow enthusiasm of those who tell us that revival hides just around the corner and that all we've got to do is sit tight, keep singing and pray a little harder!

God is sovereign and can choose to pour out his Spirit as and when he sees fit. But unless he decides to overide those lessons he is teaching us on a local scale, there is a great deal of hard work and thinking to be done if the church in Great Britain is really to get to grips with culturally relevant evangelism.

We have boldly proclaimed the 90s to be 'The Decade of Evangelism' and committed ourselves to taking the task of re-evangelising the UK seriously. Now it is time to deliver the goods. In attempting to accomplish this goal we face a great challenge. But there is a second, far less obvious, long term problem which the Decade of Evangelism poses for us. We must ask the question: For whose benefit did we invent the name in the first place? It was surely not for all those outside the church whom it is our task to reach. Few non-christians have any desire to be 'evangelised', in this or any other decade! Nor could it have been for those inside the church who are already totally committed to making disciples and recognise that, if we are to be faithful to God, every decade must be a decade of evangelism. The real impact of the title can only be intended for those inside the church for whom evangelism, for one reason or another, has not always been one of the greatest of priorities. And so we face the second challenge: if the church fails to grapple with the issues of how to reach effectively the culture in which it is set now, it runs the risk of leaving very many of its own members thoroughly disillusioned with the whole concept of evangelism.

Planting Tomorrow's Churches Today is a book which deals with the reality of the situation in which the church in Great Britain finds itself. Here you will find no empty triumphalism but only practical, thought-through principles and suggestions for the way forward. Martin Robinson and Stuart Christine show church planting to be a strategic part of the intelligent approach to re-evangelising Great Britain. The message of this book deserves to be taken seriously by all who really mean business over the Decade of Evangelism.

Steve Chalke
The Oasis Trust

INTRODUCTION

Many thousands of churches are planted in countries around the world every year. While this is true of our world as a whole, the experience of the church in Europe is much more one of decline and the closure of churches than of church planting. It is only in relatively recent years that the potential of church planting for assisting the church in its renewal has been glimpsed. This does not mean that church planting should be seen as a simple 'cure all' for the ills of the church. Indeed, church planting has its own set of difficulties which are sufficiently daunting that only those who are clearly called to this particular ministry should consider an active involvement. Nevertheless, church planting offers a potentially exciting arena in which new structures, new strategies and new forms of worship can be given freedom in which to be fully tested.

The challenge for church planters is therefore to give birth to new forms of the church rather than replicate the same structures that have already failed elsewhere. Church planting offers the opportunity to explore what it means for the church to become a genuinely missionary church with new responses to the challenge of a culture which has proved to be highly resistant to the message of the gospel in the twentieth century.

This book seeks to tackle two tasks. The first is to reflect to some degree on what it means to plant churches which will be genuinely missionary congregations. For this reason, Part One of the book seeks to give a theological rationale and an historical context for church planting. This might seem like hard work for those who have a practical inclination and who are more interested in doing the job than in thinking about the task in hand. Nevertheless, it is usually the case that our activity is strongly shaped by our theology even if we are not aware of it. It is therefore the conviction of the authors that a sound theology and an informed understanding of the historical context in which we operate will ultimately strengthen our attempts to plant churches.

The second task is to give as much practical help as possible, both at the planning stage and in the actual process of planting. Parts Two and Three seek to cover the practical issues that church planters will face. While not entirely a step-by-step guide to the practicalities of planting, there is an attempt to present the issues that church planters will face as closely as possible to the sequence in which these issues will arise for most potential planters. The single chapter in Part Four represents a call to recognise the strategic importance of church planting within the mission agendas of not only local but national church bodies. It is perhaps unusual for a single book to seek to weave together the dual concerns of theology and practical advice and yet we are convinced that nothing less than this unusual combination will be sufficient to meet the challenge of church planting in our continent.

Is this therefore a book for European readers only? Certainly it is written from a concern to see the church in Europe advance and the context for most of the practical illustrations is a European one. However, it is no coincidence that both authors have strong personal connections with the worldwide church. Martin Robinson was born in India of missionary parents, lived and ministered in the United States for a year and has travelled widely throughout the world. Stuart Christine came to Christianity while at Oxford University, has spent eleven years as a missionary in Brazil and actively maintains an extensive network of international mission links.

But the wider relevance of the issues addressed in this book is guaranteed by more than personal considerations. It is evident that a great many of the cultural obstacles faced by the church in Europe are also faced by the church in other parts of the world. Those countries outside Europe, but which belong to the English speaking world, are increasingly facing many of the same difficulties as the church in Europe. To a great extent, this is because they are part of a broader Western culture which is now strongly influenced by the secularising tendencies which first sprang from the European enlightenment of the 18th century.

Some countries, such as Australia and New Zealand, have been aware of these problems for some years. Other countries, such as Canada and the United States, have experienced the impact of secularisation on a more regional basis. Thus the eastern seaboard of the United States and the north west of that same country have long been acknowledged as regions where the church has known far greater difficulty than in the Deep South or the Mid-West. However, there is increasing evidence which suggests that in future decades no part of the United States or Canada will be immune from the kind of experiences which have been so familiar throughout Western Europe.

Other parts of the world where the culture of city life is influencing the response of city dwellers to the Christian gospel may also discover in future years that the experience of the European church will come to have an unexpected relevance for the future of the church in their lands too. Our success in planting culturally appropriate missionary congregations in Europe may well hold crucial lessons not only for the future of European Christianity but also for the activity of the emerging church around the world. This book is offered as a contribution towards achieving that success.

Part One
Laying the Foundation

CHAPTER ONE

CHURCH PLANTING AND THE KINGDOM OF GOD

Martin Robinson

Two convictions underlie the writing of this book. First, that there is today a significant world-wide growth of something that we can call a church planting movement. Second, that this is something that we can learn from and encourage. But not everyone agrees with such a perspective! Not all Christians are convinced that church planting is at all a good thing. Instead, they urge us to be more concerned with the unity of the people of God or with matters of social action by which the church that already exists can act to change the world in which we live.

Those who are convinced of the need to plant churches can and do argue that we are not faced here with an either-or situation. It is possible to plant churches and to be concerned with these other agendas. We might also want to present a whole variety of pragmatic explanations as to why church planting is a desirable activity. But we need to do more than this. We need to be sure that the activity of church planting lies not just on the practical agenda of activists but that it also belongs to the purpose and call of God for his church.

It has been said that the early Christians were expecting the kingdom but that what came was the church. This rather wry comment contains within it a great many of the questions that face anyone looking at the New Testament record for an explanation of why we might want to plant churches. We must admit that there is precious little record of any words of Jesus about church planting. Indeed, there is very little in the teaching of Jesus about the institution of the church at all! We do not see a Galilean master plan which lays out a strategy for a world-wide church planting movement.

What the New Testament does reveal is that the self-understanding of the followers of Jesus was something that developed as a direct result of their attempts to engage in mission. The more they discovered about their self-identity as the church, the more they learned about the mission in which they were engaged. Involvement in mission and self-understanding as the church were inseparably entwined in a pilgrimage of discovery.

The mission develops

During his earthly ministry, Jesus sent the disciples out on at least two missions (Lk 9:1–6; Lk 10:1–20). Their mandate was not to plant churches but to preach the gospel. Following the resurrection encounters, they were left with a commission which was clearly understandable in the context of those earlier missions: to go and preach the gospel to all nations (Mt 28:16–20). The disciples did not have to move very far away to fulfil such a mandate. The events of Pentecost allowed Peter to present the content of that early preaching to those from a multitude of nations (Acts 2:1–12).

Up to this point, the context for everything that they had done had been a thoroughly Jewish one. Those who were present from so many nations were all Jews. The only Scriptures that the disciples possessed were those of the Jewish people. Their Messiah was a Jewish figure who was only fully understandable in the context of a Jewish tradition. Jesus had ministered primarily to Jewish people, largely within the confines of the Jewish territories. While there had been some encounters with Samaritans, this hardly compromised the main focus of his ministry as one directed towards the Jewish people. Even the encounter with the Roman centurion (Lk 7:1–10) was clearly a meeting with someone who stood in the circle of the 'godfearers' (Acts 10:1,2), and as such was probably regarded by the Jewish people as at least sympathetic to Judaism. The worship of Jesus and his followers took place in the Temple and was therefore worship in which only Jews could participate.

None of this activity, however much attention it might have

attracted, looked like the founding of a new institution. It looked more like the start of another Jewish sect, of which there were already many, or possibly more like a Jewish reform movement. Even the persecution that took place in Jerusalem did not alter the fundamentally Jewish character of all that was happening. Indeed, it could be argued that the dispersal of the 'followers of the Way' only served to emphasise that this was an internal Jewish dispute. It was, after all, fellow Jews who were engaged in the process of persecution. When Saul was sent as far afield as Damascus to persecute the church, he was going not to close down any churches because church planting in that sense had not yet begun. His intention was to visit the synagogues of Damascus to root out 'followers of the Way' among the Jewish community (Acts 9:1,2).

The taking of the gospel to Samaria and Judea was also a mission to the Jews. Certainly, some Samaritans were converted, but there had never been an objection to Samaritans becoming Jews and there is every reason to believe that in becoming 'followers of the Way', the Samaritan believers were actually becoming Jews. Certainly, they could no longer accept only the books of Moses as the canon of Scripture if they were to become Christians (Acts 8:4–25). It is very clear that the Christian community appealed to the whole of the Old Testament as Holy Scripture, just as Jesus had done.

Even the spread of the gospel to the Jewish community scattered throughout the Roman Empire, and the accompanying inclusion of the 'godfearers' (Acts 14:1), did not take the mission of the church outside of a Jewish context. There is considerable evidence to suggest that the 'godfearers' played a significant part in the Jewish community. In some cases, the degree of their involvement was such that they were practicably indistinguishable from the fully Jewish participants in the synagogue.[1]

The New Testament record shows that the 'followers of the Way' were often excluded from the established synagogues in the towns where they had taken the word (Acts 19:8–10). However, we should not conclude that such exclusion then resulted in the founding of a local church radically different in character from the synagogue in which they had been worshipping. It is much more likely that what they established was in fact a messianic synagogue, much closer to the synagogues of those who call themselves Messianic Jews today than to the kind of Gentile churches that were established later. At this stage, the most that we could say about the early Christians is that they were synagogue planters, not by choice, not because of any strategy but only because of exclusion from the existing synagogue!

However, this picture of a reforming messianic but thoroughly Jewish movement was to change radically as the early communities of believers came face to face with the issue of how they should respond to the question of Gentiles who wished to become believers. The issue was dramatically illustrated in the most startling vision that has ever impacted the development of the mission of the church. Peter's mission to Cornelius (Acts 10:1–48), together with its accompanying visions and later consequences, signalled a change that was to forever alter the racial and cultural composition of the early church. Just as importantly, it was also to assist a process which had the end result of entirely refocusing the whole self-understanding of the church and its mission.

It is hardly surprising that Peter felt the need to report his encounter with Cornelius to the leaders in Jerusalem! At this early stage, they were content to simply listen to Peter's report and to observe, 'So then, God has granted even the Gentiles repentance unto life' (Acts 11:18). The significance of this event was not fully appreciated by the church at that time. However, this was not to be an isolated phenomena. In parallel with these events, the Scriptures report that while some who had been scattered by the persecution, 'travelled as far as Phoenicia, Cyprus and Antioch, telling the message only to Jews', some 'went to Antioch and began to speak to Greeks also, telling them the good news about the Lord Jesus' (Acts 11:19–21). The establishing of a significant community of believers in Antioch, consisting as it did of both Jews and Gentiles, was to be significant for the future of the church throughout the world. It was in this context that the significance of Peter's vision was to be fully explored.

The church at Antioch made two huge contributions to the developing self-understanding of the church. First of all, as the sending congregation for Paul and Barnabas, whose mission was clearly to both preach and establish new Christian communities, Antioch was to act as a model for the communities established through these missionary journeys. Therefore it was part of the expectation of Paul and Barnabas that these new communities would contain both Jews and Gentiles. This did not mean that they were establishing completely Gentile churches: such a development came later. Their early pattern was always to go first to the synagogue in each town to speak to both Jews and 'godfearers'.

Second, the church at Antioch forced the issue of whether or not Gentiles needed to become ritually Jews in order to be Christians. It was the challenge of brothers who came from Judea to Antioch and who claimed, 'Unless you are circumcised, according to the custom taught by Moses, you cannot be saved' (Acts 15:1,2), that caused the leadership at Antioch to seek a ruling from the Council at Jerusalem. One can quickly see why. The Judean brethren were calling into question the whole validity of the Antiochene experiment in mission and consequently the validity of all the mission churches that had been established through their vision.

It is possible that when the Council at Jerusalem considered this matter (Acts 15:4–35), many of their members envisaged that the number of Gentile believers would be rather small compared to the thousands of Jewish believers who formed the overwhelming majority of the Christian community. It is also possible that some Council members expected that the imminent return of Jesus would in any case settle the matter before any difficulties became too serious to handle.

The later letters of Paul tell us that the issue was not finally settled by the letter of the Council of Jerusalem,[2] but nevertheless the decision of the Council was decisive in terms of the future development of the church. Not only were the new churches that had been planted from Antioch now regarded as legitimate but, even more importantly, the Council's decision effectively shaped the future self-understanding of the church and its mission, and as a consequence allowed the notion of church planting to be given full and free rein.

The impact of the Council's decision can be clearly seen in three areas, all of which are critical for a proper understanding of church planting.

The church and the unchurched—who is included?

A primary question for anyone who is engaged in church planting is simply, 'Who are we seeking to reach?' or, to put it another way, 'Who is included in the scope of this message?' The Council of Jerusalem was implicitly claiming that the church was correct in trying to reach all who would respond. Potentially, at least, everyone is included! From our perspective such a conclusion is obvious. From the perspective of those who took part in the Council of Jerusalem it was far from obvious.

As we have seen, in the first few months of its life, it was quite possible for the community of disciples to look at the teachings of Jesus, including the Great Commission (Mt 28: 16–20), and still to see only the people of Israel. There were Jews among all of the known people of the world, and the international character of the scattered Jewish community was well known to those who lived in Jerusalem and who regularly witnessed the arrival of such people for the great Temple festivals.

The impact of these Jewish communities in the wider Roman Empire was considerable. Virtually alone among the myriads of religious and national groups in the Empire, the Jews had won for themselves exemptions and privileges which allowed them to retain their identity within a society which shared little of their values. In addition to this status, and perhaps partly because of it, Jewish communities were to be found in virtually every part of the Empire. Some scholars have suggested that the numerical strength of these communities was very significant, especially when the attached 'godfearers' are included.[3] There did not really seem to be any need to move outside of these communities in order to fulfil the Great Commission.

The decision of the Council of Jerusalem to allow Gentile believers to be part of the emerging church not only solved a practical problem in resolving the attitude of the church to those who were in some sense already related to the wider Christian community; it also contained a profound implication for those who, like Paul and Barnabas, were seeing the conversion of Gentiles, not just as a by-product of their witness to Jews, but because they had consciously seen Gentiles as the legitimate objects of the Great Commission. Their intention became not just to add a few Gentiles to existing Messianic Jewish communities but to establish churches which might be composed entirely of Gentile believers. This departure in his mission practice caused Paul to wrestle with some very fundamental questions concerning his understanding of the mission of the church.

In his letters, we see Paul grappling with the questions 'Who is Israel?' and 'What is the intention of God for Israel?' The early church had already concluded that the message of Jesus was a fulfilment and not a replacement of the message of the Old Testament. The church was indeed the new Israel but this did not imply any discontinuity with the old Israel. To put it rather crudely, the church was the same as the old Israel except it was reformed and fulfilled. Only in that sense was it the New Israel.

However, it was one thing to emphasise such continuity when all of the members of the new body were practising Jews, fulfilling all of the ritual requirements of the Old Testament. It was quite another thing when the majority of the members of the new body were not genetically Jewish and in any case did not practise any of these requirements. Under such circumstances, what could it possibly mean to describe the church as in any sense the new Israel? Paul's solution was to see the church as the spiritual inheritor of all that God had intended for the old Israel. His Gentile converts were, therefore, just as much children of Abraham as any full-blooded Jew because of their spiritual grafting through Christ. This solution made it possible for Paul and his companions to think in terms of an entirely Gentile people of Israel. What an astounding notion!

If the former people of Israel could be replaced in this way by a new Gentile people of Israel, what then was God's intention for the Jews? Paul's majestic theme, worked out in the Book of Romans, of the place of the old Israel in the plan of God for the whole of human history has never been surpassed. The scale is breathtaking. God, having used Israel as the means by which the Gentiles can hear the gospel, is going to use the Gentiles as a means of bringing the rebellious people of Israel to a realisation of his purpose for them.

Romans is, therefore, not just a treatise on justification by faith, it is first and foremost an explanation of Paul's ministry in establishing churches among the Gentiles. For Paul, his work among the Gentiles is much more than just the exploration of a new and potentially vast mission field, it is the means by which the very purpose of God can be worked out for the people of Israel themselves. In this way, the taking of the gospel to the Gentiles is not simply a passionate response to the desire to see some brought to a saving knowledge of God before the end times, it is also a very part of the process by which the end times will be fulfilled. The bringing in of the Gentiles forms a crucial part of the whole action of God in sending Jesus the Messiah. The establishing of churches among the Gentiles is, therefore, an inseparable part of the plan and purpose of God for his world. Church planting is not an optional extra for Christians, it is an intrinsic expression of the redemptive action of God in his world.

The church and the kingdom—the content of the message

Jesus came to announce the coming of the kingdom and to call for faith and repentance in relation to that kingdom. This was a message that was certainly understandable to those who were part of the old Israel. A concern for the coming kingdom was something that was part of the political and religious agenda of many groups which were active at the same time as Jesus. The call to repentance struck a deep chord in a people who were occupied by a foreign power, and felt that all of their national and religious life was under pressure.

But if the majority of those to whom the message of the kingdom was now to be preached were not Jews but Gentiles, what impact might that change of audience have on the message itself? Stripped from the national and religious context of Israel, what meaning would any preaching on the kingdom now have? To borrow a phrase from Gerald Coates, 'What on earth is this kingdom?',[4] and more particularly, how does it relate to the church that was coming into being among the Gentile believers?

It would have been possible for the concept of an imminent coming kingdom to have been preached purely in terms of the need for individuals to respond. For those who were Jews and who were already worshipping God, the call to repentance might have been interpreted simply in terms of the need to recognise Jesus as the agent and sign of a kingdom which was even then beginning to crash in upon the divided and confused world of Judaism.

The vision of Paul to include the conversion of the Gentiles in the plan and purpose of God meant that the preaching of the kingdom assumed dimensions far beyond those of simply a personal response. The scope of Paul's theme extends to a vision of the action of God which has consequences far more cosmic both in space and time than simply the response of a single generation of Jewish believers (Eph 3:1–10).

For Paul, the scope of salvation that was covered by the action of God in sending Christ can be understood only by reference not just to the history of Israel but to the whole history of man. Christ is not just the Messiah referred to in Old Testament prophecy, he is also the Second Adam. His action in dying on the cross is salvific, not just in relation to the sins of the nation of Israel, but for the whole of human sin. Christ is not just the Saviour of Israel but the Saviour of mankind.

Nor does the implication of the action of Christ end with its impact on mankind alone, it also has implications for the whole of creation. The creation itself is being cast anew as the new creation struggling to be free from the consequences of sin (Col 1:15–23). Thus the extension of the mission of the church to the Gentile world produced a degree of reflection on the significance of the gospel which would have been virtually imposssble if the mission of the Christian community had remained an entirely Jewish concern. The planting of churches among the

Gentiles, or the question of who should be included in the church's extension, therefore allowed the larger implications of the gospel to be more fully understood.

However, if the enlarging of the concept of the church to potentially include all who might respond was helpful in understanding the implications of the gospel message and the kingdom, that same enlargement also produced a real tension with regard to the church itself. Where did the church fit in relation to this message of the kingdom? Was the church only the unfortunate by-product of the extension of the gospel, a kind of evangelistic agency whose sole purpose was to be a vehicle for the proclamation of the gospel? Or was the church to be something more? Was it to be the place where this coming kingdom was going to be lived out and demonstrated? In this sense, was the church not so much the vehicle of the message as part of the message itself? Or even more strongly, was the church to be the means by which the kingdom was established, changing society until it eventually conforms to the image of the kingdom.

If we are to be in the business of planting churches we need some answers to these questions. Are we to plant churches only as bearers of the message, are the churches that we plant part of the message, or are we to plant churches because the church itself is the sum total of the message?

There can be little doubt that the preaching of Jesus encouraged his followers to believe that the end times were to arrive very soon indeed. Under such circumstances, the church was seen very much as a temporary community. Such a radical perspective tended to emphasise the church as a vehicle for proclamation, with very little attention given to the notion that the church also provided some foretaste of the heavenly kingdom.

However, the failure of the end time to arrive began to increase the relative importance of the church as part of the content of the message itself. The dominance of the church in that part of Europe which became known as 'Christendom' increased that tendency until there was a very strong sense in which the teaching of Jesus was presented as announcing the church more than as announcing the kingdom. Increasingly, the end times were seen as lying very much in the future and therefore the kingdom of God was a goal to be achieved through the work of man.[5] In such a static system, church planting was not really an issue. Certainly, new churches were built but these were not in any sense missionary churches, rather they were the provision of worship centres for those who already believed. The concept of church extension would better describe any new church building than that of church planting.

The closed system represented by the notion of Christendom was to collapse under the dual hammer blows of the post-Reformation religious wars in Europe and the coming of the Age of the Enlightenment. It is no coincidence that the collapse of the idea of Christendom took place at a time when there was an increased awareness of the world outside of Europe. It is also no coincidence that the later advent of the great evangelical awakenings of the late eighteenth and early nineteenth centuries and the related missionary movement was paralleled with a revolution in thinking concerning the relationship between the church and the kingdom.

At a popular level, the early nineteenth century saw the development of a number of movements, each of which raised expectations of the imminent return of the Lord. Theological developments were revolutionised through the work of Johannes Weiss who presented a picture of the kingdom of God as something which would only happen through the action of God without the help of man. For Weiss, Jesus and John the Baptist only announced the kingdom, they did not do anything to bring it into being. According to Weiss, the kingdom remains entirely in the future and nothing man can do will bring it into being.

This radical view of the kingdom as being entirely a future reality reduces the role of the church to merely that of announcing the coming kingdom. But, somewhat ironically, the more radical the announcement of the kingdom as something distinct from the church, the more that churches tend to be planted! Would it be entirely unfair to observe that aggressive church planting follows in the wake of a radical preaching of the kingdom, whereas those who emphasise the importance of the role of the church in relation to the kingdom are strangely slow off the mark in the field of church planting?[6]

Given some of the unhappy lessons of church history in the relationship between church and kingdom, is it possible to have a view of both church and kingdom that stimulates an approach to church planting that is vigorous but nonsectarian? I want to suggest five statements about which most of us can agree and which would allow us to construct a sound foundation for our church planting efforts.

1. The kingdom of which Jesus spoke has a future and cosmic dimension which has not yet been fulfilled.
2. Not all of the kingdom lies in the future but some of its content needs to be lived out by those members of the church who are aware of its present reality.
3. There is a relationship between the church and the kingdom even though they are not identical.
4. The church is called to announce the kingdom of God as well as to attempt to live in the light of its coming.
5. The judgement of the coming kingdom needs in some way to influence the way in which we live now in relation to our world.

We therefore cannot think about the kingdom without also thinking about the church and what it might look like. Preaching about the kingdom of God, whether we are announcing the future coming of the kingdom or whether we are seeking in some way to extend the kingdom, cannot be done without also seeing the future life of the church as in some way bound up with that preaching. Thus we need to be aware that our preaching about the kingdom is likely to cause the church to come into being. Where the kingdom is, there will be the church also, even if we cannot always say that the opposite is true.

So, the taking of the gospel to the Gentiles, the preaching of the kingdom to those peoples who have no previous knowledge of the dealings of God with Israel, inevitably leads to the creation of the church among those people. But the planting of churches outside of any attempt to make those who respond become Jews, leads to the question, 'What should such churches look like?'

The church and culture—what forms can the church take?

As the Gentile church began to emerge from its initial birth-place in the Jewish community it became clear that although there was a cultural discontinuity, there was not a complete break with the Jewish milieu of the original gospel proclamation. Most importantly of all, the emerging church claimed as its own the Jewish Scriptures. A sense of ownership with regard to the Old Testament produced a continuity with that most essential of all the distinguishing features of Israelite religion, the link between religious devotion and ethical commitment (Acts 15:24–29).

However, such an ownership was by no means an easy one even though the Gentile church was freed from any observance of the old law by the new law of grace. Tensions, illustrated in their most extreme form by the attempt of Marcion and his followers to present the God of the Old Testament as different from the God of the New Testament, continued long after the Gentile Church developed its own distinct life and witness.

The successful marriage of Greek and Roman culture to the gospel message was a critical factor in the development of the church from its position as a persecuted sect to that of the established religion of the Roman Empire. However, the degree of that success carried with it its own problems for the mission of the church. The very success of the marriage of gospel and culture meant that it was not always easy for the church to see where the gospel ended and cultural expression began. Early warnings of these difficulties could be seen in the dealings of the church with the culturally distinct manifestations of the faith in the Celtic West and Nestorian East.

More serious problems have developed as a consequence of the astonishing success of the modern missionary movement. In the last 200 years, Christianity has changed from being an almost entirely European and North American faith to a situation where for the first time in its history, it could lay serious claim to being a world faith. The cultural problems that this has brought for the church have been enormous.

Imagine the situation of the African clergyman in training for the Anglican ministry. He must learn English in order to learn New Testament Greek! In the process he is passing through a number of cultural filters. He is seeking to understand the Bible sufficiently well to be able to contextualise its message for his flock. However, first he has to understand the culture of the Bible. Astonishingly, he has to do this through the cultural filter of European Christianity, only to find that the world of the Bible is considerably closer to his own culture than that of the culture that first brought him the faith and through whose filter he first understood all that he learned.

In describing the position of the Catholic Church in Africa, the noted historian Adrian Hastings comments on the stricture of celibacy in relation to the priesthood. He makes the claim that celibacy is so alien to African culture that '... it is common knowledge in some dioceses that hardly a priest is without children of his own.'[7] All too often, the Western Church has been so bound by its own culture that it has not been able to make the same imaginative missiological leap that was made by the Council of Jerusalem and which first set the Gentile Church free from Jewish cultural norms in order to better explore the gospel.

In recognition of the problems of gospel and culture, mission publications are filled with words and phrases like, cultural adaptation, indigenisation, and contextualisation. Pages are filled with debates on what precisely the gospel is, what represents legitimate development and what becomes syncretism.

When thinking of the task of church planting, we need to be aware of the work of two men in particular who have addressed the issues of culture and the gospel. Both have been Western missionaries in India and both have been aware, sometimes critically so, of the work of the other. The first of these men is Dr Donald McGavran, founder of the church growth school at Fuller.[8]

McGavran's concern arose out of what he saw as the evident failure of Western mission in India. In his view, the primary problem was that of the 'Western clothes' in which the gospel was presented. He maintained that it was critical that people should not be asked to cross cultural barriers in order to become Christians. He laid great emphasis on the fact that the Great Commission was directed to all *ethne* or ethnic peoples rather than to 'all the nations' as most translations rendered it. He pleaded for missions to see people in terms of people groups rather than culturally diverse 'nations' which were often the product of Western imperialism. He observed that it was much easier for people to be reached by others of their own culture, especially when the cultural clothes in which the gospel was being presented were appropriate to both the evangelist and those being evangelised.

The second of these Indian missionaries is Lesslie Newbigin.[9] Although critical of some aspects of McGavran's work, he shared a concern for the recognition of culture as having the potential to both clarify and obscure the gospel. In his work on the BCC programme, 'The Gospel and our Culture', Newbigin has pointed out that Western Christianity has so absorbed the secularism produced by the Western Enlightenment that the gospel message has become obscured. Indeed, Newbigin's most biting criticism of the Western Church is that Western missionaries have often represented the greatest secularising force in the developing world. In attempting to bring the gospel, what many missionaries have actually brought is not the Christianity of the Bible but modern Western secularism.

The critiques of both these men, and indeed of many others, have shown that a distinction does need to be made between the Western adaptation of Christianity and the heart of the gospel message itself. What is not always so clear is how such a distinction is to be made. Newbigin points to the Bible as being a reference point by which our own culture, and indeed other cultures around the world, might be judged. This approach is not without its difficulties, not least because there are many cultures represented within the pages of the Bible. However, this is not the place to conduct that debate so much as to recognise the resource of the Bible as a means of helping us to resolve some of the tensions implicit within the relationship between gospel and culture.

As part of this debate, Newbigin asks the highly provocative question, 'Can the West be converted?'[10] In doing so he points out that the West can no longer think in terms of mission as something which is directed solely towards the countries of the Third World. The West is now a mission field and this is all the more serious because none of the models that we have used in taking the gospel to other lands is likely to be helpful in this enterprise. He calls such a mission, mission to the First World. This mission field is broader than Western Europe, or even Europe and the various English-speaking countries around the world. It is all those places, usually cities, where First World culture predominates. The hallmark of this culture is the predominance of a secular worldview. Admittedly, even in Europe this secular worldview is never found in a pure or pristine form. Nowhere is man entirely secular. Usually a secular worldview overlays an older pattern. It fights for pre-eminence with a deeper-rooted existential religious impulse. Such an impulse will vary depending on where in the world one looks but it is almost always a form of paganism, sometimes disguised as folk religion.

What tools are available to us in such a mission? Newbigin is concerned to create a debate that seeks to engage the 'higher ground' in intellectual encounter. But that debate is only one level in his missionary concern. Perhaps unexpectedly, Newbigin looks with hope to the local church as the place where ultimately the challenge of mission to the First World will be worked out.[11] Having expressed this hope, Newbigin is rather short on any explanation as to how this might happen.

A new kind of church

When speaking of new church planting, I have sometimes heard people object to the use of the word 'new'. 'If you plant a church, isn't it by definition "new"?' some say. I am not so sure. I have seen far too many churches planted which are not new at all! All too often what is planted is actually a replication of older failed structures and represents what we might call 'old church planting'.

Newbigin and others are clearly calling for the creation of a new kind of church, aware of its missionary call and increasingly equipped to respond to the challenge of a new kind of mission. Exciting as this challenge might be, is it not almost too much to expect a large percentage of the existing congregations in the West to become such missionary congregations? It is too early to say. However, what we can say is that when we are speaking of church planting it is the planting of such congregations that we are seeking to encourage. It is vital in grasping our concern for church planting that the call to create such missionary congregations is clearly understood.

It would seem to us to be largely pointless to plant yet more churches of the type that have already failed if we are to come to grips with the missionary context in which we are working. Such activity would not be church planting but the duplication of failed structures. In talking of planting, not just of churches but of missionary congregations, we do not rule out the possibility that many of these congregations will not be completely new, but rather the transformation of existing churches so that they become missionary congregations. However, we also recognise that in most cases it is easier to plant missionary congregations when starting with a completely new situation.

How is it that we have arrived at a situation which is so serious that even though we already have some 45,000 congregations in Britain, we have to think in terms of planting yet more congregations in order to produce missionary congregations? A report of the Missions Board of the Diocese of Southwark illustrates very well the extent of the problem facing the church in Britain. In a profound analysis it points out that all of the structures of the church in Britain are essentially pastoral, or what the report calls 'come' structures. Such structures reflect a situation in which it was assumed that everyone was at least nominally Christian. In such a context, evangelism was always thought of as an exercise in calling people back to Christ.

In the situation of the church today, it is no longer possible for us to think in terms of bringing people back to Christ or even back to the church. They have never yet been in order to have left. We are not called to be ever more effective pastors but to be missionaries. It is pointless trying to encourage yet more effective 'come' structures when what is called for is to develop 'go' structures in which the church learns afresh how to be missionaries in our own land. The planting of new missionary congregations represents a vital ingredient in developing these new 'go' structures.

What would a 'go' structure look like as compared with a 'come' structure? One way of illustrating such a difference is in relation to ministry structures. When looking at the New Testament model for ministry we read in Ephesians of the five-fold division into apostles, prophets, evangelists, teachers and pastors (Eph 4:11,12). Situations where people are all at least nominally Christian operate what we might describe as 'come' structures and so draw heavily on the ministries of teachers and pastors.

To a large extent the pastor/teacher model has predominated in the ministry of the Western Church for hundreds of years. This reality is reinforced by means of a self-perpetuating cycle. Thus, the model that is used for the selection of potential candidates is one which is looking for pastor/teacher qualities. Once in college, training is geared towards producing pastor/teacher ministers. The result is that pastor/teachers, both by gifting and training, are what tend to emerge from our colleges. Because so many pastor/teachers emerge from our colleges and then take up positions of leadership in our churches, the model is reinforced when the issue of selection is again raised.

The fundamental point of 'come' structures is that they do not know how to cope with apostles, prophets and evangelists (although those evangelists with significant pastoral and teaching gifts will probably survive). What happens to those who have the gifts of apostleship, prophecy and evangelism and want to use them in the service of the Lord? All too often their avenues for service have been rather limited. Frequently, such people have either become overseas missionaries, or they have had significant involvement in parachurch structures, or they have begun new denominations!

In creating 'go' structures, it is vital that those with apostolic, prophetic and evangelistic gifts be drawn into the local missionary congregation. Church planting of the type that we are describing is the ideal way of drawing in such gifts so that 'go' structures are created. If the West is ever to have significant numbers of local missionary churches, then church planting needs to take place on a scale that most mainline denominations have not yet considered possible. It is our hope that this book will be one small contribution in such a process.

For discussion and further study

1. What aspects of the life of your church are central to the gospel message itself?
2. Are there any aspects of the worship of your church which seem strange to those who visit the church for the first time?
3. Use a concordance to list the references in the New Testament to apostles. What are the distinguishing marks of these apostles?
4. How would you describe the operation of the ministry of an apostle today?

Notes

1. The question of the exact role of those Gentiles who were part of the broader Jewish community and who are referred to in Scripture as the 'Godfearers' has provided the basis for a lively debate in recent years. There is a useful summary of this debate written by J. Andrew Overman, 'The God-Fearers: Some Neglected Features', *Journal for the Study of the New Testament*, 32 (1988): pp 17–26.
2. The continuing conflict with the circumcision party is well illustrated in Paul's letter to the Galatians. See especially Galatians 5:7–12.
3. For an extended discussion on the numerical significance of the Jewish community including the 'Godfearers', see Adolf

Harnack, *The Expansion of Christianity in the First Three Centuries*, (translated and edited by J. Moffatt), 1904, Vol One, pp 1–18. Harnack makes the calculation that at least 7 per cent of the Empire were either Jews or 'Godfearers' and that in some of the more important provinces the percentage was much higher than this.

4. Gerald Coates *What On Earth Is This Kingdom?* (Kingsway, 1983).

5. Wolfhart Pannenberg has a useful summary of the historical debate between various views of the relationship between the kingdom and the church in *Theology and the Kingdom of God* (Westminster Press), pp 51f.

6. Pentecostals have been among the most active of church planters during the twentieth century and yet have often claimed that they are not a church at all but a revival movement! Typical of such statements is the statement by George Canty, a leader in the Elim Pentecostal Church, in which he asserts that Pentecostalism is a revival not a church and that there will be no role for the church until the Lord returns. See 'And Now Shall We Go Back to the Church of England?', *The Ministry*, (October/December 1964).

7. Adrian Hastings, *African Catholicism* (SCM, 1989), p. 13.

8. The seminal work of Donald McGavran is *Understanding Church Growth*, which was republished in a revised edition in 1980 by Eerdmans.

9. Lesslie Newbigin has written an extensive critique of the influence of the Enlightenment on Western civilisation and the relationship of the church to the presuppositions of the Enlightenment. His three publications on this topic are: *The Other Side of 1984* (WCC Risk Book Series, 1983); *Foolishness to the Greeks* (SPCK, 1986); *The Gospel in a Pluralist Society* (SPCK, 1989).

10. The question 'Can the West be converted' is asked in an article by Lesslie Newbigin 'Can the West be Converted?', *International Bulletin of Missionary Research*, XI no 1 (January 1987).

11. Lesslie Newbigin, *The Gospel in a Pluralist Society*, Chapter 18, 'The Congregation as Hermeneutic of the Gospel'.

CHAPTER TWO

WHY CHURCH PLANTING?

Stuart Christine

It's good!

For a Christian, something is good if God's stamp is on it. Church planting is good for precisely that reason; God owns it! It has God's stamp of approval on it, it's his way.

In the Christian liturgy of worship known as the General Thanksgiving, or Sursum Corda, there is a phrase that though archaic in language still conveys an important truth that helpfully illustrates what we mean by this assertion of the goodness of church planting. The worshipper is called upon to give thanks unto the Lord, and responds: 'It is meet and right so to do.'

This statement is affirmed by the worship leader with the following words of explanation: 'It is very meet and right, and our bounden duty, that we should at all times and in all places give thanks unto Thee O Lord. . . .' There then follows a recital of some of the characteristics of God and his works appropriate to the particular season of the year, that make thanksgiving appropriate.

The message is that the very character of God is what makes it 'meet and right' to give thanks to him. This very same assertion can be made with regard to the activity of new church planting: it is an entirely proper and indeed necessary response of the church to the character, works and purposes of God revealed in Jesus Christ and projected into the experience of God's people by the Holy Spirit.

The account of God's missionary commitment in history clearly declares his intention of establishing the authentic divine-human relationship as the universal experience of existence. Always personal in his focus, but developing from the individual

35

to the family, the nation and finally to that international network of fellowships known as the church, our God continues to strive, along with his fellowship people towards the fulfilment of that goal.

The missionary Paul of Tarsus clearly set out the divine objective as 'to bring all things in heaven and on earth together under one head, even Christ' (Eph 1:10). Paul recognised that to be engaged in the extension of that network of worshipping and witnessing communities was to become fully identified with this gloriously gracious and all-determining objective of God.

All four Gospels declare in their own way the dramatic requirement that humankind should accept the lordship of Jesus and in accepting it respond to it by identifying whole-heartedly with this mission of God revealed in the life and Person of Jesus. To quote just John and Matthew: 'As the Father has sent me, I am sending you ...' (Jn 20:21). 'All authority in heaven and on earth has been given to me. Therefore go and make disciples of all nations, baptising them in the name of the Father and of the Son and of the Holy Spirit. ... And surely I will be with you always ...' (Mt 28:20).

Upon the rock of the faith and discipleship that brings life with God, Jesus has promised that he will build his church (Mt 16:16), and through the presence of his Holy Spirit within his church the message and reality of the kingdom will be projected throughout the nations (Mk 13:10,11).

The proper measure of the expectations and goals of the gathered community of disciples is nothing less than the life and activity of the Spirit of God seen in the life of Jesus the Son of God.

Upon them Jesus breathes the selfsame Spirit whose coming the writer of the Gospel records as being the sign which set Jesus aside at his baptism as the agent of the kingdom of God.

It is the Spirit that drove Jesus out into the wilderness to confront the devil and who subsequently fuelled the impetus of his mission as he first demonstrated the powerful arrival of the kingdom in his presence at Capernaum. It is the Spirit that promptly pressed him onwards against the entreaties of his disciples that they should remain there to bask in glories of that 'kingdom sunrise' so as to meet the needs of the other towns and villages in the region.

This same Spirit transforms the gathered believers themselves into the agents of the kingdom. Luke records some of the events resulting from that transformation. The Spirit inspires evangelistic proclamation at Pentecost, gives boldness to witness in the face of persecution, challenges the traditional mindset of Peter so as to use him to establish the group of believers in the household of Cornelius, and mobilises the church at Antioch to commission key leaders to extend the kingdom network. This is the Spirit of Jesus at work in his body, the church. The Spirit is in the driving seat, motivating, directing and resourcing the expansion of the church, through the multiplication of churches.

It should not be surprising, then, that a renewed vision for new church planting has arisen in the wake of the renewed experience of the Holy Spirit's presence and power that has characterised so much of the UK church scene during recent years. It would rather be a matter for the gravest concern if it were not so.

Our God is on the move, today as ever establishing the divine-human relationship in the expanding network of worshipping and witnessing communities. Churches are the footprints of his progress across the landscape of humanity and history as he moves towards his goal of universal dominion. They are both signs of the kingdom's coming and the means whereby that coming touches the lives of those as yet outside the kingdom.

In the full sense of the word it would be true to say that church planting is an essential expression of the divine-human relationship established through Jesus. It is an activity which grows out of the very nature and essence of God himself. At the close of their excellent book *Creating Communities of the Kingdom*,[1] Stutzman and Schenk express this same conviction:

Surely there is no vocation, no vision, no commitment more precious to God. Surely there is nothing more significant to humanity than the multiplication of redeemed communities of people who love the

Lord with all their mind, heart, and strength, and who also love their neighbours.

It is very meet, right and our bounden duty, that we should at all times and in all places ... plant new churches. It's a *God* thing to be doing; it's a *good* thing to be doing.

It's needed

At a recent series of breakfast meetings for leaders of Baptist churches in London a survey form was distributed. Question 8 read as follows: 'Can you identify an area around you that could benefit from the establishing of a new church—Baptist or ecumenical?'

From the 700 or so responses to that question, filled in on the spot, over 100 different locations were suggested as in need of a church presence. This result was impressive not because it was the consequence of meticulous research conducted by skilled observers but rather for the very opposite reason: that it was produced by ordinary Christian folk who knew and cared about their 'patch'. They didn't need a degree in missiology to cast their mind's eye around their neighbourhood and know that in such and such an estate there was no group of Christians regularly meeting and living out before that community the life of the body of Christ.

If there ever was a time when Christian churches covered our land like a seamless garment then that day is long gone. The many factors that have contributed to the decline in the numbers of churches in the UK during this century have left the cover of Christian communities that our land possesses looking exceedingly threadbare and holey. Unhelpful theology, intractable tradition and a false sense of 'spiritual ownership' of society rendered the mainline denominations ill-equipped to respond with resilience and vigour to the traumas of war and social and economic restructuring that have changed both the heart and the face of the British nation in the course of the century.

Christian communities with their life and witness focused

upon the fixed locations of parishes and church buildings have been outflanked by a mobile population. An increasing number of parishes whose boundaries once encompassed coherent sociological areas now contain mixtures of communities often shared with neighbouring parishes, and which defy the creativity of any single church centre to minister effectively to them all. Chapels and churches once strategically placed have found themselves marginalised to a backstreet existence by housing and commercial redevelopments. Patterns of worship and witness that once were effective vehicles of the gospel in the community are retained even though the neighbourhood has changed in its social or ethnic make-up. Contact and credibility within the community are sacrificed upon the altar of conservatism within the church and although the buildings might remain, functioning as a Christian clubhouse for members who travel in from outside the area, the local community becomes in reality unchurched. To count spires as a basis for assessing the Christian cover given to an area is manifestly misleading if the pews beneath the spires are empty of the people who live within sight of the spire.

Christian mission is about people, and the church's mission task has grown more challenging in direct proportion to the increasingly varied mix of people that make up the communities of our land.

Increasing cultural diversity is one of the most significant features of contemporary society. Particularly in population centres, the pressures of urban living make it ever more difficult for people with different social and family situations to have any significant social contact. Even within a single geographical area of uniform housing, these pressures can lead to social fragmentation of the community such that it becomes increasingly difficult for a single church group to effectively relate to all of the various circles of people on the estate. This cultural fragmentation of a neighbourhood becomes more pronounced still where there is variety within the ethnic background of the residents. In a city like London with over one million inhabitants of non-Anglo ethnic origin one can begin to realise just what a complicated social reality the churches are faced with in their task of communicating the gospel in a meaningful and appropriate way to their neighbours. The question 'Who is my neighbour?' has become a critical one for churches to ask of themselves if they are serious about mission.

Where there is a good measure of cultural uniformity in an area or where new housing projects produce distinct and easily identifiable communities then people can be fairly well located according to 'geographical co-ordinates'.

Increasingly, however, churches and denominational mission strategists—if such people exist!—must take seriously the need to commit resources to people identified by social or cultural co-ordinates rather than by geographical location. The emergence of some 500 ethnic churches within London during the last 20 years or so, when the mainline churches have experienced such a drastic decline, is evidence that should not be lightly put aside when deciding the case for a greater variety of culturally specific Christian groups.

It is not uncommon for objections to be raised to the formation of such 'homogeneous' churches on the grounds that Christ and therefore the Christian church should embrace all cultures. This is a valid concern and the question of how such groups might relate to one another in the formation of larger, more mixed fellowships in order to affirm the universality of the Christian body is a proper one. It is, perhaps, for today's church one of the challenges that come in different forms to the church in every age as it is confronted with the need to adapt itself to the changing patterns of the society that it is called to serve. Perhaps, however, it is a measure of our cultural blinkeredness that we fail to recognise that in fact our existing churches rarely achieve the gospel goal of culturally heterogeneity but are in fact culturally specific. The fact this is not the result of deliberate mission policy does not alter the reality to be found in most congregations on any given Sunday. Each has its own particular style of life and language, worship and witness that is more attractive to some than to others.

It is worthy of note that very often where there are several churches within a given geographical area they are in fact all targeting, albeit unconsciously, the same section of the local community. A greater awareness of who is the neighbour that God has given a group of churches to serve could hopefully lead to a heightened sensitivity in the development of complementary church programmes and practices, with a view to helping as wide a cross-section as possible of the casualties of secularism to find healing and new life in the kingdom. Too many congregations are more or less consciously passing by on the other side, preferring the security to be found in the traditional and familiar to the uncertainties and disruptions that come with changes of direction that will bring the churches alongside the vast majority of those who live without hope and without God in the world.

God's way is to send Jesus down your street. That's the message of the incarnation. There are too many streets where the body of Christ today has never been. The inhabitants think differently, speak differently, live differently. They enjoy different styles of music and dress. In short, they wouldn't fit. Where that's true, and it will be true of some groups in every town and village in the land, it should be recognised and responded to with creative thinking as to how Christian communities could be established 'down their street'.

There is neither need nor justification for allowing our churches to continue to be shackled to culturally inappropriate patterns of life and witness that have resulted in so many communities of our land becoming effectively unchurched. In Jesus we have both the precedent and the power to develop mission strategies which will take the church where the people are today.

Church planting is precisely about the establishing of a living and relevant witness within every 'people group', so that all may be offered a realistic opportunity of experiencing the signs of the kingdom that are present wherever two or three or more meet in Jesus' name. Thousands of new 'communities of the kingdom' are needed to repossess the land so changed since the turn of the last century. Vigorous programmes of planting will be needed to retain such a presence in the public market place of our changing society as it moves into the century ahead.

It's effective

It's good to establish churches. They're needed. But would more churches mean more Christians? Is church planting an effective way of re-evangelising our land?

The recent English Churches' Census[2] has shocked many a denominational committee from out of the sleep of complacency that seems to have held such a mortifying sway over recent mission policy making. The loss of a thousand church attenders per week for the past ten years simply cannot be ignored any more than the removal of every fifth name from a denominational membership list during the same period. Even if recent denominational expectations had focused on maintenance and survival rather than any hopes of church growth—and much local and national church policy making would suggest that this has been the case—it is now quite clear that new and effective initiatives are urgently needed.

But is new church planting such an initiative? Can the haemorrhage of people out of English churches be stemmed by this strategy? It is tempting to suggest that, as in the case of the woman with the flow of blood in Mark 5:26, everything else has been tried, and so, if for no other reason, church planting should be given a chance! Happily there are more compelling reasons for making church planting a central plank in our churches' mission platforms in this Decade of Evangelism.

The Lausanne link in December 1990 helpfully reported on the findings of the American church growth research group, Barna Research, which can be summarised in the table opposite.

The table shows the gain or loss in American mainline denominational membership during the period 1970–1990. Two things are immediately clear from the figures.

The first is that despite all that is popularly spoken about the spiritual receptivity of American society many mainline churches, as in the UK, are in decline.

The second is that there are two pronounced exceptions to that trend: the Southern Baptist Convention and the Assemblies of God. The Southern Baptist Convention is in fact numerically the fastest growing church in North America.

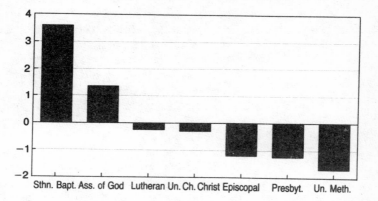

Gain/Loss in Denominational Membership
U.S.A.—1970–1990 (in hundred thousands)

Source: Barna Research.

Now, like any church group, the Southern Baptists would be the first to admit that of recent years they have had their own internal difficulties and yet they continue to grow. What is the distinctive emphasis of their mission policy that is producing such encouraging results? Let me quote from a Home Mission Board publication entitled, *An Associational Church Extension Guide*. In the very first paragraph of the introduction we are told that the purpose of the guide 'is to assist leaders in developing and implementing a comprehensive, ongoing strategy for starting and growing new churches and missions.'

Here, then, is the commitment that lies at the heart of their mission strategy—church planting. To quote again from this excellent publication:

The Southern Baptist Convention has a 'Bold Mission Thrust' goal of 50,000 churches and church-type missions by AD 2000. This goal requires a net increase of nearly 13,000 new churches during the closing years of this century.

What is evidently true of this denomination is that church growth and church planting go hand in hand.

The same picture emerges from within the experience of church groups of every shade of denominational affiliation from all around the world. The vigorous expansion of the Brazilian population and economy in the late fifties confronted the churches with a challenge as to how to respond to a population that was suddenly 'on the move' socially and geographically. Different mission postures were adopted by different church groups. Of the mainline denominations the Assemblies of God and the Baptists were committed to move with the people and to establish new churches across the changing face of Brazil. Other mainline denominations, equally long established in the traditional centres of Brazilian society, failed to make this strategic response and thirty years on find themselves largely marginalised with an inadequate church network, severely limited in their mission potential even in a time of continued spiritual receptivity.

It is, perhaps, not surprising that the lessons learned during the sixties and seventies about the relative growth rates of churches that do or do not think in terms of church multiplication as the critical parameter for evangelistic activity, continue to form the corner-stone of Brazilian Baptist denominational mission policy. This is exemplified by the Baptists' five-year national evangelistic plan aiming at the doubling of the number of churches in the five-year period from 1988 to 1992. It is notable that the goal was expressed in terms of some 3,000 new churches rather than in terms of a similar percentage increase in membership.

Mention has already been made of the sobering findings of the English Churches' Census. Similar denominational decline in the American mainline churches during the sixties and early seventies provoked an assessment of the current mission strategies of the churches concerned with a view to identifying pointers for turning the tide. Lyle Schaller, an acknowledged authority on the dynamics of church development, made the following telling observations.

Denominations that show an increase in the number of

congregations show an increase in membership. Denominations that show a decrease in the number of congregations show a decrease in membership.

Denominations that show an increase in membership show an increase in the number of congregations. Denominations that show a decrease in membership show a decrease in the number of congregations.

He concludes: 'The first step in developing a denominational strategy for church growth should be to organise new congregations.'[3] The voice of the Spirit is clearly to be heard from around the international body of Christ: reproducing churches produce growing denominations; sterile churches produce declining denominations.

By any comparison with nature or with the commercial world these conclusions seem compellingly obvious. Yet it is remarkable the distrust and resistance that the suggestion of new church planting can evoke at even senior church leadership level. If the results of the English Churches' Census provoke a radical reappraisal of current denominational mission policies and a new openness to the church planting experience of our brothers and sisters around the world, then the survey will have proved strategic indeed.

A case has been made for the crucial value of church planting for the cure of our ailing denominations. However, the salvation of our denominations cannot be an adequate motive for the establishing of new churches, whether they be Methodist, United Reformed, Elim, or any other. The Great Commission enjoins upon us the task of working and witnessing with a view to the 'cure of souls', the salvation of men and women.

Newer churches are, as a rule, more effective than older, larger ones in this task. In a study aimed at determining the relative effectiveness of churches of different age and size in bringing new people into the active life of the church, it was clearly shown that churches less than 10 years of age with fewer than 100 in average attendance are twice as efficient in reaching new people as churches more than 10 years of age with more than 100 in average attendance.[4]

Time and again the same testimony is heard from somewhat envious senior pastors of planting churches: the daughter church is growing more rapidly than we are! Recently a minister confided to me that within a month of the public launch of the new congregation the total attendance of the church and congregation was double that which the church alone had been living with for years.

It is not difficult to understand why this should be so.

- The individual members of the new group are there as a result of a conscious decision of commitment. They know why they are there and they own the enterprise.
- The experience of pioneering encourages a reliance upon God for guidance and power and progress, which has always been the hallmark of effective witnessing and vigorous spiritual life.
- Their faith is supported by the prayers and encouragement of the planting church.
- The new group has a clear goal to grow in numbers.
- They are able to tailor the new church programme to the specific needs and type of community they are in.
- They are local, familiar to and easily accessible to the residents of the neighbourhood. This is a crucial factor.
- The months of planning, praying and preparing normally engenders a strong sense of fellowship, but with an outgoing focus that warmly receives newcomers.
- They are highly motivated, expecting to have to work hard and give sacrificially.
- In the smaller group each member feels a heightened sense of accountability and responsibility to the group and its body life.

All these factors add up to a description of church life that many a leader of a long established congregation would covet, precisely because they represent the ingredients for growth.

It is the first ten to fifteen years of a new congregation's life that are usually its most efficient in producing new members. With the passage of time, objectives become obscured and motives mixed. With increasing numbers the back pew becomes the bolt hole for the casual Christian. Personal needs become the focus of concern as ownership of the church programme weakens. The vision for growth becomes defocused by the complexities of pastoral care, property maintenance, leadership restructuring and the accommodation of the different priorities of a growing membership. The plateauing out of growth is not inevitable but it is a tendency. Frequent vision check-ups are needed to correct blurring and shortsightedness! Having said all this, however, it is exciting to be living in times when more and more churches are seeking a new clarity of purpose and finding that the promise to the Laodicean church is still valid (Rev 3:14–22).

In the previous section of this chapter where the need for new church planting was set out, the issue of the cultural fragmentation of contemporary society was highlighted. The emergence of distinct, socially self-contained people groups within our towns and cities was recognised as being a characteristic of our day that complicated the mission task of the church.

It is precisely in the face of this challenge that the genius of new church planting as a means of evangelism becomes apparent. Its freedom and facility to generate ongoing witness from *within* a community, sensitive and responsive to local realities in a way that imported evangelism rarely can be, sets it apart in terms of effectiveness from other ways of witnessing.

However, the seeding and cultivation of groups of Christian believers within distinct people groups represents a genuine challenge for the mainline denominational groups of churches. Denominationalism speaks of a measure of conformity to accepted patterns of what it means to be a local expression of the body of Christ. These patterns of church life have all developed within the mainstreams of society and the leadership, language and life within the churches of a given group tend to be similar. The stereotyped image of the different denominations conveyed in the choice of photograph that accompanies the statistics of each group in the full report of the English Churches' Census is all too true a picture to be comfortable. Conformity to past practice and patterns in expressing the gospel and the corporate Christian life are great barriers to a radical programme of diversification of church types that is needed to keep pace with the development of increasing numbers of distinct subcultures within our society. Whether it's youth or yuppies, Sikhs or single parents, hard and creative thinking is the order of the day if mainline churches aren't going to loose touch completely with whole sections of society. It is arguable whether in fact the so-called new churches have been any more creative and flexible in the models of church life that have been established in their new congregations. They have, however, enjoyed the freedom to take risks for the kingdom that it is often more difficult to obtain from the permission givers and facilitators of longer established groups.

Cross-cultural evangelism, which, as we have seen, is increasingly the name of the game in our own land, is perhaps more than any other best served by a strategy of new church planting. The emphasis, however, must be on the 'new'. Charles Brock, a long-term American missionary in the Phillipines, echoes this when he describes the planter's objective as 'more than planting a church, it is planting an indigenous church'.[5]

Clones will simply serve to restore the churches' penetration of those sectors of society within which the denominations have traditionally worked. Culturally inappropriate church plants will either wither in the 'foreign' climate or will create for themselves an artificial environment supported from outside the target community, continuing to exist there but making little or no impact upon it. Such was the sad fate of many a well-intentioned but ill-conceived church plant from middle-class to council housing estates in the immediate post-war period. Sadly, one still hears of such mistakes today.

Cross-cultural church planters are one of the greatest needs of our churches in these days if the potential of this 'most effective means of evangelism under heaven'—as C. Peter Wagner delights in referring to church planting—is to be realised and the churches are to reverse the process of cultural marginalisation that has been shrinking their constituency so drastically in the post-war years.

If the church can still be compared to a boat and evangelism to fishing, then what is needed are for groups of fishermen and women to construct shallow draft boats to get them access to the backwaters and shallows of society, to cast the net where some fish are hiding and others are living by preference or through circumstance. There are numbers and varieties of fish to be found there that the deep draft denominational vessels have rarely brought on board! Culturally sensitive church planting offers the church at large just such a vehicle of evangelism. The potential for effectiveness in this most challenging task of people group evangelism is unrivalled precisely because new witnessing communities can be seeded and grown within the social and cultural environment of the new group itself. In such a way the new church becomes an authentic and resident expression of Christianity able to reproduce and spread within the people group, evangelising from within rather than perpetuating the struggle of constant cross-cultural witnessing from groups outside.

If many a denominational jury is still out, deliberating the case for the effectiveness of church planting as a response to the mission of God and the needs of the nation, there are signs that perceptions are changing. When an Archbishop of Canterbury feels able publicly to urge church planting upon his denomination, as he did at the 1991 Anglican church planters' conference, then there is every reason to hope that a fresh appreciation is dawning of the effectiveness of new church planting as an effective strategy of evangelism.

It's renewing

An increasingly godless British society needs to be confronted with the reality and the relevance of the Christian gospel. Church planting is the most effective immediate and long-term response to that need. Reaching unconverted individuals and unchurched communities should always represent the prime motive for promoting multiplication as the preferred mode of church growth.

One further encouragement to plant should be set out, however, while the question of 'why plant?' is being addressed.

It is as follows: the renewal of life brought by this enterprise of evangelism is not confined only to its target audience, the unsaved, it is shared also by those involved in it. The uncompromising and often uncomfortable demands of church planting upon a church are perhaps the best training ground for personal and communal Christian life that the church has available to it. Genuine generosity of spirit, dependence upon God, commitment to service, the readiness for radical reappraisal of the purpose and practice of church life, are just some of the attitudes that must be cultivated and will be tested in the venture of establishing a new community of the kingdom. Church planting offers denominations, churches and individual Christians alike an unprecedented opportunity for renewal in a whole range of areas that are vital for healthy spiritual life.

If the world is an arena in which God is working out his eternal purposes to bring all things under Christ as Head, then to be involved in starting a new church places you right up on the frontline of where God's action is. You'll see things happen that are quite out of the sight of those living in the world of the back pew, or, dare we say it, the committee chamber! The entire Israelite army knew when Goliath fell, but how many I wonder were close enough in support of David to be inspired by his declaration of faith in the power of God: 'I come against you in the name of the Lord Almighty . . . whom you have defied . . . the battle is the Lord's, and he will give all of you into our hands!' (1 Sam 17:45–47). The challenge of planting might make your spiritual knees shake but the shaking can do wonders for muscle tone! To coin a phrase familiar from advertising: it has the ability to reach the parts that others . . . cannot reach.

Faith, then, is tested by the exercise of church planting. It is one thing to work for developments in the life of the established church community, it is quite another to look for creation of a church ex nihilo. At least Ezekiel had dry bones to work with. A church planter can't even rely upon them! Many who have been members of groups that have church planted will testify that the experience stands out as a time when their confidence in the sufficiency of God was strengthened more than in any other period of their Christian life. Zechariah 4:6–9 became the foundation for not only the life of the new church we were establishing some years back in the town of Rondonopolis, Brazil, but of the personal life of almost all the founding group.

A shortage of people resources is the heartcry of many a conscientious church leader. In a new and growing church this shortage is acute and chronic at the same time. A properly prepared founding group will have been alerted to this reality from the outset and potential members left with no illusions as to the level of commitment required by those believing God to be calling them to form part of the core team. It is not uncommon therefore to find that the norms of discipleship that come to be accepted in newly established churches are a challenge to more relaxed standards of involvement familiar to longer established churches. Levels of giving, prayerfulness, congregational unity and outgoingness are particularly significant characteristics of a new growing fellowship that can often challenge the lifestyle typical of the mother church. This is healthy and every denomination needs the stimulus to critical self-assessment and rededication that the sacrificial service of church planting and other radical forms of Christian mission inject into its corporate life.

Shortage of labourers will not be felt only by the new group, however. Almost invariably the planting church or group of churches will have taken the step of faith to set aside key people for the work to which the Holy Spirit of God had called them (Acts 13:2). The gaps created in the frontline of leadership of these agencies will give opportunities for fresh individuals to be equipped by God and brought into leadership positions. This process of leadership renewal offers a great opportunity for the enlivening of fellowship life and thinking in the sending group. Like all opportunities it does need careful handling, however, and leaders of churches that have planted out several groups will testify to just how demanding an aspect of the whole enterprise this rejigging of the mother church can be. This is particularly true since it is very often some of the most active and gifted members that are being sent out to form the core group of the new fellowship. Patterns of worship and decision making that functioned well while those key members were present can overnight become rather lacklustre. The growing of fresh leadership and the praying for renewal of gifting from among the remaining membership must form a vital part of the preparation by the group that is planning to plant. The stimulus of the search for fresh gifting and the openness to fresh patterns of life and ministry that the emergence of such gifting can bring is precisely the process that no church can do without.

How often would you stop your car on a journey if the fuel tank seemed to be full? How often do churches fail to look for a resupply of spiritual gifts among its membership because all the necessary tasks in the church seem to be adequately catered for? It might be uncomfortable to lose a Paul and a Barnabas but we can give the 'Lord, the giver of life' the credit for knowing what he's doing! Many a commercial company has suffocated to death by stifling the opportunity for the development of junior management, filling senior posts with people who themselves had nowhere else to go. A general loss of vision and vitality in policy making and a lack of commitment and quality in production is the guaranteed result of such business practice. New church planting keeps the challenge of renewing leadership and refreshing outlook constantly before the churches.

The renewal of leadership outlook is a spin-off of the planting process that is worth taking note of, especially for those carrying the concern of the longer term well-being of the churches in our land. Those concerned for ecumenical development, for cross-cultural mission, and simply for the continued relevance of the church in a rapidly changing world will be quick to recognise the value of bringing fresh minds and hearts to the ongoing challenge of reshaping received traditions in the light of new realities. The hard theological and practical work bound up in the process of establishing new and culturally appropriate churches can become a veritable lifeline to processes bogged down in yesterday's presuppositions. Church plants can become testbeds for new insights into the question of what does it mean to be the church of Jesus at the end of the second millennium. They can provide alternative and potentially more radical and positive paradigms for church development than those that have been sought for in the church mergers of the last thirty years.

It is not without significance that the Lausanne process has given birth to the DAWN 2000 initiative with its aim of promoting the cross-denominational co-ordination of church planting as an appropriate response to the Great Commission at this stage in the church's history. When the wheels of change turn faster, the oil of renewed ecclesiological thinking is all the more essential to avoid the engine of denominational life seizing up. The process of new church planting offers just such a well of renewal in this, as in the other areas mentioned above.

It's strategic

From what we have said so far it could perhaps be thought that church planting is being commended to hard pressed denominations as a short-term panacea to see them through a particularly lean period in the spiritual history of our nation. On the contrary, however, it should be recognised that the systematic and ongoing process of establishing fresh worship and witness centres throughout our land has strategic rather than merely tactical importance. Commitment to a policy of church planting is strategic for the task of evangelism at home, throughout Europe and world-wide.

Strategic for the UK

The United Kingdom is a mission field. Responsible leadership today must, as in every generation, take as part of its sacred trust the responsibility of passing on to the coming generation a mission base that is both strong and flexible.

It is a striking fact that a high percentage of the Baptist churches functioning in the Greater London area were founded by Charles Haddon Spurgeon and his immediate associates. One is reminded of the development aid advertisement that makes the point that if you give a man a loaf you feed him for a day but if you teach him to farm you feed him and his community for a lifetime. New believers incorporated into existing churches will result in those self-same churches being in existence when the individuals are grown old and gone to glory. New believers gathered together in a new church plant will leave an additional agency of worship and witness. As a general rule it will be more strategic to establish a church than to convert an individual. The results will be more far-reaching.

Not only should the mission base of our denominations and groups be expanded and strengthened through the addition of new agencies of the kingdom, but in a climate of rapid societal change it is of strategic significance to do everything possible to ensure that the mission network will be *responsive* to change. The strategic goal should not be merely to bequeath many churches but churches that are also serviceable in the cause of evangelising the next generation.

Creative church planting that discovers new ways of being the body of Christ in a changing world will help keep the sinews of our denominations supple and more able to respond sensitively and vigorously to the as yet unforeseen challenges of tomorrow's world. Children keep you young at heart and they keep grandparents on the move and living in the present rather than the past. New churches, and the fresh theological insights that they generate, counter the tendency to ecclesiological ossification that turns structures into strictures. The legacy of narrowness and cultural insensitivity which has so much hampered the responsiveness of the churches in today's generation is not one that we should wish to pass on to our children.

Strategic for Europe

Europe has well been described as today's dark continent. History, culture and processes of economic and political development make the experiences of the churches in the UK a potentially far more appropriate source of inspiration and direction than those rooted in North American realities. Particularly in the area of establishing new churches, the relative failure of American missions in Europe has been amply documented. At a church planting conference held in Paris in 1990 the question and answer sessions were almost totally dominated by perplexed US missionaries wanting to understand why ways and means successfully applied in the States were proving so barren across the Atlantic. Although it is true that both in mainland Europe and in Scandinavia successful models for establishing new churches are emerging, it is in the United Kingdom that the greatest number and variety of models can be found. It is important that this European dimension to the significance of our churches' involvement in church planting be recognised and that helpful channels of interaction be set up to facilitate the exchange of experience and expertise.

Strategic for the world

Reaction against an often less than glorious colonial past should not blind Christians to the significant role that the UK still plays on the world scene. Both in terms of the influence Britain still exerts by dint of its economic and political resources and also in terms of the image it presents to a large sector of the world's peoples as a Christian country, our responsibility to re-establish the church in our land is a strategic one. The leavening effect of a prophetic Christian voice from within industry and government, spoken into the forums of world debate and decision, should not be overlooked, if we do indeed look to the day when all things shall be united under Christ as Head. The colonial past has made London a world focus for international travel and the cheapest centre for establishing many Two-Thirds World organisational headquarters. Important decisions are made within a national climate more or less influenced by the vigour and relevance of the Christian churches.

It is not, however, only as a crossroads of international travel, commerce, and debate that Britain remains a significant influence upon world affairs. New Commonwealth immigration has transformed the face of British society itself and made the UK a springboard for reaching back through the activities and vision of emerging Asian and African Christian fellowships into countries almost closed to traditional missionary influence. Cross-cultural church planting into the burgeoning numbers of national groups now resident in our land will enable the Spirit to accelerate this process of international missionary penetration as he inspires new ethnic origin disciples with the vision of evangelising their ethnic group overseas.

Our concern for stimulating a fresh commitment to new church planting should not then focus solely upon the effectiveness of such a policy for reaching our own generation but also the next. And beyond that in enabling us to play a wider role in missions and be good stewards of the influence and opportunity that our national history has bequeathed to us in regard to our role in Europe and the world.

It's timely

The greek word *kairos* has become part of the language of leadership in this Decade of Evangelism. It signifies a special time or season, and in the context of Christian conversation, God's special time for a particular aspect of his agenda of world salvation. Jesus, of course, based his own ministry upon the knowledge that the divinely appointed time, the *kairos* had arrived for the kingdom of God to be projected into the life and history of humankind (Mk 1:15). He passed on to his church the responsibility to continue to be available to God as the agents of this kingdom *kairos*. That fact, as we spelt out at the opening of this chapter, underlies every particular consideration of the appropriateness of the church's engagement in church planting as a means of extending the network of the kingdom.

Within every chapter of the church's history, however, different emphases seem to have been commended by the Spirit of Christ to his church as of particular moment. Among the various strands of present international experience and concern that make up the backcloth upon which more local issues are worked out, church planting undoubtedly finds a place. Throughout the international body of Christ there is a recognition that there's a time to plant and that time has arrived. The call for a new confidence in the gospel and commitment to its spread has swelled from the churches of sub-Saharan Africa and from Latin America to challenge the established churches of Europe and parts of Asia. It would be no exaggeration to identify the development of a world-wide movement of new church planting with the experience of each national church stimulating and reinforcing the activities of the others with whom they are linked. The establishment in 1990 of the International Network of Church Planters based on the work of Dr David Finnell and

Dr Ralph Neighbour Jr at the Columbia Biblical Seminary and Graduate School of Missions is typical of the emergence of national and international forums for the sharing and promoting of this aspect of the church's mission. It is noteworthy that within the first eighteen months of the launching of the Spurgeon's/Oasis Church Planting and Evangelism course in London, detailed enquiries had been received from eleven international mission agencies from as far apart as Canada, Holland, Australia, Sweden and New Zealand.

It is true to say that church planting is becoming very much the buzz word among mission leaders in the UK at present. It is equally true that not a few are voicing caution against simply jumping aboard the latest bandwagon. There is, however, an international dimension to this renewed commitment to extending the network of witnessing communities that would suggest a substantial basis to the current trend.

Jesus is recorded as affirming that 'Whoever serves me must follow me; and where I am, my servant also will be. My Father will honour the one who serves me' (Jn 12:26). We live in an age when it is easier than ever before in the history of the church of Christ to hear the voice of the Spirit speaking across national boundaries to inspire and direct its upbuilding. There is much that would encourage us to believe that the impetus for this movement of the body into church planting is coming from the Head. As such the expectancy of God's blessing upon the sacrificial ministry of church planting is a proper incentive to its undertaking. If the Spirit of Christ has shown his church both the need and the vision then in the words of the New Zealand Baptist Union call to a new commitment to planting, 'Run with it!' (Hab 2:2).

For discussion and further study

1. What aspects of the current UK social and religious scene point to the need for a renewed commitment to evangelism through church planting?
2. In what sense can church planting be understood as a particularly strategic form of mission activity?

3. Review the evidence in support of C. Peter Wagner's statement that, 'Church planting is the most effective form of evangelism under heaven.'

4. Discuss the proposition 'The renewal of life brought by this enterprise of evangelism is not confined only to its target audience, the unsaved, it is shared also by those involved in it.'

Notes

1. David Schenk and Ervin Stutzman, *Creating Communities of the Kingdom* (Herald Press, 1988).
2. Peter Brierley, *'Christian' England* (MARC Europe, 1991).
3. Lyle E. Schaller, *Understanding Church Growth and Decline 1950–1978* (The Pilgrim Press: New York, 1979), p 351.
4. Clay L. Price and Phil Jones, *A Study of the Relationship of Church Size and Church Age to Number of Baptisms and the Baptism Rate* (Home Mission Board, Southern Baptist Convention: Atlanta, 1978), pp 8,9.
5. Charles Brock, *The Principles and Practice of Indigenous Church Planting* (Broadman Press, 1981), p 33.

CHAPTER THREE

CHURCH PLANTING—A STRATEGY FOR MISSION

Martin Robinson

There is now sufficient interest and involvement in church planting at a local level to ensure that church planting will be a major issue in church life, at least during the last decade of the twentieth century and probably well into the twenty-first century. What follows details some of that activity as we survey the present scene. But it would be a mistake to believe that church planting is an entirely recent concern. Church planting has been both an issue and a practical reality at other times in church history and this more ancient inheritance inevitably influences all that we do today. It is as well to have some awareness of what has gone before.

A clash of cultures—church planting in pagan Europe

We know something of the very earliest attempts of the church to plant churches in Europe from the pages of the Bible itself. Our knowledge of church history gives a well-documented picture of the gradual spread of the church throughout the Mediterranean basin and so we know something of the spread of the church in those parts of Europe that were closest to the heartland of the faith in Asia Minor, the Middle East and North Africa. However, our knowledge of the early church in the more northern parts of Europe is somewhat scanty.

We do know that the church existed in Britain in the early third century. St Alban is reputed to have been martyred around the year 208, together with other believers. More intriguing is the suggestion made by Tertullian that the church operated in those parts of Britain not yet reached by the

Romans. Given the time of Tertullian's writing, this most probably means the parts of south-west Britain as yet unoccupied by the Romans. We certainly know of the existence of the church in the fourth century because British bishops attended the Council of Arles in 314.[1]

Following the action of the Emperor Constantine to radically improve the position of Christianity in the Empire,[2] we can assume that the Christian faith had found a widespread acceptance, at least in the Romanised parts of Britain, by the middle of the fourth century. However, before the end of the fourth century the arrival and eventual dominance by new and pagan peoples, the Angles and the Saxons, called into question the very existence of the church in Britain, because the invaded British do not seem to have communicated the faith to their new masters.

In Wales, great saints were being produced who ensured that the faith was deeply planted in the consciousness of the people but, as David Edwards points out in his book *Christian England*, there is no record of a single Welshman who was ever a missionary among the English during this time. The task of converting the English and planting churches among them was left to others.

The fifth century was not a good time for church planting in any part of Europe. We call it today the beginning of the Dark Ages. Not just Britain but most of Europe was being invaded from the East by pagan peoples. It seemed to many who were living then that the great triumph of Christianity in becoming the official religion of the Roman Empire, with all that such an achievement represented, was to be swept away. Many concluded that the coming of the Lord was imminent, the end of all things had arrived.

At such a time there arose a remarkable band of church planters who travelled throughout Europe. We know these men and women today as the Celtic saints. Although we know the names of hundreds of these church planters through the parish churches which bear their names, little is known of the lives of many of these pioneers and nothing at all is known of the many in their monastic bands whose names do not appear on any church.

What we do know is something of the character and consequence of their work. The Celtic missionaries operated
initially between Brittany, Ireland, Wales and Scotland. Later,
their activities spread to many other parts of Europe and even
on some occasions to North Africa, Iceland and Russia! The
Irish Sea and the river valleys that flowed into it formed a useful
means of communicating with the various Celtic communities in
much the same way that the Mediterranean acted as a means of
communication for the earlier Roman Empire.

The Celts were monastic missionaries who used a self-
replicating/discipling model for their mission. Typically, one
man would gather twelve others around him to act as his
helpers. Many of these twelve would in turn leave at some point
to found their own communities, also gathering twelve disciples
in order to repeat the process. Their lifestyle was simple in the
extreme. They practised a unique blend of scholarship spirituality
and practical involvement with the lives of those they sought to
serve. Much of this blend was bound together with a strong
knowledge of and love for the Bible. They were very committed
to the poor, normally practised believer's baptism by immersion
and, moreover, often attracted attention by the signs and
wonders that seemed to flow from their ministry.[3]

Theirs were gathered churches, the buildings simple in design
and materials. Women were not unknown as part of their
communities. There is even one report of a woman as bishop!
Their interaction with the cultures that they worked among
produced very different churches from the urban, Romanised
churches that seemed to fail so easily following the collapse of
the Romano-British civilisation. They tended to build churches
which were rooted in the countryside and reflected far more the
clan structure of the society that they worked in.

It was from their monastic base in Scotland that their
missionary enterprise in England began. At the height of their
activity, Celtic missionaries could be found in almost every one
of the kingdoms in England other than those in the extreme
south-east of England.[4]

The continental or Roman mission inspired by Pope Gregory
was taking place in the south-east of England during the very

same years that the Celtic monks were making such an impact in other parts of England. This parallel development was producing a very different type of church. Certainly its originators were also monks with a love of learning and spirituality but their fundamental ethos stood in stark contrast to that of the wandering Celts. Both Celtic and Roman missions recognised the authority of Rome in some sense and both had many more points of agreement than disagreement, especially in doctrinal matters.

The calling of the Synod of Whitby in AD 664 to resolve those differences that remained seemed to revolve around apparently small matters. The differences over the calculation of the date of Easter and the wearing by priests of the Roman tonsure would seem to us to be relatively small matters, all the more so when one remembers that many parts of the Celtic Church in Ireland and elsewhere had already accepted these points.[5] However, what was really at issue was a more fundamental clash of culture. The Celtic Church, built as it was around the principle of the gathered church, and which baptised individuals who owed allegiance to a bishop who was more of a spiritual father than an administrative figure, found it hard to accept the rather more static church represented by these Roman missionaries.

The original intention of the Roman mission had been to establish two archbishoprics, one in York and the other in London. These cities were not chosen at random, they were the former centres of Roman Imperial rule. The establishing of the southern archbishopric at Canterbury rather than in London reflected the harsh realities of the opportunities that were actually available to those missionaries. What a contrast between these choices and the Celtic refusal even to make their centre in the capital city of the king who invited them to Northumbria but to choose instead the island of Lindisfarne as their mission base!

The Roman mission was not centred on community so much as on the office of the bishop. Theirs was a territorial and hence an administrative approach, centring first on the urban areas of population and only moving later to subdue the countryside.

One gains a sense that the Celts were baptising individual disciples, the Romans were baptising the prevailing culture. Such a contrast almost certainly represents an exaggeration but nevertheless there clearly was a difference of ethos, strategy and method between Celtic and Roman missionaries.

The years that lie between the initial missionary success of both the Celtic and Roman missions reveal much further drama in terms of the challenge of converting the invading Norsemen and then later of harmonising the slightly different practice of the faith as represented by the native English and the invading Normans. However, the fundamental pattern had been set in the early years of mission and church planting. What followed was essentially a matter of the gradual extension of the territorial parish system originally envisaged and begun by Theodore, Archbishop of Canterbury from AD 669. The structure of the medieval church was determined largely through the gradual acceptance of this system. Its impact on English church life has been so profound that by the end of the medieval period (usually dated as AD 1500), 23 per cent of all the churches that are still in existence today had been established.[6] Given that by the year 1500 there were virtually no churches other than what we would now call Anglican churches, the really significant figure is that 53 per cent of all Anglican churches that exist today were planted before the year 1500.[7]

However, before we become completely convinced of the success of the Roman model in English church life we need to remember that while it is certainly true that it was the Roman approach that predominated after the Synod of Whitby, we can also say that the themes represented by the parallel (and earlier in many parts of Britain) approach of the Celtic missions have continued in less obvious ways and have tended to surface at various times of missionary challenge in our land.

Reformation inactivity

Those of us who are part of the Reformation inheritance might be tempted to look back on that period and see it as the release of a huge amount of religious energy. Clearly there was a great deal of religious fervour present at that time. However, what we also need to note is that there was very little church planting energy released as part of the Reformation. Perhaps we should not be too surprised by such a realisation. After all, what we are describing is the reformation of something that already existed and not the creation of something new. The focus of the struggle of the Reformers in the sixteenth century was the practice of the parish church and not the creation of new churches.

The Commonwealth period allowed some fairly radical elements contained in the Reformation to take up residence in many parish churches. It is possible to see a number of fonts in English churches today which had apparently been pulled out of their original location by detachments of Commonwealth soldiers using ropes and horses. Such men were evidently not much in favour of infant baptism!

Following the restoration of the monarchy and the ejection of the more radical Anabaptists, together with the rise of movements such as the Society of Friends, there followed the establishment of separate churches which were organised on a gathered church principle. The difficulties faced by these groups were considerable. Not only were they viewed with great suspicion by the emerging rural squirearchy, but significant legal restrictions were imposed relating to where their buildings could be located. The intention of this legislation was to ensure that their buildings would not be located near population centres. Such restrictions made church planting extremely difficult.

Added to the obstacle of opposition to their very existence by the authorities was the onset of a spiritual malaise among churches of every denomination. Nonconformity, as it was now called, suffered from a kind of hyper-Calvinism which regarded evangelism as entirely the concern of God and not of man. The likelihood of such groups engaging in radical church planting was not too great. This inactivity during the period represented by the Reformation and its more immediate radical inheritance helps to explain why only 6 per cent of the churches in existence today were planted in the years 1500 to 1799.[8] This contrasts sharply with the almost 15 per cent of all our present churches begun in the 200 year period 1100 to 1299. This period of inactivity was to change dramatically in the face of the dual impact of a rapidly changing society and the emergence of the Wesleyan revival of the late eighteenth and early nineteenth century.

The rise of denominational pluralism

The revivals of the early nineteenth century did in some cases lead to the renewal of existing parish churches. However, in many more cases, the major consequence was the creation of new denominational groupings, each with their own chapels. This was not just a bad case of sectarianism. The vast population movements brought about by the depopulating impact of the agricultural revolution and the demand for labour in the new towns and cities of the industrial revolution meant that often there was no place of worship near where people lived until the chapels came into existence. These new gathered churches met both religious and social needs in the emerging working- and middle-class populations that they served.

During the first half of the nineteenth century, some 12 per cent of all the churches in existence today were established.[9] The second half of the nineteenth century saw an even greater upsurge in church planting as the nonconformists were joined by the Anglicans and then the Roman Catholics in some very extensive efforts to establish congregations near where people actually lived. Twenty-six per cent of all the churches still in existence were planted in the second half of the ninteenth century.[10]

The notable activity of the Roman Catholic Church during this period is largely explained in terms of the large influx of Irish labourers that took place during this period, combined with the introduction of legislation in 1829 that gave freedom of worship to Catholics and so allowed the establishing of Catholic churches. Anglican activity is generally supposed to have been a response to the shock suffered by the Anglican establishment following the publication of the 1851 census. The census revealed that only 25 per cent of those in worship on the census Sunday had been in an Anglican church. The nature of the established church was being seriously called into question. What a contrast to the year 1740 when only 2.5 per cent of the population were estimated to be nonconformists and Roman Catholics hardly existed at all outside of a few wealthy aristocratic homes![11]

The shock waves induced by the census returns were given a practical outlet because of the reforms undertaken by the Anglican Church in the early part of the nineteenth century. These reforms, together with the church planting zeal of the developing Anglo-Catholic Oxford Movement, also facilitated some of the Anglican expansion of church planting activity. The following figures represent numbers of churches planted which are still in existence today. They do not take account of the many churches, especially Free Church congregations, which were planted during those years and have since closed. Anglican churches planted in the period 1850 to 1899 stand at 3,091 compared with some 1,474 churches planted in the previous half century. Similarly, Roman Catholic activity went up from 344 plants in the first half of the century to 918 in the second half of the century. But so too was Free Church activity expanding. Their 2,927 churches planted in the fifty-year period to 1850 became an amazing 6,037 in the fifty years from 1850 to 1899![12]

The twentieth century—new patterns emerge

We are accustomed to thinking of the twentieth century as a period of decline for almost all churches. Certainly, in general terms, the percentage of the population that attends church on a weekly basis towards the end of the century is only approximately 25 per cent of the percentage of the population that attended at the beginning of the century. It is also true that the huge increase in church building that took place among the historic Free Churches and the Anglicans during the latter part of the nineteenth century has not continued during the twentieth century.

That does not mean that there has been no church planting taking place. What is true is that the pattern of church planting in the twentieth century has been markedly different from that which has gone before. Moreover, we have to admit that the church planting which has taken place has been more than offset by church closures. Nevertheless, it is important to note some of the key factors which mark church planting during this century as different to that of the previous century.

First, the average size of all congregations has gradually declined as the century has continued. Inevitably this has had its impact on congregations which are newly planted. Church planters from the church growth school often make the general point that the growth of a new congregation in its first two years of life is critically important in determining the ultimate size of the group that will be planted. The general decline in congregational size has a tendency to influence both the expectation of what size a new congregation will grow to and also the size of the group that is sent out to plant. Smallness seems to have become part of the mindset of British church life. Such a mindset deprives church planting of much of its potential impact.

Second, a great deal of the church planting that has taken place in the twentieth century represents the growth of denominations that did not exist at the beginning of the century. There are 2,475 Anglican congregations which have come into existence between 1900 and 1989. However, there are almost certainly more than this number of Pentecostal churches, all of which have been planted this century. When one adds the large number of house churches which have been started since 1970 then it is clear that a very high percentage of the total Free Church figure of 7,640 new congregations now in existence which have begun this century have in fact been started by new denominational groups and not by the historic Free Churches which were so active in church planting during the last century.[13]

Third, the Roman Catholics, who have until recently avoided the decline of other denominations largely through continued immigration patterns, have played an increasingly important role in the total number of congregations begun this century. The total number of Roman Catholic churches now in existence and started since 1900 numbers 2,371. Although this is slightly less than the Anglican figure for the century so far, the Roman Catholic total since 1950 exceeds the Anglican total by 1,147 to 981.[14]

Fourth, some of the new starts this century are ecumenical projects, and although those in new towns represent completely new congregations, some in older towns have only been achieved through the closure of two or possibly many more congregations to form a new church. Certainly there are arguments in favour of such developments, but it is a factor which has not been present in previous centuries and although such congregations may well see evangelistic growth, their formation is not generated entirely by such a consideration. Still other of the new starts listed in the figures given above are in fact buildings which replace church buildings damaged in World War II.

Lastly, there is increasing evidence that although the shift in population this century has not been as dramatic as the move from a rural to an urban culture was in the previous century, nevertheless significant population movement has taken place and is continuing. There is reason to believe that the church planting which has taken place this century has not kept up with such population movement. In addition, there has been some degree of flight from the inner cities since World War II, especially, although not entirely, on the part of the historic Free Churches. This has led to many inner city areas becoming significantly underchurched. When one adds to this reality the presence of at least three million people from Muslim, Hindu and Sikh backgrounds, many of whom live in the inner city, the need for missionary congregations in our inner cities becomes ever more clear. In short, the experience of the twentieth century to date reveals the need for church planting but not necessarily for the replication of existing church structures.

Present developments in church planting

Church planting among the newer denominations—the only means of growth

As has been suggested in the preceding paragraphs, for the many newer denominations that have emerged during the twentieth century a fairly aggressive programme of church planting represents almost the only means of effective growth. We use the phrase 'almost the only means of growth' because in fact most groups do begin with at least some transfer growth, quite often in the form of whole congregations, but certainly in the transfer of the original leadership group and initial core of members.

The three white-led Pentecostal denominations in Britain, namely the Apostolic Church, the Elim Pentecostal Church and the Assemblies of God, represent some of the more established of the 'newer churches'. These three groups together represent more than 1,000 congregations, most of which have been planted this century. However, the church planting experience of these three groups is markedly different.

The Apostolic Church, the oldest of the three original Pentecostal groups, began in 1908 in South Wales. By 1920 links had formed with similar groups in Glasgow, Hereford and Bradford, and thus began a church planting impetus so that by 1939, over 200 churches had been planted in the United Kingdom. In addition, a great deal of church planting took place in the context of a vigorous overseas mission movement. Following World War II, growth slowed with only twenty-four churches being planted from 1945 to 1985. Since that time there has come a renewed interest in church planting and a further seven churches have been planted between 1985 and 1990, with more planned for the decade of the 1990s.

The Elim Evangelistic Band began in Northern Ireland in 1915 as a group which was self-consciously attempting evangelism through crusades and follow-up church planting. The outstanding ministry of George Jeffreys brought significant growth to the movement especially during the 1930s. The unfortunate rift between Elim and Jeffreys, which resulted in the splitting away of some Elim congregations and the formation of the Bible Pattern Church under Jeffreys' leadership, caused the momentum of the Elim movement to be halted somewhat during the 1940s. A steady programme of church planting brought continued recovery and growth for Elim following this unfortunate division. However, the onslaught of the secularising shock of the

1960s, so serious for nearly every denomination, caused a further loss of momentum for the Elim movement. The 1970s saw a recovery of growth, with over fifty new congregations beings established in the period 1975 to 1980.

A very recent restructuring of the movement into regions has assisted an additional emphasis on growth based on church planting. There is a national strategy which calls for the planting of 400 congregations during the decade of the 1990s. This national strategy sounds very ambitious for a denomination which had 350 congregations at the time when the plan was announced, however, during 1990, some 46 congregations were planted and there is little doubt that the leadership of Elim believe that their goal is realisable.

One important ingredient in such growth has been the appointment of regional superintendents whose task it is to give flesh to the overall goal of planting new churches. One example of these regional plans is that of the north-west region. The programme is called Breakthrough 2000 and is challenging the existing 65 congregations in the region to plant 100 further congregations before the year 2000. The programme does not just set goals, but has a clear planning basis for attaining the goals that have been set. The regional superintendent, David Tinnion, is himself a proven growth leader as are the other regional superintendents. Elim's largest congregation, Kensington Temple, has also been a pioneer in church planting and has established more than forty congregations in the London area in recent years. The appointment of leaders who have demonstrated their ability to see churches grow rather than simply to administrate represents a key to the early success of Elim's current church planting initiative.

The Assemblies of God came into being in 1923 with seventy existing Pentecostal congregations. Most, though not all, of their present 560 congregations represent church plants. In common with Elim, the Assemblies found the 1960s to be a difficult time. In addition, their structure of congregational autonomy made them much more vulnerable than Elim to congregations leaving to join the house church movement during the 1970s and 1980s. Despite church planting activity, overall growth of a dramatic nature has therefore proved to be very difficult in recent years. In the decade up to 1988, 132 churches were planted but 77 congregations either left the denomination or were closed. Despite these disappointments, the situation would clearly be much more serious if no church planting were taking place.

At this time there is no actual national strategy which is directly related to church planting. As one might expect with a congregational structure, most church planting is taking place through the initiative of individual progressive congregations. However, there has been some reorganisation of the national structure in the hope that a more dynamic set of co-operative relationships can be encouraged at a regional level. To some extent this change has been influenced by developments at Elim with which there is often a healthy interaction of ideas.

The significant growth of the predominantly white-led Pentecostal churches has been paralleled and outpaced by the unexpected growth of the Afro-Caribbean churches, most but not all of which are Pentecostal. There are a small number of denominations which cannot be described as entirely black-led but which nevertheless have a significant number of black leaders. The largest group in this category is the Seventh Day Adventist Church but there are also smaller groups such as the Seventh Day Baptist Church. All of these churches have grown through church planting.

There are now over 1,000 congregations and about 250 separate denominational groupings in this very diverse community of churches. The two largest Pentecostal churches, the New Testament Church of God and the Church of God of Prophecy, have not grown quite as rapidly in recent years as they did during the 1960s and 1970s. In part this reflects their increasing difficulty in reaching black young people born in Britain, but it also reflects their success in penetrating a single section of the total community in Britain and their almost total failure to reach people outside of the black community.

A number of new Pentecostal and or Holiness-type churches with a largely white leadership have come into being during the 1980s. The Fellowship of Pentecostal Holiness Churches have begun a church planting programme, so far largely in the London area. The Four Square Gospel Church began as an organised church in Britain in 1988. They so far have nine churches (not all through church planting) and have a goal of forty churches by the year 2000. At the present time they think it likely that this goal will be exceeded. The Victory Church, Hampstead, is not strictly a classical Pentecostal church but nevertheless has its origins in classical Pentecostalism. It has grown to the point where its original congregation has more than 1,000 people in worship. It has since planted two new congregations and clearly has the potential for many more church plants. Interestingly, although as we have noted these churches have a largely white leadersip, their churches have a strong inter-cultural dimension. One wonders if there might in the future be enough such 'bridge churches' to help the black-led churches to escape their cultural captivity.

The Free Methodist Church which also stands in the Holiness tradition predates the above churches by a few years. They began in England in 1971 as a reaction to liberalism in the mother church. Initially five churches were planted and they presently have a total of fifteen congregations and continue to grow through a system of planting and transplanting.

Church planting among the 'new churches'—an engine for growth

The description 'new churches' seems to be one that is replacing the earlier description of these churches as the 'house church movement'. In part this reflects the reality that few such 'new churches' now meet in houses but more importantly it reflects a new self-understanding among the former house church leaders themselves as to the nature and direction of the churches that they lead. This group of churches are described separately from the very diverse group in our first category simply because the rapidity of their growth combined with their present size and the undoubted gifts and resources contained within this movement give them a very special opportunity in terms of church planting.

Although one can see the early roots of the new churches

stretching back into the 1950s, the majority of new churches came into being in the 1970s and 1980s. As with many other groups, their early membership was drawn from other existing churches. However, in the case of the new churches this simple and in many ways unremarkable reality was given a controversial edge because of their articulated self-understanding as restoring the New Testament Church in terms of doctrine, ecclesiology and daily living. The thrust, therefore, was a conscious criticism of existing churches with the accompanying message that those who were in the existing churches needed to come out of those structures and into the new wineskins that God was bringing into being. But it also needs to be remembered that some of the early leaders, including Gerald Coates, did not leave their respective churches, but were asked to leave as a direct result of their experience of Spirit baptism. Such treatment went some way towards their initially critical view of the historic churches.

It is not the purpose of this book to document or comment on the origins of the new churches. However, it is clear that the ideological concerns of the 'new churches' placed them in a situation of conflict with many existing churches but particularly with those in the Pentecostal and charismatic movements who felt hurt by what they felt were unjust criticisms.

With so much energy going into a form of 'come outism' it is hardly surprising that the many new churches which were created in the early days seemed to those outside the movement to consist of those who had been attracted from other churches, often causing very painful local divisions. Nevertheless, from a strictly church planting perspective such developments, while understandably hurtful in some instances, are not necessarily negative. The creation of hundreds of new fellowships with ostensibly flexible church cultures carries the potential for effective outreach to social groups who might never have considered being involved in any of the existing churches in a given area. There is considerable evidence that in many cases this has certainly happened.

The 'new churches' (how long will they be new?), by virtue of their present newness are still capable of considerable change.

It is fascinating to reread Andrew Walker's *Restoring the Kingdom*[15] (Hodder & Stoughton, London, 1985) and to observe how much has changed in the last six years. It is clear that the kingdom rearrangement of the early years has now largely ended and that a very large percentage of the growth of the new churches is through primary evangelism. It is also clear that the various networks that exist among the new churches have become much more clearly defined. Gerald Coates believes that many of the independent churches which lie outside of the networks are rather static and he is almost certainly correct. The networks are much more self-consciously planning for growth and in most cases church planting is envisaged as the means for accomplishing growth.

There are currently some 1,000 churches which can be described as belonging to the new churches which, together with a further probable 1,000 non-networked churches, comprise some 250,000 members. There are at least twenty-five identifiable networks within the new churches. The most significant in terms of both growth and church planting are Harvestime, originally based in Bradford but now moved to Leicestershire, Ichthus Christian Fellowship in London, the Pioneer teams originating from the Cobham Christian Fellowship, Team Spirit also based in London, Terry Virgo's New Frontiers teams based in Brighton, and the groups associated with the Bristol Christian Fellowship.

Church planting among the historic churches—providing for the faithful?

As we have indicated in the figures given earlier, the historic denominations have continued to church plant throughout the whole of this century in the sense that they have built new church buildings, and as a result of this process, new congregations have been established in various parts of the country. However, most of the historic churches, with the notable exception of the Roman Catholics, have closed more churches than they have opened during this century. Moreover, even when church planting has taken place, it has not happened on anything like the scale that it did during the last half of the nineteenth century.

One is left with a sense of the historic churches retracting in those areas where the general population has either declined or remained static and failing to keep up with the growth of population in other areas. There are still many Anglican parishes with more than 10,000 people to a single church centre. Even in the case of the Roman Catholics, the dominant theme is the provision of more worship centres for those Catholics who have moved away from the initial centres of immigration and for whom there is no nearby Catholic church. Church planting seems to be largely a matter of making provision for the faithful rather than being understood as an evangelistic strategy. There are now some clear signs of a change in this perspective.

We cannot make the claim that any of the larger historic churches have a clear national strategy for church planting. Indeed, despite the presence of Rob Frost and his Seed teams among Methodists and the activity of the Gear grouping in the United Reformed Church neither denomination has any official church planting strategy.

The position among the Anglicans seems to be gradually changing in this regard. The strategic foundation for change was laid in the 1970s by David Wasdell. His study papers, publicised by the Archbishop's Commission on Evangelism in the 1970s (ACE), argued the basic point that the penetration of a parish diminished significantly once the parish reached 2,500 people. Given that the average size of an Anglican parish is closer to 8,000, David Wasdell was arguing strongly for smaller parishes or for additional worship centres within a single parish.

This initial research was strongly reinforced by the pioneering work of Ian Bunting at Chester le Street. Ian Bunting's approach of planting multiple congregations within the parish has since been copied elsewhere. The story of Chester le Street is well documented in the book *Ten Growing Churches*, and the book itself has helped to inspire other experiments along similar lines.[16]

The work of co-ordinating, publicising and encouraging other initiatives has been ably pioneered by Bob Hopkins, a non-stipendiary curate at St Helen's in Lancashire. Bob has been the driving force behind a number of church planting conferences for Anglicans. The first was held in 1987, with additional events in 1988, 1989 and 1991.[17] The majority of these events have been held at Holy Trinity, Brompton, which reflects the commitment of that church to a church planting programme. One conference was held at St Andrew's, Chorleywood, which has been in close relationship with the work undertaken by Bob Hopkins. Christ Church, Chorleywood, is Bob Hopkins' sending church.

George Lings has collected a great deal of data on Anglican church planting. This data clearly shows that the majority of church plants so far take place within parish boundaries. It is hardly surprising that this is so since the difficulties involved in planting across any kind of ecclesiastical boundaries in the Church of England are considerable.[18] The need to encourage such church planting is clearly a priority for all of those leaders associated with the Anglican church planting conferences. Holy Trinity, Brompton, has engaged successfully in cross-parish and even cross-diocesan planting. Charlie Cleverly of Cranham, who has planted within parish boundaries, argues passionately for planting across parish boundaries in his book *Church Planting Our Future Hope*. Bishops David Pytches and Brian Skinner of St Andrew's, Chorleywood, have run into some controversy engaging in cross-parish planting. This controversy surfaced at the 1991 church planting conference. The same bishops also argue passionately in print for a more relaxed view of parish boundaries in their book *New Wineskins*.[19]

It remains to be seen to what extent the pressure group that is represented by the Anglican church planting conferences can influence the long-term policy of the Church of England in terms of seeing church planting as part of a dynamic thrust of missionary activity. Certainly the advent of the Decade of Evangelism has helped. The 1989 conference saw two diocesan bishops and one suffragan bishop present (other than the authors of *New Wineskins*).

It has proved to be highly serendipitous that one of the diocesan bishops present in 1989 was George Carey, then the Bishop of Bath and Wells. George Carey was also a major speaker at the 1991 Anglican church planting conference, but this time he came as Archbishop of Canterbury. The attendance was well up on previous years! Such connections can only help, but radical, missionary church planting, together with the support system that would be needed to make it work, are still a long way from being part of official Anglican policy.

In some ways, the Baptists are nearer to making church planting part of their overt strategy for mission. Once again, the initiative for a strategy of church planting has come from individuals rather than from the denominational structure.

Key individuals have been Peter Nodding of West Bridgeford in Nottingham, Harry Weatherley, who was until recently the Baptist Union's Yorkshire missioner, Stephen Ibbotson of Harris Street Baptist Church in Peterborough, and Steve Chalke of the Oasis Trust based in London. Oasis have played a key part both in training and in the practical provision of help in the form of Frontline teams. Although Frontline teams have not planted completely new churches, there is a strong argument for the case that their work in older churches has amounted to church planting in some situations. All Frontline volunteers receive at least one day's training each week in the area of practical ministry. As one might expect, a proportion of volunteers do offer themselves for full-time ministry after completion of two years' teamwork.

Allied to the Frontline training is a training course in evangelism and church planting which represents a partnership between Oasis Trust and Spurgeon's College. The course requires a two-day-a-week attendance at college with the other days being spent in a supervised placement. The course is distinct from the normal training programme for Baptist ministry. This recognition of the different kind of training required for church planting from that required for the pastoral ministry represents a breakthrough for training among the historic denominations.

Spurgeon's and Oasis have been able to act as catalysts for church planting in the denomination, which has helped to move church planting out of the realm of purely local initiatives to something more like a national initiative. This wider activity is represented particularly through the formation in 1990 of a network for Baptist church planters. A great deal of the initiative for this development came from Spurgeon's students, some of whom edit and administrate the network's bulletin, *Bacup*.

The developments at Spurgeon's have been sown in fertile ground as far as the denomination is concerned. There has been a very constructive relationship in London with the area superintendent, Douglas MacBain. The Evangelism Secretary for the Baptist Union at the start of the initiative was David Coffey and he welcomed these moves. David Coffey became General Secretary of the Union during 1991 and his place as Evangelism Secretary has been taken by another very supportive person, Derek Tidball, who was President of the Baptist Union in 1990. These warm institutional ties lead one to suppose that it might not be too long before there is a more official Baptist Union strategy for church planting. Should this turn out to be the case, the Baptists will be the first of the major historic denominations to adopt such a policy.

Most of the smaller historic denominations also have no recognisable church planting strategy, with some interesting exceptions. Of these exceptions, the Salvation Army is the most recent exponent of a church planting policy. According to a statement by Major John Dangerfield, the Salvation Army's national officer for church growth, the Army has adopted a plan of opening new centres, at least two for every one of its twenty-four divisions. Five plants in Scotland, three in England and one in Wales have already taken place. Seventeen centres were earmarked for opening in 1991. The Salvation Army has placed a major emphasis on church growth teaching during the 1980s and looks to be close to reversing what is now more than half a century of radical decline. It may well be that the adoption of a church or corps planting strategy will tip the balance for the Army in producing its first significant growth as a movement in recent years.

Two much smaller historic denominations have also had some experience of church planting during the last decade. The Fellowship of Churches of Christ came into being when the older Association of Churches of Christ of which they had been a part, and which dated back to 1842, was dissolved in 1979. Forty-two of these seventy-five congregations joined the United Reformed Church, a number of others either closed, joined other denominations or remained independent. Twenty-five congregations formed the Fellowship of Churches of Christ in 1979. Aware that their former Association had been in considerable decline since 1930, the new Fellowship adopted a 'plant or die' philosophy. With few resources at their disposal, they managed to plant around fifteen new churches, not all of which survived but most of which did. All of the churches in the Fellowship are small, but interestingly even within a ten-year period, the average size of the newly planted churches slightly exceeds that of the older churches. The attempt to continue to plant goes on but even at this stage it is clear that there are some significant cultural differences between the newer and the older churches. This does raise a question concerning the extent to which the historic denominations can absorb new wine in their old wineskins. How flexible will the wineskins of the historic denominations prove to be? The Old Baptist Union with its fifteen congregations has attempted three church plants in recent years and has encountered similar difficulties to those experienced by the Churches of Christ.

The emergence of a church planting movement

So far we have looked at church planting developments in terms of the various denominational compartments to which they relate. However, this approach stands in danger of obscuring the various complex and increasingly important links which are forming between many of these initiatives.

The catalysts for the development of a church planting movement have made unusual partners. The Anglican church planting conferences have been a very important early catalyst. The 1989 conference held at Holy Trinity caused at least one of those attending to ask the question in an article which reported the event, 'Is a church planting movement coming into being?' The conference communicated the sense that, although this was an event largely for Anglicans, they were just part of something much bigger that was just beginning to emerge. Those who have given the primary leadership to this event have been important link people with other catalysts.

A second key ingredient has centred on the activities of Youth With a Mission (YWAM). Throughout most of its existence YWAM has seen itself as an interdenominational evangelistic agency working among youth. Following a crucial conference held in 1980, YWAM became committed to church planting at an international level. One of the important expressions of this change of policy in England was the creation of a training school for church planting teams which was located in St Helen's, Lancashire, under the direction of the Anglican Bob Hopkins.

YWAM had a second important contribution to make by virtue of its involvement in the March for Jesus organisation (MFJ). Following the increasingly high profile of its annual marches throughout the British Isles, the MFJ leadership inevitably began to ask the question, 'What next?' Gradually there emerged a vision for a large-scale programme of church planting. This development formed as a vision for the planting of enough churches throughout the nation to produce at least one evangelical church for every 1,000 people in the population. The inspiration for this concept came in part from the Dawn 2000 strategy propounded by Jim Montgomery and implemented with dramatic effect in the Philippines. The figure of one church for every 1,000 people came directly from this programme.

The vision of MFJ was for a national programme which would enjoy the co-operation of denominational church leaders. In the meantime, a local expression of the Dawn strategy was developing at a town level in St Helens. This initiative was brought together by a YWAM team member from New Zealand, Phil Pawley, who had received some exposure to the Dawn strategy in his own land. It also included Bob Hopkins and the local church that he works with in St Helens.

The MFJ team was very anxious to involve as broad a group as possible in the Dawn strategy. As part of this attempt to broaden involvement, a number of semi-informal discussions with church leaders led to the calling of a consultation on church planting which was held in February 1991. This event was jointly sponsored by the Bible Society, the Evangelical Alliance and March for Jesus. Approximately seventy church leaders from nearly twenty different denominations met together in a time of very frank sharing of their plans, their successes and their failures.

Prior to the church planting consultation the MFJ team had drawn up plans for the launch of a Dawn 2000 movement under the title Challenge 2000, and these plans were made known at the consultation. As a result of the consultation, the steering group for Challenge 2000 was widened. The first project for this group was to hold a major church planting conference in Birmingham in 1992 with the intent that this should act as a catalyst for a broader church planting movement.

It is still too early to say exactly what will develop as a result of the Challenge 2000 initiative. What we can observe is that there are a number of key people and organisations which seem to be cross-fertilising many of these initiatives and that these individuals are drawn from a fairly good spread of denominational backgrounds. The right ingredients for the development of a genuine church planting movement would certainly seem to be present.

For discussion and further study

1. What plans has your own denomination or group of churches for church planting?
2. What goals has your local church set in the area of church planting?
3. What other new churches have been planted in the vicinity of your local church? Have you been able to make a study of any new churches in your area?
4. What scope might there be for working with Christians of other traditions on a church planting project in your area?

Notes

1. David Edwards gives a useful summary of the position of Christianity in Britain during this period in his book *Christian England* (Collins Fount, revised edition, 1988).
2. For a fuller account of the legislation of Constantine with regard to Christianity see J. W. C. Wand, *A History of the Early Church to AD 500*, pp 131–135.
3. For a fuller account of the lives of the Celtic saints see Daphne Pochin Mould, *The Celtic Saints Our Heritage* Clonomore and Reynolds, 1956).
4. See Margaret Deansley, *A History of the Medieval Church 590–1500* (University Press, 1981), p 47.
5. See David Edwards, *Christian England*, p 57.
6. *Prospects for the Nineties* (MARC Europe, 1991), p 23.
7. *Ibid*, p 42.
8. *Ibid*, p 23.
9. *Ibid*.
10. *Ibid*.
11. The substance of this paragraph is taken from a lecture given by Derek Tidball at a British Church Growth Association Conference, Bridges for God, held at Queen's College, Birmingham, in 1987.
12. *Prospects for the Nineties* (MARC Europe, 1991), p 23.
13. All of the above figures cited in this paragraph are taken from the above.
14. *Ibid*.
15. Andrew Walker, *Restoring the Kingdom* (Hodder & Stoughton: London, 1985).
16. Eddie Gibbs (ed), *Ten Growing Churches* (MARC Europe, 1984).
17. A book has been published from papers presented at the 1991 Anglican church planting conference, edited by Bob Hopkins, *Planting New Churches* (Eagle, 1991).
18. See the book on this issue by Bishops Skinner and Pytches, *New Wineskins* (Eagle, 1991).
19. *Ibid*.

CHAPTER FOUR

THE IMPETUS OF CHURCH GROWTH

Martin Robinson

Jim Montgomery, in his book *Dawn 2000: 7 Million Churches To Go*, acknowledges his debt to the church growth movement with these words:

> I was sent to study at the Institute of Church Growth during our first furlough in 1963...the course was life-changing. The fledgling church growth movement provided all kinds of insights and tools for the discipling of nations.[1]

In a variety of ways, all of the significant church planting initiatives outlined in Chapter Three owe a debt to the pioneering work of Donald McGavran and the church growth movement that he fathered. Any serious student of church planting therefore needs to understand something of the major contribution that church growth thinking has made to the practice of church planting.

Church growth as a movement began on the mission field in India, during the active missionary service of its founder, Dr Donald McGavran. When church growth was first developed in the United States during the early 1960s, its insights were taught almost exclusively to those working in overseas mission situations. Gradually, and especially following the publication of McGavran's book *Understanding Church Growth*, there came a realisation that the church growth insights that were being effectively used overseas would also be of value in the United States. During the late 1970s church growth ideas spread to Europe and to other parts of the world which had not previously been thought of as mission fields.[2]

McGavran was insistent that evangelism did not consist only of an individual making a decision for Christ. In India, he had studied the impact of people movements and had spent some time thinking about the process by which whole villages had come to Christ. These whole village decisions were neither the result of gradual individual conversions nor were they the imposition of the will of the leaders or even of a converted majority. They were the result of multiple decisions whereby the impact of some individual decisions, combined with group discussion and debate over a period of time, convinced a whole group of people of the validity of the Christian faith. The result was to create what we might call a 'changed truth horizon', which in turn created an extremely receptive environment in which others could also make decisions for Christ. The place of the Christian community, the church, in this process was crucial.[3]

When a whole community made a decision for Christ in this way, the church that was then planted in their midst tended to look rather different from the churches led by missionaries. In other words, a dramatic process of inculturisation had taken place whereby the message of the gospel and the forms by which it was lived out were adapted to the needs of the community in question. A key ingredient in this process was that it was those from the community or village itself that were explaining the faith and leading others to Christ.

McGavran's radical and controversial concept of the homogeneous unit principle arose from this kind of study. In essence, he made the simple observation that most people come to Christ as a consequence of the witness of someone else from their own culture and class or social grouping. Moreover, churches which express a single culture or social group can often penetrate that same community more effectively because the gospel and the church that flows from it are effectively inculturised.

McGavran never said that the homogeneous unit principle always applied in every situation or that every missionary strategy should be formed around this insight. Nor did he suggest that such an approach was problem free. Others have been very quick to point out the problems of such a strategy, even accusing McGavran of racism.[4] This is not the place to continue that debate but what we can say is that there is an essential link between McGavran's concern that everyone should be able to hear the gospel without having to cross a cultural or social barrier in order to become a Christian, and church planting. If someone is to hear the gospel in appropriate cultural clothes then there needs to be a local expression of the church which is appropriate to their culture.

Further church growth thinking expressed this concern by claiming that people tend to become Christians when three conditions are met. The conditions are those of proximity, congruency and utility. Proximity is clear enough. It simply points out that the church needs to be sufficiently local for people to feel some degree of identification with it as part of the community and, at an even more basic level, to be able to get there. The theme of congruency points to the need for the church to relate strongly to the culture and needs of those it seeks to serve. Utility is a more complex theme which has to do with the general way in which a set of religious beliefs are regarded more widely by society. Clearly, the advocacy of church planting flows strongly from the themes of proximity and congruency as a way of making culturally relevant churches available to as many local communities as possible.

As we have indicated, the new discipline of church growth produced a strong critical response as well as an enthusiastic circle of admirers. In the years since the first controversy in the 1960s, church growth has both become more sophisticated in response to these criticisms and has also developed a number of newer cutting edges. Commenting on this process in *Christianity Today*, Ken Sidey says:

> The church-growth movement itself has matured, fine-tuning its formulas and abandoning some of its early excesses. And it has learned to articulate its principles more clearly.[5]

The same article makes it clear that much of the thinking of the church growth school has become part of the accepted currency of mainstream church life:

After a wave of church-growth bashing in the seventies, many of the movement's ideas have become virtual givens in today's discussions of church vitality. Demographic charts and membership projection graphs have found their way into pastors' studies and board meetings in churches of almost every description. ... The change of attitudes reflects both the recognition by church leaders of the movement's real contributions, and the refinement of church-growth ideas by its own practitioners.

Part of this refinement has come about through the development of other cutting edges that have flowed from church growth practitioners. The same article quotes the church growth researcher Peter Wagner as saying, 'I don't think there's anything intrinsically wrong with the church-growth principles we've developed, or the evangelistic techniques we're using. Yet somehow they don't seem to work.' This is undoubtably an overstatement on Wagner's part since it is possible to point to significant numbers of churches that have used church growth methods on a consistent basis and have seen regular and sometimes dramatic growth as a consequence. What Wagner rightly points to though is that the early church growth insights were not sufficient by themselves.

Wagner's attention had been drawn to the dramatic growth of many Pentecostal churches early on in his church growth career. This interest led him and John Wimber to explore the concept of the marriage of Pentecostal experience with church growth thinking to produce a movement which has been variously described as the 'Third Wave' movement and the 'Signs and Wonders' movement. Closely related to this concern has come a more recent interest in spiritual warfare and prayer. Larry Lea, the senior minister of the Church on the Rock in Arkansas has pioneered some of these concepts in close contact with Peter Wagner.

Other church growth enthusiasts have developed specific strategies for reaching the completely unchurched. Notable among these has been Bill Hybels of Willow Creek Community Church, located in the suburbs of Chicago. Bill Hybels and his team recognise that the concepts that they have developed are most effective when used in new church planting situations. The

Dawn movement, already mentioned at the beginning of this chapter, has formed another strand in terms of developing church growth insights solely in the context of national church planting strategies. These developments have all offered additional cutting edges to the original church growth impetus, but all owe a debt to church growth as a discipline, interacting with church growth to create a significant resource pool for church planting activities.

Key church growth insights

The most important church growth insight for church planters is the place of demographic research in the selection of a location for a new church plant. The question of demographic research is so critical that the whole of Chapter Seven in this book has been devoted to exploring this vital ingredient. However, there are also a number of additional key church growth insights that are important for church planters. For this reason it would be important for any group wishing to engage in church planting to be exposed to some systematic church growth teaching. The most comprehensive and available source for such teaching in the UK is the weekend church growth course offered by the British and Foreign Bible Society (in Scotland the same courses are available through the National Bible Society of Scotland). A number of Bible colleges offer similar courses, while Spurgeon's College incorporates church growth teaching in its church planting course. A number of other organisations in the UK offer training which has some relationship to the issues raised by church growth.[6]

The following summary represents some of the key concepts that church growth offers to potential church planters in addition to the question of demographic research.

1. The Great Commission calls to us to make disciples, not just converts. A disciple is one who seeks to follow Christ in an active way, seeking to work out the implications of faith rather than becoming simply a passive believer. The way in which converts are nurtured and fully integrated into the

body of Christ as functioning members of that body is explored as part of this concern. Concepts related to nurture, such as the interplay of different sized groups (cell, congregation and celebration), have been pioneered by church growth thinkers. The importance of developing multiple friendships as part of the process of incorporation features in much church growth literature.[7]

2. Church growth advocates the need to seek the receptive. Such teaching points out that the Holy Spirit is already at work with people in a given community, preparing them for the message that we will bring. Our priority, therefore, needs to be to find ways of discovering who these people are.[8]

3. Churches do not grow and decline by accident. The factors which cause decline or assist growth, some of which are unique to particular cultures, have been researched as part of this concern.

4. The part played by every member of the body of Christ is critical. It was noted early on by church growth researchers that the mobilisation of members is a key hallmark of growing churches across all cultures. This observation has given rise to a great deal of teaching in the area of gift discovery, gift deployment and gift development.

5. There is a recognition that growing churches are heavily dependent on the contribution of gifted leaders. The way in which leadership styles change as churches grow, the importance of team building, the need to be skilled in the introduction of change and the way in which leadership gifts interact with each other have all formed major areas of research and teaching.[9]

6. The need for an evangelistic strategy as opposed to the search for the 'good idea' that will work is advocated by church growth. The concept of evangelism as comprising presence, proclamation and persuasion elements as part of a related whole has become almost synonymous with church growth teaching.[10]

So far so good. Church growth offers a highly developed and sophisticated framework of study which can help potential church planters to be much more effective than they might be otherwise. But the critics of church growth have a point when they suggest that all this seems rather mechanistic, too reliant on methods. What about prayer, the walk of faith, the unexpected that comes when God speaks to us in new ways, the place of revelation and prophecy? What happens when, to quote again the words of Peter Wagner, we diligently try all these techniques and 'they don't seem to work'?

No greater contrast between the potentially dry approach of church growth methodology and the inspirational approach of prayer might be expected when we talk about the final insight of church growth, the place of planning. Yet, as we will see, there is not necessarily a conflict between these two approaches.

Planners and prophets

All too often in the Christian community, such matters as the setting of goals and objectives have been seen as somehow unspiritual as a discipline. By contrast, the approach of prayer and of prophetic insight are often seen as more truly spiritual. So the planners and the prophets are pitted against one another, the one apparently operating in the carnal flesh the other in the heavenly realm, truly discerning the will of God. This is clearly an unhelpful dichotomy. Jim Montgomery has this to say about planning:

> It can also be an intensely spiritual activity. It can be done with much prayer and seeking of God's will. It can be an expression of deep faith that God in His power can use His children to accomplish much more than experience would indicate. It can be an honest attempt to obey more effectively our Lord's command, to be a doer of the Word and not a hearer only.[11]

Successful church planting requires both the planner and the prophet, and both need to be infused with something of each other. Sometimes the planner proposes a tentative plan while the prophet needs to listen carefully to what God is saying. On other occasions, the prophet needs to speak out and the planner needs to be ready to give creative form to the words that are spoken. These apparently contradictory emphases not only need each other, they can be a tremendously powerful blend.

Although I do not feel very comfortable with the clever phrase often quoted by church growth enthusiasts and attributed to Robert Schuller, 'If you fail to plan, you're planning to fail', nevertheless there is a certain truth in his assertion in the sense that we all engage in some degree of planning, the only question is the degree to which we are consciously aware of what our plan is. Without a conscious awareness of our plan we can hardly assess its strengths and weaknesses. Even worse, without some articulation of our plan it becomes difficult for us to communicate to others what it is we are attempting to achieve.

Planting any church is always a significant undertaking! There are many planning techniques available to us but whichever one we choose, the heart of all good planning lies in the attempt to break down the size of the task into manageable parts. This procedure not only allows us to manage the task in hand but also to utilise the various gifts that the individuals working with us are able to offer. A good plan decides on who does what, by when, the means by which they will accomplish it, and makes some assessment of the resources that they will need. As we plan, it is essential that we maintain a healthy balance between prophetic insight and planning competence.

The planning process

Although, as we have said, ther are many planning techniques, the following process is one useful method for approaching the planning process.

1. Face the facts

What facts do we need? Most of the facts that are needed for church planting are outlined in Chapter Seven of this book. However, the really critical question is not the quantity of information that you have, useful as this may be, but rather the way in which you use the facts that you have collected. It is essential to interpret data with a creative mind and a listening ear.

The congregation with whom I worship began to collect some demographic information on the community to assist the focus of their mission. Although we had always known that there were a good many older people in the community, it was not until we had completed some door-to-door calling, which recorded the age group of those that we were calling on, that we began to realise how many older people were living in the immediate vicinity of the building that we use for public worship. The question then arose, how was the new information going to affect our basic strategy? We therefore began a process of prayerful reflection. Given that our church is largely composed of people in the thirty and forty age group, was God calling us to a ministry that would reach the large numbers of older people in the community or was he giving that task to others?

We made an assessment of the situation of other churches in the area and soon realised that although they did have many more older people in their churches than we did, nevertheless, the total number of older people in all the churches did not amount to much more than a fraction of those who live in the surrounding area. This then forced us back to our original question, what was God calling us to do? We decided that the next step was to try to assess why it was that few older people came to our church. We looked at what they had said about us during our calling programme. Most had known of our existence and many had identified us as a church 'for young people'. We did not know how that perception had arisen but it was fairly accurate given the age group that attended.

Where to next? More prayer, followed by the question, 'Then why do those older people come who do attend our church? Do they have something that marks them out as different?' More prayerful reflection told us that all of the older people in our church do have something in common—they are all old in years but young in heart! We therefore came to the conclusion that God was calling us to a specific ministry to those older people who are young at heart.

I tell this story not because I want anyone to copy what we have done but because it illustrates the relationship between the gathering of facts, prayerful reflection which involves more listening to God than talking to God, and a process of honest questioning. These are the vital ingredients in the process which we have called 'facing the facts'.

2. Establishing objectives

The key ingredient at this stage of the planning process in establishing objectives is to ask, 'What are we here for?' and, 'What kind of church do we want this to be?' This second question will be answered to some extent by decisions that lead to the choice of model for the church plant, the choice of the sponsoring body, the target area and the team composition. However, once the actual church plant is being planned the general answers that have already been given can now become even more specific. A way of helping to make them more specific is to formulate a statement of purpose for the church. It can be very helpful to make sure that such a statement appears on all of the printed material that the church uses. A statement of purpose begins by saying, 'This church exists to. ...'

I recently visited the second largest church in North America, with some 15,000 attending its three weekend services. One of the members spoke to a gathering of pastors and told them that the statement of purpose of that church was so well communicated to the members that every member could tell you what the mission or purpose of the church was.

A second way of helping such a process is to understand the way in which the churchmanship of your own tradition is being consciously adapted to meet the needs of the situation in which the church is being planted. Usually, a particular community has strong underlying currents which affect the way in which people regard what you are trying to accomplish. You need to be sensitive to these themes by means of prayer and prophetic insight.

One small example of such responsiveness is that a strongly liturgical church may need to pay great attention to the simplification and explanation of its liturgy. A more informal church will need to be aware of the strength of its own unwritten liturgies which will have been brought unconsciously from previous situations. Above all, it will be necessary to 'read' at a deep level the needs of the community and to be flexible enough to make changes where necessary. The precise needs of your community may mean that those with a tradition of clerical dress will need to do without it from time to time. My own tradition is one which abhors clerical dress and yet I have been involved in church planting in areas where at least a clerical collar has been essential in communicating that our worship place is a safe place to be.

The fine tuning of objectives calls for a continuing flexibility and constant openness to change. God seems to be always a God who delights in surprising us by what he asks of us!

3. Set goals

When using techniques such as goal setting, it is vitally important to remember that techniques can make valuable servants but dreadful masters. I remember the experience of an American pastor who was working for a short time in a British church. He suggested that the church hold a short crusade or mission and then he set about organising the mission using a set of procedures that he had used on many previous occasions. Part of the process included the setting of a goal for the number of converts that the crusade was going to produce. The pastor asked each church member to place on a piece of paper the number of converts that they believed would come as a result of the mission. Some had great faith and put down fairly high numbers, while others seemed to have almost no faith at all and did not think that any converts would be made. Unperturbed by any reply, no matter what the number, the pastor proceeded to add up all of the numbers to produce an average figure. He confidently announced that the resulting average figure would be the number of converts produced by the crusade. Not a few of his church members and certainly some of the leaders were somewhat incredulous concerning his approach and questioned him about its scriptural basis. He cheerfully admitted that there was no basis in Scripture but that nevertheless it had worked every other time that he had done it and therefore no one needed to be concerned. Feeling a little uneasy, his church members accepted his assurances and the crusade went ahead. In the event there were no converts at all and the shattered pastor returned to the United States somewhat earlier than he had previously planned.

This somewhat unfortunate approach to goal setting does not mean that there cannot be more helpful approaches. Bracknell Family Church holds regular guest services to which members of the congregation are encouraged to bring their relatives, neighbours and friends. The church sets goals for the number of visitors that they believe will attend at each service. However, these goals are not just pulled out of thin air. They are the end result of a process by which people are encouraged to write down the names of those people that they hope to invite to the next event. It is on the basis of these realistic intentions that goals are set. I do not mean that this is simply a matter of adding up the names and using the total as a goal. Clearly, there is no guarantee that every person will actually come or indeed that others who are not known about in advance might decide to come. Nevertheless, there is some relationship between the goals that are set and the plans that are being made to implement those goals.

The Bible Society's training course, 'What Makes Churches Grow?' includes a helpful selection on goal setting which outlines five characteristics of good goals. The course recommends that good goals should be:

1. Relevant—the goal should have some clear and direct bearing in terms of achieving the overall objective that the church has set.
2. Measurable—it should be possible to know when and how the goal set has been accomplished. (This is generally the ingredient of goal setting with which Christians seem to have the most difficulty.)
3. Achievable—there must be some relationship between the goal being set and the resources that the church has even if it is only a faith resource.

4. Significant—it is important to set goals that are seen to be stretching the church in some way.
5. Personal—we ought only to set goals that involve ourselves in some way and not just set goals for others to accomplish.

Clearly, prayer must form an important part of the goal setting exercise both in terms of the selection of actual goals and in providing the means by which any goal is reached. Prayerful goal setting can be used for large matters, for example, you may decide that your local church should plant five new churches in the next ten years, or in smaller matters, for example, you may decide that your church will recruit ten new children to your Sunday school during the next year. But whether large or small, it will sometimes be the case that you will not necessarily accomplish your goals. This should not invalidate your goal setting but cause you to prayerfully reflect on why you did not succeed. (Step 5 in the planning process comments more fully on this latter point.)

4 Make plans

All too often, Christians have a tendency to act as though the process of setting goals is the same thing as seeing those goals fulfilled. There seems to be a feeling that the act of setting goals represents the end of the process and that somehow the goals will be achieved purely because they have been agreed on. The reality is somewhat different! It is essential that we move quickly from the setting of goals to an active planning process that will decide on how these goals are going to be realised.

There are two key considerations in this planning step. The first is that of resources. In deciding how we are going to accomplish our goals we have to be able to assess the resources that we have at our disposal to see whether or not they are going to be sufficient to accomplish our goal. More often than not the most important resource that we need is not that of money or a building so much as people. Who do we have with the gifts that we need and do they have a sense of call and vision to pick up the particular responsibility that we have in mind? If we do not have such people we have two choices. We can either pray that God will send the people that we need, or we can change our goals! I never cease to be surprised by the number of churches that I come across who have prayed in the people resources that they have needed when all else looked hopeless.

This does not mean that physical resources such as money, equipment and buildings are not also important. There is nothing more frustrating for individuals than to be given a task and then to be denied the other resources that they need to be able to fulfill the task that they have been assigned. For example, I frequently come across churches who have good musicians but then fail to provide proper sound equipment for their musicians. Perhaps this is because those who are not musicians do not really appreciate the true costs involved in producing good music transmission. Realism in resource allocation is essential.

The second consideration in planning is that of proper delegation. It is very rarely the case that one or two individuals can complete a complex goal by themselves. A major project may require the active participation of the whole church if it is to be successful. It is therefore crucial to engage in a planning exercise that breaks the task down into identifiable parts and then to assign a planning process to each one of those parts. For example, a church may have decided to engage in a programme of door-to-door visitation. The planning process for this activity could be broken down into three groups, one for recruiting and training the callers, one for administration of the programme and one for the co-ordination of prayer support. Each of these groups will need to have a timetable for accomplishing their part of the plan so that the various responsibilities will work together to accomplish the goal. It can often be helpful to put these parts into a visual format so that each group can see how their contribution works with the other parts to allow the goal to be fulfilled. (See the diagram opposite for an example.)

5. Assess the results

I know of an Anglican parish church who decided to plant a new congregation in another part of the parish. The original group normally numbered around 160 in worship. They selected

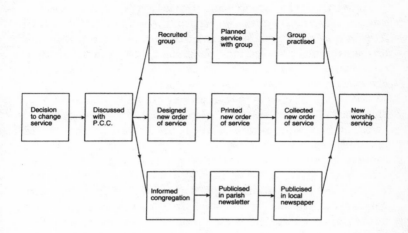

approximately twenty-five people who lived in the part of the parish where they wished to plant a new church. They engaged in a time of planning, which included the setting of goals, and especially goals relating to the number of people they believed would come to the first service. They had set what they believed to be an ambitious goal in relation to the size of the parish church and the size of the core group. In the event, 250 people came to the first service, a total which greatly exceeded their original goal!

In a world as uncertain as the one in which we live, we will not always meet our goals. Sometimes we will exceed them and perhaps more often we will fall short of the goal that we have set. Failing to hit our goal is not as important as being ready to ask some hard questions about what actually happened. Did we set the wrong goals, or did we fail to plan adequately? Even if we achieved everything that we set out to achieve, are there nevertheless some things that we could have done better?

The completion of a project for which we have set goals is the ideal time for us to begin a new planning process, to bring all of our plans before God in prayer, to listen carefully to the changes that God wants to bring, to see what God has taught us through the exercise that we have already engaged in and to rethink our objectives in the light of our experience. Making this kind of honest assessment is in fact a new kind of facing of the facts and so brings us full circle to the beginning of a new planning cycle.

This is often a critical time because even after the completion of a successful planning cycle, there is a natural tendency to slip back into the old habits in which there was an absence of planning and so a tendency to be reactive (ie, reacting to events) rather than to be pro-active (ie, seeking to shape events through our active involvement). A conscious determination to plan on a regular basis helps to break a reactive ministry pattern. Important as this lesson is for all ministry, it will never be more important than in the process of church planting that begins with a decision to plant and ends with the actual launch of the new congregation. The physical realities that face us when planting a new congregation bring an obvious demand for a planning process. The successful completion of a new church launch should spur us on to consider what new vistas God wants us to plan towards.

For discussion and further study

1. As an individual, are you naturally more inclined to prayer than planning?

2. If you are hoping to plant a new church, is there a good balance between those that plan and those that pray in your core group?

3. Can you think of projects in which you have been involved which would have benefited from a greater planning input? If so, what might you have achieved beyond the results that were actually produced?

Notes

1. Jim Montgomery, *Dawn 2000* (Highland Books: Crowborough, 1990), p 26.
2. The two best British works on the church growth movement are Roy Pointer, *How do Churches Grow?* (MARC Europe; first published by Marshall Morgan and Scott, 1984) and Eddie Gibbs, *I Believe in Church Growth* (Hodder & Stoughton, revised edition 1990).
3. Serious study on this process was first undertaken by the Methodist J. Waskom Pickett who was assisted by Donald McGavran. Waskom's work was published under the title, Christian Mass Movements in India, Lucknow, India: Lucknow Publishing House, 1933.
4. The *International Review of Mission* devoted the whole of its July 1968 edition to the subject of church growth. These articles sparked of a lively though short-lived debate.
5. Ken Sidey, 'Church Growth Fine Tunes Its Formulas', *Christianity Today* (24 June 1991).
6. Organisations offering training on church growth-related topics include Bible Society, MARC Europe, Administry, CPAS, and Scripture Union. A number of other organisations offer training to their own volunteers on church growth-related topics. These include Oasis, British Youth for Christ, and YWAM.
7. Church growth research in the United States suggests that when someone has made more than six friends in a church within the first six months of joining that church, then the likelihood is that they will remain in membership. The less friendships that they develop in that crucial period, the less likely they are to remain in membership.
8. This issue is dealt with in more detail in Chapter Twelve of this book.
9. See David Cormack, *Team Spirit* (MARC Europe, 1987).
10. This concept was first explored by Ralph Winter and now forms part of the Bible Society church growth course, 'What Makes Churches Grow?'
11. Jim Montgomery and Donald McGavran, *The Discipling of a Nation*, (Overseas Crusades, 1980), p 130.

CHAPTER FIVE
HOW DO OTHERS PLANT?
Martin Robinson

Church planting is taking place with ever increasing pace across our world. Even in Britain, the momentum is gathering. A great deal of successful church planting has already happened and we are able to learn some lessons from the successes of others. There really is no limit to the number of ways in which new churches can be planted. However, there are a number of approaches which are more common than others. It can help potential church planters to see what others have done already, to think which method looks most like the model that you are planning and to reflect on the advantages and disadvantages of each approach for your situation.

You don't have to read too many books on church planting before you realise that there are a wide variety of models available and that almost every writer has his own list and his own terminology. At first sight there seems to be little in common between these lists and there is certainly no agreed terminology.

How can we find a way through this maze of models? First, almost all writers make a distinction between the planting of a completely new work and church planting which is in some sense an extension of the work of an existing church. Some would call this the difference between pioneer planting and mother-daughter planting. Others use the technical terms sodality and modality, which simply means that specialist church planting agencies (sodalities) usually engage in pioneer work, whereas by definition, congregations (modalities) have to be involved in mother-daughter church planting initiatives.

Clearly, the New Testament's description of the kind of

church planting engaged in by Paul and Barnabas shows it was of the pioneering type. This rather rough and ready distinction is somewhat complicated in today's world by the existence of denominational structures. Often, church planting in an area where a church already exists is still described as pioneer planting because the group that is doing the planting has no existing group nearby even though there may be plenty of other churches around.

Second, although the terms used by different writers to describe the church planting models of pioneers and extenders vary considerably, nevertheless the basic descriptions of these models reveal a common set of approaches whatever name each writer gives them. The precise name that is used is not as important as the nature of the approach itself.

The contribution of church growth

The church growth school has almost certainly produced more work on the question of church planting than any other school of mission thought, and partly for this reason the basic models used in this chapter draw very heavily on categories which were first devised at the School of World Mission in Pasadena. These same models have since been adopted by the church growth teaching programme of the British and Foreign Bible Society (BFBS) which we will use as our primary headings in this chapter. The BFBS listing of models also makes the basic distinction referred to above between pioneering church planting and church planting through the extension of the work of an existing church, but uses the terms church planting by groups and church planting by churches.

Two other more recent attempts to list church planting models need to be noted. Bob Hopkins has written two booklets in the Grove Booklet Series on the issue of church planting. The subtitle for his first booklet is 'Models for Mission in the Church of England'. He lists ten different models, most of which fit fairly well into the categories in the BFBS listing, but all of which, as the title suggests, relate strongly to the particular structures found in the Church of England. Peter

Wagner, who teaches at Fuller, has recently produced a book on church planting.[1] As we might expect, his book contains a listing which draws largely on the Fuller School of World Mission list but which has one significant difference which we will comment on later in the chapter.

Church planting by churches

Autonomous daughter churches

There are at least four ways of creating autonomous daughter churches, each of which has the intention that within a fairly short space of time, the new work will have its own finances, organisation, authority structure, pastoral care, evangelistic programmes and possibly its own distinct worship ethos. In short, as the subheading suggests, it will be autonomous. But why separate a group as decisively as this?

There might be many reasons for such a distinct split. The distance between the daughter church and the sending church might make a continued supervision from the mother church unworkable, the mother church might lack the gifts and/or call among its staff members to exercise long-term oversight, the gifts of those doing the planting might be such that a 'hands off' approach might be more effective, a tradition of congregational autonomy might push people's expectations in this direction, or quite simply there may be sufficient tension in the arrangement that separation is both desirable and inevitable. What, then, are the four types of autonomous daughter church?

Church planting by hiving off At one time, this was the most common form of church planting engaged in by nonconformist churches. In the nineteenth century, a strong mother church would often give birth to many daughter churches by hiving members off. Frequently, the mother church was in the city centre, and as cities grew the church members of the city church spread far and wide. Visionary pastors were often quick to seize the opportunities for church planting that such population movement brought.

The widespread tendency in some communities for people to

go to church by car (even when they worship at a church nearby!) means that the pressure to begin other churches by hiving off is not as strong today. However, there can be factors other than accessibility which might encourage churches to hive off.

First, although many Christians might be willing to travel relatively long distances in order to attend a church with which they have strong personal ties, it is not always possible to persuade neighbours or other contacts in the immediate community to make the same journey. The creation of a new church in an area where a sizeable number of other members from the same church also live can significantly increase the evangelistic potential of those members. This is especially so when those members live in an area which has its own distinct identity, separate from and different to the area where the sending church is located. The planting of a new church produces the possibility of multiplying many more evangelistic contacts through the creation of community programmes that it would be almost impossible to maintain from a distance. Most communities need the church to have a high local profile in order for them to take the church seriously.

Second, there may be a group of people attending the church who live relatively nearby but who would prefer a different style of worship that, for a variety of reasons, cannot be accommodated in the present church structures. I am not suggesting that church planting should be used as a way of lessening potential conflict in a church although it might have that side effect! Rather, there may very well be an evangelistic opportunity in terms of reaching completely unchurched people in the very same community by using a different style of worship. It may simply be the case that the existing church is having a significant impact on those others in the community who already have some kind of church contact and that this successful ministry would be jeopardised either by a change of style or by accommodating a secondary focus. Above Bar Church in Southampton, which has grown significantly in recent years, is about to engage in a church plant which will have the specific intention of reaching those who are completely unchurched.[2] The new church will necessarily have a different feel to its worship and philosophy of ministry compared with anything that currently happens at Above Bar.

Third, it may be that even a growing church is not able to meet the needs of a particular socio-economic group nearby. It may take a different kind of church in terms of building, worship style, leadership, ministry and even size, to be effective in reaching out to that missing group. Perhaps there are already some in the church who are from the target group who can be hived off as mature Christians to begin a different style of church.[3]

Church planting by colonisation As Peter Wagner suggests, the colonisation approach represents a much more radical form of hiving off.[4] Colonisation can be said to take place when those that are being sent out actually move home to a new target community.

Such a move might mean such a long distance transfer that those who are committed to be part of such a project would need to obtain new jobs as well as new homes. This radical commitment tends to be made when a specific area has been identified by the group either as an area of great need, or of great opportunity, or both! New towns, inner city areas, and large council estates represent some of the target areas chosen by churches as places which can best be reached by encouraging groups of families to move home and establish a new work. In Britain, church planting by colonisation has been attempted by some of the networks among the new churches, in particular by the Harvestime group.

Sometimes, the colonisation would be close enough that people could commute to existing jobs while transferring their home. This would be likely to happen if a large new housing area was being constructed at the edge of, or near to, an existing older community.

Church planting by adoption In 1985, St Barnabas in Kensington occupied a church building that was intended to seat 1,000 but the congregation had dwindled to less than 20. Just three miles away, Holy Trinity, Brompton, had grown to around 1,300 people. Was there any possibility of help? Following discussions with the bishop and others, some 100 people were sent out from Holy Trinity under the leadership of John Irvine. Today the congregation has risen to some 800 people.[5] A successful adoption had taken place! This does not mean that there was no pain in such a process both for the receiving church, which saw its churchmanship radically altered, and for the sending church which lost many of its talented leaders.

Holy Trinity has engaged in a number of such adoptions and the vicar, John Collins, has commented on the cost in terms of leadership, money and misunderstanding. Reflecting on the financial drain, John Collins has written, 'I remember when my entire mail for a year seemed to be requests to transfer convenants to St Mark's Battersea Rise!'[6] Some accused Holy Trinity of building an empire, to which John Collins has responded:

> This 'empire' has cost the church £120,000 a year; it has cost all our best leaders whom the church has nurtured; and in fact is no empire at all, because the new churches are totally independent, operating in their own deaneries or dioceses.[7]

Some may wish to argue that this process represents a church renewal rather than a church plant but, in reality, the degree of change that is required in such a project makes this in effect a new church plant.

Church planting by adoption can also help in a variety of other situations. Sometimes, the founding church doesn't actually send out a group of its own members to begin a new church but is approached by an existing group of people to oversee a project. This could be the adoption of a group of people who have moved to an area and who feel the need for some support in terms of advice and counsel, or it may be a small church which stands in danger of closure but which is too far away for members to be transferred to it asks to be adopted by a larger church with whom they have had contact. In some of these arrangements, there might be a considerable distance involved and the mother church might only be able to give advice and occasional resource in the form of occasional preachers, musicians and other team members.

On other occasions, a church will be planning to plant in a particular area only to discover that a very sympathetic group of Christians already have a home Bible study group or some other such meeting in the target area. In such a situation, it makes sense to explore the possibilities for adoption.

I know of a church where the entire leadership phoned the young pastor of the church concerned and told him that they were leaving and would hand over all responsibility to him. They had not fallen out with the pastor so much as with each other. The shepherds deserted the flock! The young pastor was not really able to carry the load on his own and, without outside help, the church would certainly have collapsed completely. An adoption strategy can often lead to the successful replanting of a church which would otherwise not exist.

Church planting by accident The term 'accidental' is really a euphemism for an unplanned church plant but one that takes place when a church split occurs. Why are we mentioning such a process if it is unplanned? You would hardly want to plan or, even worse, to deliberately choose such a church planting method! At the same time, we have to be realistic and recognise that such things do happen. Although doctrine and/or worship style are often cited as the cause for many church splits, more often than not, some kind of personality clash lies behind most divisions. I mention this not to condemn so much as to be realistic about the possibility of contructing creative ways ahead in terms of rescuing something for the kingdom out of such a situation. We don't want to plan for a split but creative planning once such a situation has arisen can be crucial.

Peter Wagner quotes no less an authority than Donald McGavran and George Hunter as suggesting that church splits often lead to two congregations, each of which prosper and both of which together are larger than the original congregation.[8] Fortunate indeed are those who experience such an outcome! Perhaps that does happen in those parts of the world where the soil is fertile for church planting. I suspect that the experience of many churches in the United Kingdom is that the total witness for the kingdom of God is diminished by such a split. It is rare for either group to prosper and both factions may eventually die as a consequence of a debilitating split.

This does not mean that such an outcome is inevitable. The quality of the leadership of the churches that are involved in any kind of split will be severely tested. More often than not it calls for an act of real kingdom statesmanship for leaders to attempt to rise above such situations and try to use them creatively. An agreed, if sorrowful, parting of the quality of Paul and Barnabas is preferable to the acrimonious tearing of a congregation, with members being canvassed and forced to take sides in a situation where they will probably have divided loyalties. The temptation for those in leadership of the church that is being taken from is to want to hold on to all or most of those who are going. It might be better not to seek to hold on but to be concerned with the right evangelistic strategies to replace those who are going. The impact of those who are going is often to unsettle some members who will not subsequently stay with the departing group. It is far better for those who are going to think in terms of the new people that they might attract rather than to seek to justify the rightness of their going by pointing to the number of people who share their inherent criticism of the existing church by leaving also. The more statesmanlike the going the more likely will be the healing at a later date. Splits which take place with both congregations staying in the same denomination are much easier to heal than when the new church also leaves the denomination.

Semi-autonomous satellite churches—the strawberry runner method

The concept of a large mother church planting semi-autonomous satellite congregations which meet in larger area celebrations can be witnessed in many countries around the world. South American congregations have been particularly successful in using this model. In Britain it was almost unheard of before the early 1970s, and when it first took place, the term 'strawberry runner' was first coined to describe what was taking place. The phrase was applied to the pioneering work of St Mary's Anglican Church in Chester le Street, County Durham, first under the leadership of Patrick Blair, rector from 1971 to 1978 and then under Ian Bunting, rector from 1978 to 1987.[9]

The concept as developed at St Mary's was to form area worship groups which were in effect separate worship centres in the geographically distinct parts of the parish. Six centres were established in the parish in addition to that of the original worship centre. By this means, weekly attendance grew dramatically to some 600 people.

A quite different expression of the 'strawberry runner' principle, which has been pioneered across an area much bigger than that of an Anglican parish and which has more of the hallmarks of some of the South American examples, has been that of Ichthus Christian Fellowship.[10] Beginning as a single congregation in Forest Hill, south-east London, in 1974, Ichthus has now expanded to include forty congregations which operate as three area groups for larger celebration meetings. Attendance is conservatively estimated at 2,300 and continues to grow strongly.

In the case of both St Mary's and Ichthus, even though each of the local worship centres might have their own leaders and even on occasion staff delegated specifically to each centre, nevertheless, they are served by one central administration. The staff members and leaders are all ultimately accountable to the one corporate leadership. The leaders and staff could therefore be moved on the basis of strategic decisions that would be taken by the whole team.

The pioneering work of Ichthus has inspired others to imitate their model elsewhere, while the work of St Mary's, Chester le Street, really forms the basis for a whole variety of church planting models within the Anglican Church which can loosely be described as church plants within the parish. Bob Hopkins describes three variations of the 'plant within a parish theme', of which the strawberry model forms just one. The essential feature which marks out all of these churches is that no matter how many places of worship they might have, the model contains an interesting mix of features, some of which would lead one to say that this is just one church with many meeting places while other features might lead one to say that these are autonomous congregations which are centrally served.

We might be better able to understand this curious mix by remembering that in some situations, the strawberry runner model might represent an excellent approach for initiating church plants but might need to be seen as a transition model for some churches. Interestingly, there is a significant review of the model taking place at Chester le Street at the present time.[11] It is likely that some church plants will become completely autonomous parishes while others may relate more strongly to the mother church. It is still too early to say what might happen in the Ichthus version but, as time passes, it may well be that local plants will look increasingly like autonomous congregations in what is effectively a regional denomination with something more like a presbyterian style of church government.

Multiple site churches

Congregations which are organised on a multiple site principle share many of the characteristics of the strawberry runner model but are much more clearly one church meeting in several locations. There is one membership roll, one organisational structure and one leadership. Even the preaching staff rotate so that each 'congregation' shares members of the same staff rather than having staff members delegated to them. In one multiple site church that I know, each of the congregations receive exactly the same sermons, preached on a rota system to ensure that each group obtains essentially the same teaching. Such a system works well when the original building becomes too full and when there is a perception that evangelism would be more effective through the use of multiple sites. Most of these situations would also tend to meet as a single church on a regular basis.

One might want to ask why a church would want to work in this way rather than plant autonomous or semi-autonomous congregations. The answer is usually related to the degree to which there is a perceived advantage in retaining a strong single identity. This is most helpful in the situation of an Anglican parish where there is a strong parish identity. However, this approach to church planting is not limited to Anglican churches. Zion Baptist Church in Creech St Michael, Taunton, is using this approach as part of its church growth strategy. So far it has planted one other congregation and others are planned. The two congregations meet separately in the morning but have a joint service together in the evening. It is probably too soon to judge how successful this approach will be in the longer term. It would be all too easy for an Anglican parish using this system to retrench to the parish church when times become difficult, while there have not been enough non-Anglican examples of this approach to know how successful this method might be. It is hard to see how one could prevent a non-conformist version of this model becoming a number of autonomous churches over the longer term, with the various churches being bonded through a peculiar form of local presbyterian government.

Church planting by multiple congregations

There are two potential ways of tackling this model. One would be for a single church to develop separate congregations, each of which meet at different times in the same building. The intention of each congregation would be to develop its own staff and programme in order to meet the needs of radically different socio-economic groups. One very well known example of such an approach is that of the 'nine o'clock' service at St Thomas, Crookes, Sheffield.[12] Unlike many churches, the nine o'clock referred to is pm not am! This is just one of a number of worship services, each of which is designed to meet the needs of very specific groups that the church seeks to reach. The nine o'clock service was first developed to meet the needs of the unchurched urban young, many of whom frequent the club land of Sheffield. It began in 1986 with some fifty young people. Within 5 years, there have been occasions when attendance has reached 500.

A second broad approach is for the additional congregations to be completely autonomous, possibly even of another denomination, but the goal of reaching distinct socio-economic or ethnic groups remains the same. It was quite common in Britain in the 1960s and 1970s for white-led inner city congregations to have shared building arrangements with one or other of the many emerging black-led congregations that were then growing so strongly. In many cases, the black-led church who came as guests to share the building have become owners of those same buildings and so there is now no longer a shared building arrangement.

It is far less common in Britain than it is in the United States for congregations to deliberately seek to create separate congregations where the leaders are initially financed directly by the mother church and which seek to minister to the needs of a distinct ethnic group. There seems to exist in Britain a feeling that somehow every racial group should always worship in a multiracial setting even if it can be demonstrated that such an arrangement lessens the evangelistic impact of the church.

There are some isolated examples of the development of separate worship services where language rather than race is the issue. For example, I know of a Chinese church which has two worship services, one in English which tends to meet the needs of second generation Chinese and the needs of Chinese students from a variety of countries who may not speak Cantonese, and a second, Cantonese-speaking service for those older Chinese who are mostly from Hong Kong and many of whom are involved in the restaurant trade.

There is a need to review our practice in this area of church planting. We have to admit that we have been very unsuccessful in reaching many ethnic groups on the basis of our existing evangelistic strategies. Strangely, we are quite prepared to spend vast sums of money in training and supporting personnel to go overseas and attempt to win people to Christ from the very same ethnic groups who are now on our doorstep but, so far, nothing like the same funding has been available for ethnic church planting in Britain. We would hardly commend our overseas missionaries if they created European churches as a strategy for reaching those of other cultures and yet we do not have any significant mission plans for the creation of ethnic congregations in Britain.

One wonders what would have happened to the mainline denominations if they had developed a mission strategy for meeting the needs of Afro-Caribbean peoples when large-scale immigration to Britain first began in the 1950s. Remember that some 90 per cent of West Indian people were affiliated to a church when in the West Indies and the majority of these people belonged to Anglican, Methodist, Baptist and other mainline churches when they actually arrived in Britain. Can you imagine the leadership and spiritual resources that might have been available to existing church fellowships if they had devised a mission strategy for reaching out to such people using the already available black leadership? Some might argue that to have formed separate congregations on the basis of race would have been to create a system of religious apartheid, but has the alternative really been any better?

The best that has often been managed has been to opt for a rental of the building to growing black-led groups. Admittedly, even these shared building arrangements have not been without their tensions! I remember preaching in a white-led congregation during their rather poorly attended evening service. A black-led church was using the attached church hall for their somewhat more exuberant style of worship at the same time. As the white congregation sang their ancient hymns, they could hear the sound of tambourines and lusty singing wafting in from under the door. It sounded as if it would have been much more exciting to have been in the church hall!

These kinds of arrangements do not have to be limited to the provision of worship services for different groups in the inner city. It can often be the case that shared building arrangements work well for the planting of new churches in new housing areas. Once again there can be some tensions. I visited one church where both congregations shared a building and used it at the same time on a Sunday morning. The sanctuary was divided with a well sound-proofed screen to allow both groups to worship without disturbing each other. The idea was that after worship, and on many other occasions, the screens came back and provided a large area for a whole variety of activities. Other facilities in the building were, of course, all shared on a permanent basis. However, in this particular case, although the screen was sound proof, it wasn't smell proof and the nonconformist end of the building was often invaded with all kinds of unfamiliar smells of worship emanating from the Anglo-Catholic smells and bells end of the sanctuary!

In areas where high land costs make church planting a very costly business, this kind of shared building arrangement can sometimes allow churches to be financed where none might otherwise be built. Even if funds are available for one building, a shared arrangement might allow the provision of a building which is much larger or better equipped than if a single church were financing it. In addition to the benefit of saving on initial capital costs, there can be considerable saving in terms of running costs thus releasing funds for mission that might otherwise be spent on fabric. A shared building might also encourage the churches who use it to engage in other activities together that they might not be able to finance individually. Some churches can add youth workers, or counselling services on a co-operative basis whereas such facilities would not have been possible working separately.

In other situations, some churches have money but limited personnel who have an entrepreneurial spirit, whereas some churches are blessed with some very imaginative 'self-starters' but lack funding. Putting these two ingredients together in a shared project might allow Christian work to go forward in a way that would not take place otherwise. I know of a church building that belongs to a small and declining mainstream church with an elderly congregation. If that church closes, it is unlikely that any other group would be able to buy it because property prices are so high in that area. It would almost certainly be bought by a property developer and the opportunity for Christian witness in the area would be severely diminshed. As it is, they have allowed two other groups to use the building at another time and the new groups are growing significantly. At this point, it is even conceivable that the growth of the other two groups who use the building will encourage the original church to be more creative and hopeful in terms of their own activity. What might have been just one more closed church may well end up as three thriving groups in one place due to the generous spirit of the original group.

Churches planted by groups

Churches planted by a mission team

The concept of church planting using teams is something that is being used more and more widely in Britain today. Some of these teams are large and short term, others are somewhat smaller and stay together for several years. Some of the new church networks are using this approach to great effect. It is also an approach that has been pioneered by Youth With A Mission, notably in partnership with Bob Hopkins.

Bob, together wth his wife Mary, have been responsible for training teams of YWAM volunteers at their centre in St Helen's, Lancashire. The background to Bob and Mary's commitment to team training lay in their own participation in a team ministry. In his second Grove Booklet on church planting subtitled 'Some Experiences and Challenges', Bob describes how a team of five people were formed to go and work with Holy Trinity Church, Par Mount, St Helen's, in what was 'effectively a church planting situation'.

This was clearly a formative experience for those who took part and has since led to the concept of 'seed teams'. Essentially, seed teams are composed of approximately six people who raise their own support to go and work for a time in a church which, like Holy Trinity, becomes effectively a church plant situation, or in completely new situations. An important aspect of the seed teams is that they often operate cross-culturally, primarily in urban priority areas.

Clearly, teams can be used in a large variety of situations and do not have to be limited to cross-cultural situations. The advantage of teams in terms of pioneer work is that they can provide enough of a core group to model what it means to live the Christian life and to live as the church in a way that it is very difficult for an individual to do. Teams are expensive to send if one agency is sending them, but where people raise their own support, then they are often capable of attracting funds that would most probably not be used for any kind of mission work. It is simply the personal connection, with the individual raising the funds, that stimulates a great deal of such giving. Teams can therefore be very helpful in terms of generating funding for church planting.

My observation of teams over a twenty-year period suggests to me that many team members will stay in one or other of the situations in which they initially work as a church planter. This is especially true of those who join the team as single people and then marry a partner in the church where they are working. It is most unusual for exactly the same team to start one situation and then move on intact to another. Even if some of the team moves on, there will almost certainly be some extensive personnel changes.

Planting churches using a catalytic church planter

Perhaps we could call such a person a catalytic converter because he or she will almost certainly have strong evangelistic gifts! He may well build up a team around him but in the first place starts just as an individual. In all probability a person with this ministry will exercise it by moving to a new community and, by simply sharing his vision of what he hopes to see achieved, he will gradually attract a group of people around him who are inspired by that vision.

Church planters of this type do not usually stay for a long time with the churches that they start so that the quality of the team that they build around them is critical to the long-term success of their venture. Since the catalytic planter normally has strong evangelistic gifts, he normally needs to attract those with teaching and pastoring gifts to the team in order to establish the converts that are being made. The kinds of relationships that are being formed in the group will say a great deal about its long-term viability.

One question to ask would be, 'To what extent are the relationships in the group all with the leader and to what degree is the group beginning to relate to each other?' Usually the initial relationships are multiple individual relationships centring on the catalyst. There are usually few interacting relationships in the group. The successful operation of pastoring and teaching gifts will cause the group relationships to develop so that each person is fully integrated in the group. When this is happening, naturally, then, the catalyst can often be free to move on or to change his role in the group.

These kinds of people are often very creative, highly self-sufficient people. Their creativity can either be suppressed or enhanced through the quality of relationship that they enjoy, or do not enjoy, as the case may be, with some kind of church planting agency. A good relationship with a church planting agency (denominational or otherwise) will help to provide the flow of other gifts that are needed in the team. It may also assist the group's confidence when the time comes for the catalytic planter to leave, and can be helpful in suggesting options for the next church plant.

Catalytic planters represent a resource of great value for any group of churches. However, their motives are often misunderstood, which can sometimes lead to tensions with their brethren in the denomination that they come from. Mentors who can ease their way in the denomination are needed if these kinds of people are not to be burnt out.

Church planting using a founding pastor

Sometimes a group of people wishing to start a church in a given community has already been located and a pastor is sent in to start the work. On other occasions, a team is sent in, perhaps with a strong evangelist in the team who may or may not be the founding pastor, and when the team moves on, the founding pastor stays to develop the church that has been started.

Two issues arise for the founding pastor. First, as the needs of the church change, can he adapt in terms of his ministry gift area? If the founding pastor has an evangelistic gift and uses it in order to establish the church, is he able to draw in the necessary pastoral gifts and yet still maintain his evangelistic ministry? The deeper question here is how strong are his overall leadership gifts? If his leadership gifts are strong then he will be able to lead the church and use his ministry gifts, whether evangelistic or pastoral, as appropriate in the context of the broader framework of leadership that he is creating.

Second, as the church grows can his leadership gifts keep pace with the congregation? Some leaders are able to take relatively small groups of people and build them into viable churches but cannot take them beyond the size of group which allows personal contact with all the people in the church. This is not so much a matter of leadership gift as of leadership style. Often the solution is for that person to move on and to allow the church to call someone else who has a different leadership style that will enable the congregation to continue growing.

However, sometimes, the founding pastor is able to change his or her leadership style and grow as a person with the church. On some occasions, this process will stretch the founding pastor almost to breaking point. Robert Warren of St Thomas's, Crookes, Sheffield, spoke at an Anglican church planting conference on how at certain critical points in the growth of his congregation he had felt that he could take the church no further and therefore that it was time to leave, only to be told by his congregation that they simply insisted that he stay and continue to grow with them!

Founding pastors are often the kind of self-starters who will take a part-time job in order to allow the work to begin. On many occasions, other members of the family will take paid employment in order to allow the founding pastor to give all of his time. Such sacrificial commitment is to be admired, but it can be taken advantage of to the ultimate detriment of both church and pastor. The church may lose the best asset it has by simply taking such sacrifice for granted. One man who had been a founding pastor of a number of churches commented that the worst paid pastor of any church is always its first pastor!

Planting churches with independent church planters

There are those unusual individuals who are not supported by any church planting agencies or denominations, who work entirely alone in planting churches. I am not aware of large numbers of these people, and certainly I have not seen many who are successful planters in Britain, although I am aware of a few. Many of the people that I have observed in this category have been Americans, and nearly all of these people have not really succeeded in their goal.

It may be that this kind of planting is only very successful in

situations where the level of receptivity to the gospel is somewhat greater than that which we have witnessed in Britain in
recent years. Certainly, I am aware of far more examples of the
success of this kind of church planting in other lands. One very
notable example is that of a Scotsman who went as a sole self-
supported missionary to Ghana. Not only was he successful in
planting a church, but he is the founder of what has become a
very sizeable denomination in Ghana, all the more interesting
because it is regarded, rightly so, as an indigenous church and
not as a mission church. Perhaps it is the ability of individuals to
produce such a degree of indigeneity as compared with the
efforts of mission agencies that commends the independent
church planter as having a valid approach to church planting.

Crusades and events

This has been a very common method of church planting for
Pentecostal churches and for a number of other smaller denominations, notably the Seventh Day Adventist Church.
Although some details vary from group to group, the basic
ingredients of this approach are as follows.

Ideally, there will already be some mature members of the
denomination in question living in the target area. These may
be few in number, possibly less than twenty people. However,
quality is more important than quantity for this group. A target
area having been selected, a very high profile crusade, or
convention, will be held in the area. House-to-house visitation
by teams, press advertising, posters, handbills, the introduction
of high quality music groups, choirs and, most important of all,
an acknowledged evangelist follow. Often divine healing is
strongly profiled as part of the event. The intention is to see at
least fifity people, and hopefully more, converted through the
campaign which will typically last between one and two weeks.

In the meantime, a long-term pastor will already have been
selected to work with the original group and with the new
converts. Usually, a meeting place will also have been chosen in
which meetings will continue after the crusade or convention
has ended. In some cases this will be a redundant church
building purchased for use after the event. If the crusade is

successful then a church of approximately seventy people will have been created (the original group of twenty and fifty new converts) almost overnight. In recent years, the Elim Pentecostal Church has maintained two national crusade teams as a primary means of new church planting.

The intention from the beginning to establish a new church as a consequence of a major crusade or event is an important element in the successful follow-up of converts. I recently heard someone who had been an evangelist with the Reinhard Bonke team in Africa explain how he had come to see the value of church planting when he had returned after some years to the places where crusades had earlier produced large numbers of converts, only to find that few of these converts had become established in existing churches. Deliberately planting new churches that will be a good match for the cultural fit of those who are being targeted in a crusade can represent a responsible way of caring for converts.

Other approaches

Peter Wagner no longer lists crusades and events as a means of church planting in his book on church planting, which otherwise is similar to the above listing. Instead, he has a category which he calls the apostolic church planter.[13] Under this heading, he describes how some of the new church networks, having planted a church themselves, use the congregation as a sending body for other teams of church planters. Wagner says, 'The new church is typically not a satellite, but an autonomous church. It has its own legal standing and owns its own property. However, the pastor and the church remain under the ultimate authority of the Apostle.[14]

Wagner makes the additional point that there is considerable overlap with this model and the colonisation model. It seems to me that there really is no difference between these two models and that this last category of Wagner's, properly belongs under this heading. The fact that the churchmanship is an interesting mix of congregationalism and a form of episcopacy does not really make this an entirely different model. Indeed, there are some older denominations or, if one prefers, movements, that have almost identical structures.

The value of support

No matter what church planting model is selected, there are two factors to be aware of:

First, it is all too easy to duplicate the structures that we are familiar with. However good they might have been elsewhere, or even in another age, they may not necessarily be appropriate structures in the situation you are in. It will be a constant battle to think in fresh ways but it is almost certainly essential to do so. Looking at what others are doing will help you in this process.

Second, church planting is never easy and it will require a great deal of support to be effective, especially when the church plant is a long way from the sending church or group. One way of providing support for church planting is to use the cluster approach. This means that you will plant a number of churches which are relatively close to each other. The resultant fellowship, solidarity and practical support that the various plants can offer each other may well be crucial to their success. The Free Methodist Church, whose church planting activities are described in Chapter Three, have had notably more success with their cluster planting of churches in the north-west of England than with their few attempts to plant congregations in other parts of the British Isles far removed from the majority of their congregations.

We can be thankful to God that so much has already been initiated in the field of church planting that we are not short of successful church plants to offer as signs of vitality. Hopefully, the experiences of others will inspire you to choose the methods that will work best in your given situation.

For discussion and further study

1. How many successful church plants have you studied in depth?
2. Can you identify a model which fits closely with the kind of

church plant that you had in mind? Are there any differences and, if so, what are they?

3. Are you sure that you have the right personnel for the model that you most favour?

Notes

1. Peter Wagner, *Church Planting for a Greater Harvest* (Regal Books, 1990).
2. The story of Above Bar Church is told in Eddie Gibbs (ed), *Ten Growing Churches* (MARC Europe, 1984). The church plant referred to has been greatly influenced by the ministry philosophy of Willow Creek Community Church.
3. One example of a church plant which is reaching a radically different socio-economic group is described in Bob Hopkins (ed), *Planting New Churches*, (Eagle, 1991), under the title, 'Planting in a Newcastle Urban Priority Area'.
4. Wagner, *op cit*, p 62.
5. The story is told in *Planting New Churches*, under the title, 'Planting from Holy Trinity Brompton'.
6. *Ibid*. pp 99f.
7. *Ibid*, p 100.
8. Wagner, *op cit*, p 65.
9. The story of Chester le Street was first told in *Ten Growing Churches*.
10. The story of Ichthus Christian Fellowship was first told in Roger Forster (ed), *Ten New Churches*.
11. For further reflection on this review see *Planting New Churches*, pp 148ff.
12. The story of St Thomas is told by the vicar Robert Warren in his book, *In the Crucible* (Highland Books, 1989). Further reflection on the model is found in *Planting New Churches*, pp 49ff.
13. Wagner, *op cit*, p 73.
14. *Ibid*, p 74.

Part Two
Preparing the Way

CHAPTER SIX

PREPARING TO PLANT—THE ROLE OF THE SPONSORING AGENCY

Stuart Christine

... 13,000 new churches and missions during the closing years of this century. Thousands of churches are needed to sponsor and guide the development of these new churches.[1]

Churches, like cornfields, do not just appear: they need to be planned and prepared for, planted and cared for.

It's true that 'wild oats' do spring up in fields and hedgerows, and no doubt help meet the needs of birds and fieldmice, but there would be no credibility in an agricultural policy that proposed to feed towns and cities on the basis of such uncertain and meagre production!

It is no more acceptable for the church of Jesus to expect that the spiritual needs of our country's millions of unchurched can be met on the basis of the spontaneous emergence of new churches, fired into life through a personal vision here or a chance coming together of like-minded souls there. It is to the shame of the churches that in certain instances the Spirit can find no other way to light the lamp of witness, particularly among minority ethnic groups, than by firing the hearts of ones and twos while churches with thousands live on in cold indifference or ignorance.[2]

It is the job of *churches* to plant churches and to do so not on the basis of spontaneity but as the outworking of strategy. Church planting on a scale adequate to meet the spiritual needs of our people must be driven not by individual personalities but rather by institutional policy. Churches need to be into positive family planning rather than wild oats!

The purpose of this chapter is to give helpful guidance to

those churches and denominations prepared to take up their calling as agencies for multiplying communities of the kingdom.

It's natural to want to reproduce!

> God blessed them and said to them, 'Be fruitful and increase in number; fill the earth and subdue it (Gen 1:28).

It's the most natural thing in the world for God's people to multiply their local family units, for churches to want to reproduce themselves and bring the land under the influence of the Lord. Multiplication is one of the keywords of the opening book of the Bible and it's hardly surprising to find that this modus operandi of the Spirit of God continues to characterise the dynamics of God's purposes for his people in the new creation also.

The parenting of new congregations, whatever the model of planting pursued, is a natural instinct of those born again by this Spirit and gathered by him into local Christian families. Single churches, local groups of churches of the same or of different denominational backgrounds, and the mission departments of larger national churches are all able to co-operate with the Spirit of Jesus to bring into the world new and vigorous congregations.

Patterns of parenting can vary

The pattern of parenting or sponsorship will depend upon the group involved. The Southern Baptists quoted at the beginning of this chapter identify several sponsor models:[3]

Primary sponsor: a church that starts and nurtures a mission congregation. Generally the mission congregation operates within the constitution of the primary sponsor. The primary sponsor usually holds legal title to mission property, approves major decisions, and records membership.

Co-sponsor: a church that contributes significantly to the financial support of a mission congregation located nearby or in another state. The co-sponsor may send workers for special projects.

Support sponsor: a church (or agency) that provides financial and prayer support to assist a primary sponsor in starting and developing a mission.

Sister church: a church that enters into a nurturing relationship with a newly formed church. Both groups can realise benefits from the alliance.

Whatever approach to congregational reproduction is most suitable to the ecclesiastical traditions and theology of the group concerned, it is essential that the role of the planting agency is recognised and affirmed as a vital component in the equation of multiplication.

Particularly when the glamour and excitement associated with the new work itself tends to divert attention away from the older established fellowship, it is of the greatest importance to remember that healthy children are only produced when there is commitment and capacity for birthing and rearing on the part of the parental unit.

The importance of proper preparation and commitment to this task is well attested by those who have lived through the trauma of the birth and infancy of a newly planted congregation. A telling comment surfaced in a survey conducted among newly planted British churches by the Administry organisation.

> For the work to take off there needs to be a much more positive attitude from the mother church who seem to view it as a nice little project which is a good thing as long as they don't have to be involved.[4]

These comments recorded from two New Zealand pastors reflect the same concern:

> When churches are planted without a very strong relationship with another (mature) church the likelihood of growth is greatly diminished, because the support networks are not in place.

> The key to sustaining church planting is the availability of healthy home churches, providing leadership resources, training, healthy models, and programmes.[5]

One goal but different starting points

Local Baptist church leaders attending a breakfast meeting recently were posed the question, 'Is church planting under consideration by your church?' As might have been expected, responses varied, reflecting the spectrum of spiritual vigour and mission commitment and experience of those present, but one answer stood out from the rest: 'We have Ichthus to do that sort of thing for us don't we!'

In a sentence, the important point was made that when it comes to new church planting, different churches and denominations are starting from very different places.

New church groups

It is a fact that while some groups like the Ichthus Fellowship have built up a reservoir of experience, know how and models, many of those in leadership within the mainline denominations have never been down the church planting road and are, in consequence, unsure of the route and of the difficulties likely to be encountered on the way. A century of stagnation and decline has resulted in a serious loss of memory about the dos and don'ts, whos and hows of establishing new congregations. What was common knowledge among churches at the close of a Victorian era characterised by expansion has become shrouded in uncertainty and acquired a mystique that makes many a church question whether church planting is something for them.

The new churches born through the house church movement or among ethnic communities are in fact well placed to engage in vigorous planting. Many, by virtue of their origins, have experienced the challenges of starting from scratch, unencumbered by buildings and traditions that so easily limit vision for what the church can do and how it might develop. A commitment to grow, strong leadership able to enunciate clear policy for all to own and a confidence in God and his gospel make an excellent seed-bed for the multiplication of worshipping and witnessing units. Church planting is both the experience and *expectation* of such groups. Spiritual status is attributed to those who are called or committed to it. Some groups affirm it to be the very raison d'etre of their association together.

Older denominational groups

While most older church groupings could trace their own origins to such movements, the dynamics of mission have in many instances been smothered by the demands of maintenance and, as with most skills, so also the skills associated with establishing new congregations, when no practised, are lost.

This situation is well illustrated in the history of the Association of Baptist Churches in the London area. The very first sentence in the constitution of the London Baptist Association, re-established under the influence of Charles Spurgeon in 1865, affirms that it was the purpose of the Association to plant new churches. A survey of the church planting activity of the Association since that date is instructive, highlighting in a way not difficult to interpret how national trauma, sociological change and a period of unhelpful theological emphasis can submerge the founding vision and drain the mission energy from a group.

It is, however, a matter of great significance and encouragement that, breaking all the precedents of church history, Baptists have recently begun to grow again. The invigorating influence of the charismatic renewal movement must certainly be the prime factor in this turnaround. The renewed commitment to mission that has grown out of this has, however, until recently been focused in the restructuring and return to growth of existing churches, while evangelism through new church planting has been slower to gather momentum.

Lack of leadership know how must be one of the principle reasons for this. The launch of the Spurgeon's/Oasis church planting course in 1989 and the formation of the Network of Baptist Church Planters in 1990, together with informal links with the new churches' networks, is already restoring church planting wisdom to the denominational consciousness and will guarantee a dramatic increase of evangelism by this method up to the close of the century. The promotion of similar programmes of 're-education' among other mainline groups can be seen to be having a similar effect. And it is vital, for a number of reasons, that this 'most effective form of evangelism under heaven' is re-established as an acceptable and familiar mission option for the older denominational groups. The fact is that notwithstanding the exciting growth of the new churches, it is still the older groupings that have the most people, plant, presence and prestige as representatives of the Christian faith throughout our land. Certainly, the denominational establishments lack the vigour and purposefulness that characterises many new church groups, but our God is in the 'dry bones business'. The experiences of renewal of recent years should encourage us to believe that God has not written off the vehicles of faith that have carried the gospel across the bumpy roads of this century and up to the present.

Ecumenical groups

Ecumenical groupings represent a further category of church base from which church planting ventures are being launched.

As with all church planting ventures, the potential for the development of a lively and effective witnessing congregation will depend to a large extent upon the motivation and philosophy of ministry that lie behind the enterprise. Too many ecumenical projects have been launched as expressions of Christian unity or as survival packages for declining causes with little else in common save for their inviability as independent entities. The clarity and unanimity of evangelistic purpose that is so necessary for growth is not always easy to establish among a group that draws its ethos from a variety of different church traditions, each with its particular theological emphases. While wholeheartedly affirming the need to 'think ecumenically', it is worthy of note that no less an ecclesiastical diplomat than Archbishop George Carey has conceded that:

We are at the heart of a problem that I frankly don't know the answer to. It seems to me that the most successful types of church planting come from churches which have a clear cut identity; usually evangelical/charismatic.[6]

Equally, the spiritual energy associated with effective pioneer workers is usually intolerant of the bureaucratic controls sometimes associated with jointly owned ventures. This tendency to overcontrol is well illustrated by a case of which I learned recently. A proposed local ecumenical plant in Wales recently became bogged down by decisions not to move into a new estate until all the financial resources for the initiative were guaranteed. In the meantime, an Elim church had come to the estate and formed a church in a school which was progressing well. The maintenance of 'spiritual momentum' is an important dynamic in the building of a new growth-oriented congregation and local leadership must have freedom to act without undue constraint if this is to be achieved.

George Lings, writing from an Anglican perspective, has made the comment that, 'Too often ecumenical instruments are thought too cumbersome and too readily perceived as mergers of failing companies, hardly a base for vigorous growth.'[7]

It is also vital to preserve the freedom of the new group to develop patterns of ministry that are responsive to the needs of the local community rather than to the practices of the sponsoring churches. Again, this is a criterion for the parent/child relationship that ecumenical steering committees sometimes find it hard to fulfil as different representatives seek to remain true to their particular traditional heritage and understanding of what represents an appropriate congregational ministry style.

In spite of the cautionary tone sounded so far, however, it can be affirmed that there are examples of formally constituted LEPs (local ecumenical plants) that have experienced growth and become effective worship and witness centres in the local community. Jonathan Edwards, until 1990 Baptist pastor responsible for one of a number of ecumenical plants on new estates in the Bury St Edmunds area, has spoken enthusiastically of the effectiveness of establishing a common Christian witness in such new areas. He has offered some general guidelines for moving out into planting from the starting point of ecumenical commitment:

● Spend time to ensure good communication among those involved at every stage of development.

- Ensure that the common calling of those who will join the planted church is Christ-centred and not merely ecumenical.
- Be ready to learn and to be changed by the experience.
- Keep in touch with the parent denominations whether they want it or not!
- Ensure that the local church is allowed to develop in its own way under the lordship of Christ.

The advice offered by one diocesan board would, perhaps, reflect the general attitude prevailing in regard to choosing an ecumenical starting point for a church plant. 'Ecumenical involvement should be assumed from the start wherever possible. However, it is unwise to formalise an LEP until the enterprise has become well established.'[8]

One goal but different pathways

Not only do different groups begin from different starting points in terms of experience and mission outlook, they must also traverse different ecclesiastical terrain to actually get to the point of launching a planting project.

The decision-making process

The decision-making, permission-giving mechanisms of different churches vary and present different challenges to the would-be church planter as he works to lay proper foundations of approval and support to establish a new congregation.

'Think before you leap!' began Dr Carey in an article entitled, 'Church Planting—Anglican Style'.[9]

Many of us do not seem to know the rudiments of procedures for appointments in the Church of England. Last Monday I had a phone call from a NSM clergyman who claimed to have had a brilliant idea for a neighbouring parish. 'My idea is this,' he said, 'There is really no need to put another full-time chap in there. I will gladly take it over and bring in a dozen or so of my friends.' . . . He was not asking, Who are the patrons? What would the PCC think about his idea? What is deanery and diocesan policy? We *must* understand the laws of the church and the constraints under which we operate to discover what is possible or not.

We might have some sympathy for the enthusiastic clergyman so roundly rebuked, but the fact is that every church group operates according to a mutually agreed set of rules and regulations that determine how things can be done, and Dr Carey's reminder that 'we must understand the laws of the church and the constraints under which we operate' is a valid one. Although the principles of church planting are universal, the practice is denominationally conditioned, and the tighter and more centralised the denominational structure is, the more difficult it will be to gain approval for innovative proposals. Local independence and responsiveness are often sacrificed in favour of security and uniformity. Although there have undoubtedly been periods in the history of the church when security has been the order of the day, it must be seriously questioned as to whether highly centralised systems of government are viable in a period of rapid change. The lesson of the dinosaurs, whether reptilian or political, is that evolution is a process that is ignored at one's peril.

The prospective planter would do well to draw up a map of the decision-making process through which he will need to take his proposal, and think long and prayerfully about the best way to negotiate each feature on the landscape.

To illustrate this, the relatively simple case of the normal decision-making process for an autonomous Baptist church will serve.

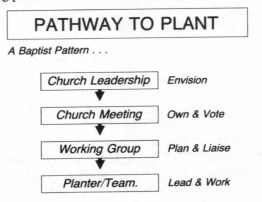

PATHWAY TO PLANT

A Baptist Pattern . . .

Church Leadership	*Envision*
↓	
Church Meeting	*Own & Vote*
↓	
Working Group	*Plan & Liaise*
↓	
Planter/Team.	*Lead & Work*

Other ecclesiastical constraints

David Pytches' comment about parish boundaries being the condom of the Anglican church, impeding natural reproduction, has already passed into church planting folklore. It succinctly highlights a particular constraint that those working with that particular church grouping need to take seriously. The fact that the newly appointed Archbishop Carey devoted almost his entire address to the issue at the 1991 Anglican church planters' conference confirms the sensitiveness of the issue. The way through that particular thicket of parochial inviolability, he suggests, is by a strengthening of the role of the bishop as strategic director of mission throughout the diocese.

Churches that express their 'denominational life' more as independent units within a voluntary association will rejoice in the freedom of action that such a system allows, but can conversely suffer from the limitations of isolationism and a very locally focused mission vision.

For some, their very understanding of what is involved in the establishing of a church can put a question mark against church planting. An example is cited by Peter Wagner.[10] Asking why a certain presbytery in Texas was planning only a single plant for the 1980s he was told that at a cost of about $500.000 a church that was all they could budget for. Shortly after, at a seminar for pastors of the Assemblies of God in North Carolina, he was informed that the planting goal achieved in the 1970s had been eighty-five new churches. Asking how much each was estimated to have cost, he was told, 'Each one cost about $2,500'! The difference didn't lie in what the final costs of church establishment, buildings and ministry would be, but rather in the fact that the Presbyterian approach required that the whole sum be available upfront while the Assemblies of God leadership expected the new church itself to discover and generate the funds necessary for its establishment. The consequences of the different approaches for the growth of the denominational group are obvious and serve as a lesson in how *not* to assess the costs and difficulties of a mission task.

Some mission agencies have found themselves constrained by

their own constitutions that were drawn up in days when both vision and reality were different from those prevailing today. Campus Crusade would be an example of such a group. Extensively and effectively acting as a mission agency around the world, church planting had not been perceived as an appropriate mission option for inclusion in their founding charter. Faced with a growing appreciation of the value of gathering new converts into communities for mutual support, teaching and witness, Campus Crusade overcame the self-imposed constraint by simply redefining, calling such Christian communities, 'home fellowship groups' instead of churches!

Different starting points and different routes into planting mean that there can be no single pathway for everyone to follow. While general principles may serve to illuminate the way ahead, specific guidelines need to be laid down according to the position of the group proposing to plant. And because many church groups have forgotten their way around this terrain there is a lot of exploring and basic map work to be done, especially in the major denominations.

The emergence of denominational church planting networks able to stimulate discussion and pool experience appropriate to each particular church situation is therefore to be encouraged, especially during this period of rediscovery.

Of particular importance, however, in every situation where a group is planning to sponsor or parent a plant is that a group be set up to work through precisely the issues indicated above.

The make-up and function of this group is the subject to which we shall now turn our attention.

The planting project steering committee

Planting project steering committee, church mission development council, church planting task force are all titles that I have encountered to describe the group whose job it will be to help the parent body think through, and prepare for, the issues involved in the planting project.

Its function

Specific aims of such a group could well include:

- To liaise with the leadership to ensure that appropriate biblical teaching is given to enable the church to appreciate how new church planting fits into the purposes of God and the particular mission of the local church.

The following series of ten titles are suggested as highlighting the areas that could helpfully be dealt with in helping to create a spiritual climate suitable for growing the vision for a planting project:

1. Mission unlimited—the mission commitment of God the Father.
2. Jesus: Good News down your street—the missionary principle of incarnation.
3. The Holy Spirit—managing and motivating God's mission team.
4. As the Father has sent me, so I am sending you—the role of the church in God's mission.
5. Mission marks: vision—illustrated from Acts.
6. Mission marks: faith—illustrated from Acts.
7. Mission marks: prayer—illustrated from Acts.
8. Mission marks: generosity—illustrated from Acts.
9. Mission marks: partnership—illustrated from Acts.
10. Mission marks: perseverance—illustrated from Acts.

- To arrange visits to the proposed target area for church members. This would be with a view to helping them sense the degree of need and of focusing prayer and concern for the community there.
- To suggest a programme whereby the church's understanding of contemporary church planting is increased. Possibilities would include seminars, perhaps stimulated by material available through the central mission department of the denomination or an informed outside speaker, visits from groups of the same denominational background that have

already gone down the planting road, recommendation of
helpful literature and so on.

● To anticipate questions that the leadership and membership
of the parenting church will want answered in order for them
to be able to take an informed and wholehearted decision
about whether they should proceed with the plant, and if so
how.

For example:

Why is a new church needed?
What is the reaction of other churches in the area?
How much will it cost to set up and for how long?
Where and when will the new group meet?
Who will lead and who will be involved in the plant?
How will worship, the sacraments, funerals and so on, be handled?
How will the gaps in the sending church be refilled?
How will the new congregation relate to the existing church?
What about membership, will there be one role or two?
Will the congregation have financial autonomy?
Where will decision-making power lie?
How will the lines of communication be kept open?
How will differences of opinion with the church be dealt with?
Is the ultimate goal one of independence or not?

It is of the utmost importance to make sure that everyone
involved has the same expectations regarding the approach to
be adopted, the timescale and the final objective of the plant.

● To serve as a forum or meeting and discussion point with the
core group of the new plant as the practical issues involved in
forwarding the progress of the plant become clear and as the
philosophy of ministry to be adopted is thought through.
● To co-ordinate the parent church's involvement in the pre-
launch process of publicity, evangelism and prayer.
● To liaise with the leadership to ensure that a suitable programme of teaching, encouragement and training is prepared
to help the sending church recover from the loss of members
who move to the new congregation.

Its composition

As a working group the membership should not be too large. Two or three representatives of the parent body leadership, the proposed leader and another couple of people belonging to the core group of the new congregation are probably a good basic group, with the power to invite other church members with particular expertise to share in the sessions from time to time as appropriate.

Where non-local church co-sponsoring agencies are involved, such as groups of churches or denominational mission departments, then a suitable representative of such bodies should also be included.

What is important is that from the outset the whole church and all other sponsoring agencies should be aware that such a group is meeting on their behalf with a view to helping everyone to think through the issues. Prayer for the work of the group and regular opportunities for both formal and informal reporting on progress should be built into the ongoing life of the parent body.

Whatever such a group is called and whatever the precise terms of reference adopted, the function of ensuring a thorough, sensitive and positive review of the issues involved in undertaking a planting project is of vital importance. Earlier in this chapter, the importance of obtaining informed and widespread commitment to the venture from the membership of the planting body was stressed and is worth reaffirming here. The counsel of the pastor of an independent church in Kansas concisely articulates the need: 'Make sure the mother church has the vision, not just the pastor.'[11]

The Antioch church—a biblical example

The response of the Antioch church to the church planting mission of Paul and Barnabas models the importance of expressing the ongoing corporate commitment of the planting church to the mission group.

Mutual commitment

Fasting, praying and the laying on of hands are all corporate acts of commitment towards the mission group as it sets out.

To understand the significance of this threefold commissioning it is worth noting that the same three elements are employed by the apostles in *their* commissioning of the elders in the newly formed churches in Lystra, Iconium and Pisidian Antioch (Acts 14:21–23). The word translated, 'appointed' literally means 'stretched out their hands upon', and the significance of the ceremony is explained by the words, '[Paul and Barnabas] committed them to the Lord in whom they had put their trust.' This understanding of the sending church's action towards them is confirmed by verse 26 which describes their return to Antioch, 'where they had been committed to the grace of God for the work.'

The act of commissioning is therefore clearly portrayed as a wholehearted affirmation of the planting church's support for, and ownership of, *the work* of mission that the Spirit of God had called it to engage in through the agency of the particular individuals being set aside.

The Spirit challenges the church to confirm his calling of the mission group (Acts 13:2) and to *release them* (Acts 13:3) (the distinctive meaning of the Greek word rather unhelpfully translated as 'sent them off' in the NIV), so that he can send them on their way (Acts 13:4).

The fact that the group feel both constrained and content to report back to the sending church (Acts 14:27, 28) confirms that though being released for the Lord's work under the guidance of the Spirit, the sense of partnership in the work is by no means terminated with the releasing and departure. It is interesting to note that the Greek vocabulary used of their 'reporting back' is very reminiscent of the phraseology used to describe the enthusiastic reporting back of the disciples sent out by Jesus in Mark 6:30. The local church, the local 'body of Christ', had sent out its apostles and was now receiving their reports just as the Lord himself used to.

Generosity

The generosity of spirit and confidence in God displayed by the Antioch church has been a particular source of challenge and encouragement to churches considering the planting option. Founded itself around AD 37 as the agency of the kingdom in what was then the third largest city of the Roman Empire, the church at Antioch faced an enormous local evangelistic task. The Roman historian Seneca expressed one opinion of the quality of moral life in this huge population centre when he compared immigration from Antioch to Rome in terms of Syrian sewerage emptying into the River Tiber upon which Rome stood. Yet, in spite of the enormity of the mission challenge on their own doorstep, we find this Christian church, a mere nine years old, confident enough in the good purposes of God for them that they are prepared to release two out of their five principal leaders and workers for mission outside their own 'patch'!

In the closing section of an article dealing with the mothering of new churches, published in *Leadership* magazine in 1985, a collection of 'Free advice to Mothers and Daughters' is set out, gathered from pastors of churches involved in parenting a plant. I would, from my own experience, identify fully with the editor's summary of the advice received: 'The majority attitude is perhaps epitomized by the Florida pastor who wrote, "Be bold, brave and generous".'[12]

Parenting has always been about self-giving and it is as true in the church as it is in the home. To become a church that the Spirit is able to use in a church planting ministry then there must be a genuine belief in the words of the Lord that it is more blessed to give than to receive!

Dealing with the doubters

The experience of Moses when he carried out a feasibility study for the invasion of Israel is recorded in its all too familiar detail in Numbers 13:26–33. Many a church planting proposal has foundered upon the rocks of doubt and fearfulness ever since. Peter Wagner has rightly stated that 'the greatest barriers to church planting are in the mind',[13] and it is in the hearts and minds of church members that the church planting battle may need to be fought first before you are even able to get the troops out of the barracks!

Some of the objections or concerns commonly voiced are rehearsed here:

- 'We would offend the church(es) who already consider the targeted area as "their patch".'

Opposition to new church planting very often stems from negative experiences of insensitive initiatives or of 'sheep stealing'. A commitment to consultation, mutual respect and a clearly stated objective of reaching the unchurched and not 'poaching' the members of others, can go a long way to allaying such fears both amongst the planting church membership and the churches already present in the targeted area.

- 'We don't believe that there is sufficient potential in the targeted community to produce a church that will be able to sustain itself.'

Many unchurched groups, especially in ethnically diverse inner city or scattered rural areas, go unreached in consequence of the difficulties of sustaining effective witnessing groups able to speak out and live out the gospel 'where they are'. These difficulties can and are being overcome in the cell, congregation, celebration model of church life. Structures can be developed that can integrate small, culturally and locally focused witnessing groups or cells into larger, financially and socially viable fellowships.

- 'There is no site or building available for use in the targeted community.'

Church planting is about building a witnessing community not a suite of premises. The testimony of some black church leaders is worth noting here. In the early years of the post-immigration struggle to establish churches, when meetings were based in halls and centres used by the community, growth was vigorous and membership commitment to evangelism significantly greater than since the churches have begun to ensconce themselves within 'dedicated' buildings. From the standpoint of the unchurched community the accessibility and acceptability of a meeting place is more important than whether or not the premises actually belong to the Christian group.

- 'We'd surely do better to try to lend a hand to some of the small struggling churches in our area than start yet another that would be in competition with them.'

The goal of the revitalisation of a declining work is a laudable one but easier said than done. Renewal of church life will invariably involve changes in leadership and lifestyle for the struggling group, since by definition the current patterns of church life are failing to impact the community in an effective way. Unfortunately, it is a sad fact that many such congregations are unwilling to let go of ways that though they might have served the kingdom well in the past, no longer do so. It must be asked if it is good stewardship of kingdom resources to perpetuate ineffective activity. Sometimes a cure is not possible and there must be death before resurrection can take place!

- 'We're not able to fill our own premises, what's the point in trying to start another church?'

It is quite proper for every Christian church to be concerned about the effectiveness of its existing evangelistic programme and be committed to keeping it under constant review. Christlike concern for the immediate locality will certainly not, however, be a barrier to an equally Christlike concern for and commitment to other areas where there is no witnessing community able to bring to its residents a realistic opportunity of an encounter with the gospel. The challenge of Acts 13 mentioned above is worth citing here.

- 'We aren't large enough to be able to send off thirty or forty folk to begin a new church.'

There are many different ways of going about planting a new church. To establish a new garden you can either transplant ready formed plants or you can put in seeds. It's true that transplanting will get you off to a flying start and that the transplanted plants will perhaps be more likely to survive an unfavourable climate, but the ready grown plants you want aren't always available and even if they are you might not be able to afford them. The quality of what you are putting in and the way it is looked after are what really matters.

● 'Our aim is to develop a large, strong church with resources to provide effective facilities for a broadly based mission programme that can really address the needs of the community. To plant out would weaken that base.'

There is great merit in seeking to develop a church with sufficient resources to project kingdom values and presence in an attractive and highly visible way into the local community. The geographical and social limitations upon the effective extent of a single church's ministry should not, however, be overlooked. Size that can be an attraction to one can also be a barrier to another. The question of accessibility even in the motorised age is also a pertinent issue since not all can drive, nor do all have access to the family car on a day when it might normally be used for other leisure activities. The importance of a local church fellowship that relates to local people and speaks about God in the accents of the locality should not be underestimated. For many it is an attraction, and for some groups, especially those culturally different to the majority of members of a large thriving church, it may be essential if the gospel is to have a chance.

● 'We have never undertaken such work before. It would surely be more prudent to do what we already know what to do and leave church planting to groups that are more experienced in such things.'

It is important that we avoid fuelling the myth that church planting is for specialists. Wherever in the world the church is growing, ordinary believers in Jesus are proving that this just isn't so. We are fortunate to live at a time and in a country where their testimony can so readily come to our ears, encouraging us to be less cautious of the world and more confident in the gospel. Mission, by definition, takes place in the very uncertain and risky environment of the world that crucified Jesus, and Jesus himself forewarned his disciples that not every investment of their time and energy would be met with acceptance by the local community. That didn't stop him, however, from sending them out, nor from commanding them to pray for the Lord of the harvest to raise up many more such as they. Nor did it stop the disciples returning with joy at the successes that they did experience. William Carey's well known and well founded call to Christian confidence is worth quoting here: 'Expect great things from God, attempt great things for God.'

Also, it is essential to remember that residues of doubt and a sense of insecurity among the membership of the planting church may well be grounded in genuine concern for the best use of kingdom resources and in bad experiences of similar ventures in the past. Whatever their origin, however, they are readily exploited by the spiritual forces opposing the extension of the kingdom. It is the common testimony of church planters that manifestations of spiritual opposition in the early stages of a church plant are a reality that cannot be ignored. It is well worth spending the time necessary to allay ungrounded fears and to avoid sustaining casualties and damage from 'friendly fire'.

Postnatal preparation—the consequences of planting for the parent body

Planting should be mutually beneficial

The expectation for congregational growth in a church planting project is usually focused exclusively upon the new work being established. The 1991 Administry survey on church planting has recorded, however, reassuring evidence that growth is not only found in the new centre but also stimulated in the parenting group.[14]

This trend is particularly noticeable when one of the motives for planting out is the fact that the worship space available in the sending church had become over 80 per cent occupied and the departure of the planted group released additional space for growth. Problems of leadership saturation, especially among multi-talented suburban memberships, can also be relieved by the siphoning off of gifted individuals into leadership responsibilities within the new group. This exodus of talent can shift leadership logjams that stifle the emergence of gifts among newer members of a congregation. Fresh blood in leadership can result in fresh vision and initiative, creating the conditions needed for a revitalisation of the ministry of the mother church.

George Ling has noted similar evidence 'that the churches that plant new congregations set in motion a dynamic, both in the sending and the new church, which tends towards further growth and planting.'[15] Similar examples can be found cited in a wide range of literature from the UK and US.[16]

Planting fatigue

Not all planting is done from positions of strength, however, and in any event if the members being sent out are quality Christians representing the cross-spectrum of gifting needed to develop a new church then their going will inevitably be felt, both at the leadership and the fellowship levels.

Planting fatigue is a condition that can begin to show itself in a church particularly when it is not large or when repeated plants have been undertaken. Stephen Ibbotson testifies to the growth of such symptoms in the Open Door Baptist Church in Peterborough during the process of establishing its four satellite congregations. Post-natal care of the parent is a crucial issue that any leadership team proposing to plant out should consider and prepare for before giving birth.

Vision and direction may well need to be rediscovered after the demanding goal of establishing a new congregation has been achieved and the group has left. Prayer, encouragement and training will be needed to refill leadership positions left vacant and a wise leadership team will have set the processes of renewal in motion even before the mission group has left. The spiritual balance of the remaining congregation may also have been altered by the departure of the enthusiastic pioneers. The process of rebuilding the dynamics of worship is a particularly crucial one which, if not attended to, can easily lead to post-natal depression particularly among the remaining leadership.

A further area of special concern arises if the planting model adopted involves continued close fellowship between the centre and its new satellite. In this case considerable energy and creativity will need to be expended on developing these inter-church links. Many churches that have intended their planted congregations to continue in an *interdependent* relationship with them have failed to recognise the amount of work required to make such a relationship work, and sometimes suffered painful separations in consequence as the desire for *independence* has grown within the new group.

Parents need to know when to become grandparents

Although mission vision should in no way be lessened in the parent church it is worth recognising that the expertise for planting will tend to become concentrated in the newly planted congregations. They've done it, learned from their mistakes and probably possess leaders most able to repeat the process elsewhere. It is not surprising that it is often in the first five or six years of its life that a newly planted congregation is found to be most capable of itself planting out a fresh group! Bearing both this and the question of planting fatigue in mind it is probably wise for a parent church to consider the value of channelling some of its mission resources through its existing plants. Enabling them to go on reproducing grandchildren, could in many instances be preferable to becoming locked into an unhelpfully intense period of child-bearing that might prove damaging to the parent's health.

For discussion and further study

1. Discuss the pros and cons of different patterns of sponsoring parenting new plants.
2. In what ways can the history of a denominational group influence its responsiveness to the possibility of developing a policy of church planting?
3. Identify the particular stages of discussion and decision making necessary to implement a programme of planting in your own denominational group.

4. Which passages from the Acts of the Apostles might be helpful in illustrating the various qualities of church life necessary for a church to be a 'good parent' in a planting project.
5. Discuss the relative importance of issues that a church planting steering group would need to deal with in a situation of which you are aware.

Notes

1. Southern Baptist Convention, *Associational Church Extension Guide*, p. 11.
2. George Lings, 'A Time to Plant—Recent Church Planting Statistics' in *Planting New Churches* (Eagle, 1991). Page 165 shows that according to his analysis of Anglican church planting from 1967 to 1990, no plant was motivated by the need to meet an 'unreached people group'.
3. Southern Baptist Convention, *Guide for Planting Congregations* (Home Mission Board, New Church Extension Division, 1991), p. 18.
4. 'Get Up and Grow!', Administry Resource Paper, 91:3 (August 1991): p. 15.
5. Both quoted in Bruce Patrick, *Multiplying Congregations* (Baptist Union of New Zealand, 1989).
6. George Carey, *CWN* (20 October 1989).
7. George Lings, *CWN* (6 October 1989).
8. Issued by the Mission Group (formerly the Diocesan Board for Mission and Unity) of the Southwell Diocese, January 1989.
9. George Carey, 'Church Planting Anglican Style', *Church Growth Digest* (Winter 1988/89).
10. Peter Wagner, *Church Planting for a Greater Harvest* (Regal Books, 1991), p. 39.
11. 'Mothering a New Church', *Leadership* (Winter 1985): p. 104.
12. *Ibid.*
13. Wagner, *op cit.*, p. 27.
14. 'Get Up and Grow!' *op cit.*, p. 8.
15. George Lings, *op cit.*, p. 8.
16. See also, George G. Hunter III, *To Spread the Power* (Abingdon Press), p. 116; and David Goodyear, 'One Plus One = One', *Church Growth Digest* (Winter 1990/91): pp. 1, 2.

CHAPTER SEVEN
WHERE TO PLANT?
Stuart Christine

The church was situated in one of the most densely populated areas of Western Europe. The sixty or so members had taken a fresh look at what they had always considered their 'patch' and decided that it was three times larger than the area they could hope to reach effectively through their evangelistic programmes. They realistically redrew the boundaries and set to work to plan an evangelistic strategy that could really make an impact on the community immediately around the church. However, their survey of the area had also highlighted two quite distinct estates where no Christian community was based. They decided to establish one. *But which area should they go for?*

At the 1991 Anglican church planters' conference the Archbishop had urged churches to offer resources for mission to their bishop to encourage the development of coherent diocesan church planting projects. Elsewhere another church group was already moving in this direction of strategic mission co-operation. A strong suburban church had offered to underwrite the establishment of a new congregation and its representatives were meeting with an advisory group set up to consider the possible locations. *The agenda was headed 'Where to plant?'*

I have just put down this week's edition of *The Baptist Times*. A short article on the back page had caught my attention. Entitled 'Planters Meet', it reported on a well attended consultation in the north of England aimed at encouraging and informing the growing church planting movement among Baptists. The closing sentence set out an astounding projection: 'The association could easily have 200 churches by the end of the decade.' It is evident that the delegates at that meeting were beginning to look at their localities in new ways, seeing opportunities for multiplication and identifying spiritually barren communities like fields in need of planting. *They were taking seriously the question of where could they plant.*

No 'no-go' areas

Jesus affirmed that there are no boundaries to our God's concern for humankind. 'The field is the world' (Mt 13:38), and all authority in heaven and on earth has been given to him. There is to be no corner or community within which the lordship of Jesus is not to run. No 'no-go' areas for the kingdom. Luke's account of the early years of church growth are a record of the Spirit of Christ impressing this breadth of vision into the hearts and minds of a leadership with many good reasons to be a great deal less expansive in their objectives. A handful of uncertain provincials in a cultural ghetto faced with prejudice and persecution seemed an unlikely group to take on the world. And yet the Spirit would let them settle for nothing less. The expansion of the church was driven by the conviction that 'God . . . now commands all people everywhere to repent' (Acts 17:30), and 'wants all men to be saved and to come to a knowledge of the truth' (1 Tim 2:4). Whether speaking to the debating society in Athens or whether in private exhortation to his disciple Timothy, Paul knew that he just didn't have the option of a defensive or survivalist mentality. Like Peter before him (Acts 10), Paul had been brought to realise that the boundary fences had been flattened by the wind of the Spirit and that all of the devil's backyard was scheduled for repossession by the rightful owner!

And yet there were decisions to be made and priorities to be acknowledged in deploying the resources of the kingdom in this process of occupying the land. The Spirit of Jesus would not allow Paul's church planting team to enter Bithynia (Acts 16:7). Paul himself elected not to stop in Neapolis upon arriving in

Macedonia, but rather to travel on to establish his first European mission centre in Philippi, 'a Roman colony and the leading city of that district of Macedonia' (Acts 16:11,12).

So the question is posed to us both from our own experience and from the accounts of the expansion of the early church: Where to plant? What are the criteria? Where is the Spirit of Jesus directing today? How much weight should be given to socio-economic factors such as those that set Philippi apart from Neapolis?

A recent Brazilian Baptist home missions campaign took as its motto the words of the Lord to Joshua: 'There are still very large areas of land to be taken over' (Josh 13:1). The detailed analysis that follows in Joshua 13–18, and especially chapter 18, outlining what remained to be done, stands as an example to ourselves as how to address the serious task of identifying the key communities that should form our prime planting objectives today.

Favourable factors

Three contemporary developments among the churches of the United Kingdom make this task a good deal more viable than it would have been even as recently as the late 1960s. They are increased spiritual confidence, increased community conscious-ness and increased interchurch co-operation.

Increased spiritual confidence

Particularly, though not exclusively, through fellowships in-fluenced by charismatic renewal, and vibrant ethnic church groups, a new spirit of confidence for mission has been injected into the life of our national Christian community. Prayer walks and praise marches publicly affirm the Christian conviction that the love and lordship of Jesus extends to every home and high street. Creative and sacrificial inner city ministries echo the same refusal to give up our population centres to powers that defy the One who stands eternally committed to the poor and oppressed. Oasis Frontline teams, Methodist Seed teams, Operation Mobilization Love Europe teams and others bear witness to the increasing numbers of young people prepared to take their faith out onto the streets.

'From maintenance to mission' is a phrase that has found its way onto many a denominational agenda and is beginning to represent a real, though gradual, change of outlook for many British churches. This attitudinal shift provides a springboard for fresh assessments of our churches' effectiveness in projecting the gospel into the communities of our land.

Increased community consciousness

Mission audits and community surveys have become the order of the day. Almost every denominational group has developed a pack of material to assist local churches in the process of taking an in-depth look at themselves and the community in which God has set them to be his witnesses. The development of the so-called 'church growth' movement has been influential in prompting the churches to respond more intelligently to the changing realities of society. Whether or not the vocabulary of marketing so unashamedly adopted by George Barna in his excellent book, *Marketing the Church*, finds a comfortable place in the language of Zion, the work of men like Donald McGavran, Peter Wagner and many others has provided the churches with new tools to help tackle the task of restructuring goals and programmes for mission in ways responsive both to the love of God and the needs of the local community.

Of particular importance for the task of new church planting was the impact of the missiological research conducted by MARC in preparation for the 1974 Lausanne Congress on World Evangelisation that helped to establish the concept of 'unreached people groups'. The recognition that there exist many socially and culturally distinct groups within areas traditionally thought to have been adequately covered by existing church missionary activity has provided a great incentive to apply the same research techniques to discover sectors of the communities surrounding our local churches that are going untouched by the life and truth of the Christian gospel. Greater objectivity in the assessment of the appropriateness and effectiveness of evangelistic programmes has led many churches, like the one referred to in the opening paragraph of this chapter, to recognise the limitations that both geography and cultural diversity place upon the ministry of any one church and review their mission policy accordingly. The research conducted by George Lings on the relationship between parish size and congregational size among Anglican churches exemplifies the value of careful church and community analysis in uncovering geographical areas and communities of people who are in reality going unreached by current ministry. Research is the enemy of complacency and cover-up alike, and the extent to which the churches have been falling short of their mission responsibility and indeed their mission potential is becoming painfully clear. It is a cause for gratitude, however, that the insights of church growth research that reveal the bad news also helpfully point the way ahead. That's good news that our churches are more able than ever to tune in to.

Increased interchurch co-operation

Perhaps the dawning of the realisation that British Christians live in a post-Christian age, members of a society that rarely even pretends to live by Christian values, has given the ecumenical movement its most positive focus: that of co-operation in mission. In any given area, all those who own the name of Christ share in the responsibility to make his life a challenging reality to the whole community in which they are set. Initiatives such as the Billy Graham crusades, Spring Harvest, Oasis' Christmas Unwrapped programmes, and the declaration of the Decade of Evangelism have become vehicles for moving the churches forward in recognising and responding to that responsibility.

In assessing the appropriateness of establishing a new Christian community in a particular area, due consideration must therefore be given to the extent and variety of Christian activity already being sustained there through the ministry of existing churches. Responsibility for mission is indeed shared by all but it must be recognised that not all share the same capacity for, understanding of, or commitment to mission.

Variety of spiritual emphases, and indeed of spiritual vigour, is a reality that should not be denied. It is, however, a reality that needs to be responded to with due sensitivity by those keen to pursue a policy of new church planting. If the Holy Spirit has been prompting one group to co-operate with him in establishing a new worshipping and witnessing community, it is presumptuous to think that others might not have sensed a similar prompting. Neither should the envisioned group feel free to pursue autonomous action when it is possible that it is the Spirit's intention that they should become his channel for inspiring the others of Christ's body into mutually beneficial co-operation for the kingdom.

It is a real tragedy when the birth of a new church brings joy to members of the unchurched community and yet resentment or misunderstanding among the churches. Sad to say, a careless disregard of the proprieties and possibilities of interchurch consultation led to several such tragedies in the early days of the new church planting movement. The legacy of these bad experiences has been to reinforce the fears and prejudices of those who for reasons of personality, or experience, or theology, find this approach to evangelism a difficult one to embrace. The teaching of Paul in Romans 15 is apposite here and can encourage those who enjoy the exhilaration of new-found confidence in the gospel to respond with sensitivity to those whose experience of church life in an antagonist society has been less positive. It can be extremely threatening to find that an attractive and lively group has suddenly arrived to tempt away your most able leaders and call into question the understanding of the gospel and your approach to ministry upon which you have based years of sacrificial service. Considerate consultation at the very outset of the process of evaluating the potential need for planting in a community can allow the growth of a relationship that builds up (Rom 15:2) rather than of a confrontation that the Enemy can use to rob the kingdom of the unity of love and purpose that the Spirit is so richly able to bless.

Perhaps the most common concern felt by existing groups upon hearing the news of a projected plant is that the result will only be to slice the 'Christian cake' more thinly. When churches are already struggling with depleted memberships to maintain ministry the new church can easily be perceived in life-threatening terms. No message needs to be repeated more regularly and with greater sincerity than that the purpose of the new work is to reach those who have no Christian allegiance, those who are unchurched. Many church planters find it helpful to assure leaders of existing congregations that they will positively discourage any transference of membership that is not supported by the existing church. Probably it is true to say that not a few planters wished that they had in fact adopted such a policy, as much for the well-being of the new church as for that of the existing one. It is not uncommon for new churches to attract reactionary, difficult and unstable members from surrounding groups who bring their problems with them to disrupt the aims and unity of the developing fellowship.

Not only can the new plant be presented as non-threatening, however, it can and should be presented as a means of raising the general profile of Christianity within the neighbourhood, to the benefit of all the churches. Have you ever wondered why you get roads full of shoe shops, or whole floors of shopping centres devoted to fashion outlets? The world of commerce has long since recognised the marketing value of concentrating retail outlets dealing with similar merchandise in the same vicinity. The concentration heightens the consumers' awareness of the product and of its value. Increased Christian activity will likewise help put Jesus back on the map!

There are also great potential benefits for the new group in establishing good fraternal links with existing churches. Community contacts can be provided and introductions given that can open the doors to fruitful areas of ministry: the prayerful support of a wider body of God's people as the new group engages the powers of darkness that would oppose the extension of the kingdom; the insights into community dynamics gained through years of presence that can suggest fresh and effective ways of getting into the life of the community.

Recent church planting by denominational, new church and ethnic groups has taken far more seriously the responsibility and potential of positive consultation. Some measure of co-operation without compromise is very often possible and when possible always desirable.

The review of background issues that we have just carried out provides the incentive to press on to lay down some guidelines for uncovering the local information necessary to come to well informed decisions about where and what to plant.

Faith, facts and feasibility—stepping stones in the pathway to plant location

Identify the possible target communities

It is worth making clear what may seem to be an obvious point right at the outset of any planting project: we are called to reach people, not places. It is helpful therefore to identify possible 'locations' in terms of the community of people which the new church will be aiming to evangelise. Very often the target community will in fact all be resident within a particular geographical area. They may not, however, represent all of those living there. For instance, the purpose of a new church might be to try to reach a subsection of the population that existing ministries are not getting through to. It is also becoming increasingly common to have as the target community a particular 'people group' whose members live across a wide area, such as many immigrant or refugee groups, or a new church specifically dedicated to communicating with young people. Such churches would tend to attract interest from an area much more extensive than that which a local church might normally count as its patch.

The clear identification of the community which the new church would be aiming to reach is then an important first step in the planting process. If a number of different possibilities are being considered then each option must be identified in target community terms. Clarity in this issue will tend to bring clarity into the thinking about virtually all of the issues of leadership, meeting place and ministry that will need to be dealt with later. It will make possible the identification of the resources needed to reach the particular group and so make it far easier to decide how feasible it might be for the planting agency to go ahead with that particular possibility. Lack of clarity will make the choice between possible plant locations more uncertain and ultimately lead to the emergence of a group that doesn't have a clear understanding of what it ought to be doing or what its goals ought to be.

It might be that as the community survey proceeds the definition of the particular target community will need to be refined, but at least be sure that you begin by knowing who are the people that the new church will be aiming to reach.

Once the possible target community or communities have been identified two key questions must be posed and answered.

The first is: What can we find out to help us decide whether or not we ought to be aiming to plant there?

The second question, asked once we are convinced that it is right to go ahead, is: What can we find out that can help us to know how to go about setting up a church that will have every chance of being effective at reaching the group in view?

The first question can be answered without entering into the detailed community survey work that answering the second will entail and should therefore be considered as Stage 1 in the process. The aim at this stage should be to get a green, amber or red light regarding the sense of rightness of a particular planting proposal.

Even though the leadership group of the planting church or agency might be already convinced of a particular course of action, it is valuable to work through the steps of this first stage both to clarify the leadership's grounds for their conviction and also as a means of sharing in a clearly structured way the reasons for the proposal with church or council members and other local Christian groups. It is vital that ownership of the planting scheme is as wide as possible even among those who will not be directly involved in the plant, and the Stage 1 process will encourage this ownership to develop.

Stage 1. Where shall we plant?

Four questions can help determine the rightness of a particular planting proposal. They have to do with possibility, vision, need, and receptivity.

- Is there a possibility of planting?
- Is there a vision for planting?
- Is there a need for planting?
- How receptive to the planting initiative is the target group likely to be?

Stage 1—WHERE TO PLANT?

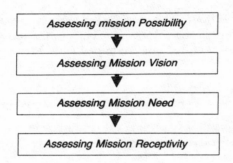

Possibility Often the possibility of starting a new work is suggested by a particular opportunity for action. Any reasons that would commend the project as opportune or feasible should be listed. They might typically include some of the following:

- Keen members living in the area concerned.
- The availability of a suitable meeting place.
- An invitation from another interested group to join them in such a venture.
- Or simply that resources have been allocated for such a project in line with mission policy.

Paul certainly knew how to grasp an opportunity when it arose, such as in the 'chance' encounter with Aquila and Priscilla in Corinth that allowed him to form a base upon which to found the church there (Acts 18).

What is generally desirable and what is specifically possible are not always the same, however. It is perfectly proper to ask whether or not a plant is actually possible or not. For even where there is vision, need and potential receptivity if the resources are not available then the project must wait. Paul certainly knew the frustration of circumstances combining to prevent him taking up particular opportunities. He was persistently hampered in his wish to revisit the newly founded church at Thessalonica by unspecified circumstances that he attributed to the work of Satan (1 Thess 2:17,18). On another occasion he was able to perceive that it was the hand of God that was closing the door to his proposed course of action (Acts 16:7).

Reasons for questioning the feasibility of the proposal should therefore also be listed and examined with due realism:

- No suitably gifted leader.
- The group targeted is too culturally different.
- Not sufficient support from within the fellowship.

Too few members or financial resources in the sponsoring group should rarely be accepted as deciding factors if other indicators are positive. The church that says 'When we get to such and such a size then we will plant' may be expressing a spiritual conviction about God's guidance to them or may be reflecting an attitude that assesses kingdom possibilities in terms of human resources. A large fellowship that turns away from planting might be genuinely affirming its conviction about the greater effectiveness of a larger 'high-impact' church able to offer a great variety of ministries or may simply be exposing an unreadiness to give away resources that might call for a revision of their own lifestyle as a church.

What is suggested at this first stage is only a general review of those particular opportunities that are prompting the church to consider the planting possibility. Later study might make things look more or less feasible, but it is a natural place to begin.

Vision Vision is a perception of God's possibilities. Men and women and young people of vision are those whom the Spirit has enabled to capture a picture of what God's future for a church, organisation or person could be. A vision is not the same as a dream. A vision and a visionary takes realities seriously—human reality and divine reality. A vision starts with today's realities but is not limited by them, rather it reaches ahead in conviction, seeing the shape of the something greater that God has in prospect for tomorrow.

Church planting is, above everything else, the work of God and so it is absolutely essential that the church planting project is clearly seen as part of God's agenda for the sponsoring group. Time and again in Paul's experience and in his writings he points to the call of God as the anchor and guarantee of ministry (Acts 18:9; 2 Tim 1:6).

The following questions might helpfully be answered in aiming to get a balanced and objective sense of the Spirit's guiding in regard to a particular planting possibility:

- Do any individuals have a 'vision' for planting in the target community?
- How has the vision come?
- To what extent does the church or mission group to which these individuals belong share the vision?
- How does this vision fit into the general understanding of how the Spirit is moving the church forward?
- What 'signs' are there that the 'hand of God' is upon the proposed venture?
- What is the reaction to this vision of other Christian groups both inside and outside the target community?

It is quite proper that a personal vision or conviction of God's leading should be tested by the group affected and, once again, there are clear examples of this procedure being followed in the development of Paul's church planting ministry.

Acts 13:1–3 offers an example of personal guidance being tested and confirmed by the leadership of a local church. There has been a popular tendency to understand the words of the Spirit, recorded in verse 2, as 'coming out of the blue', so to speak, to an unsuspecting leaders' meeting. A closer examination of the text suggests, however, that the leaders were meeting specifically to consider a sense of call to mission that Barnabas and Saul had felt earlier and had referred to the council for confirmation. The verb 'to call' in verse 2 is in the perfect tense. The use of *proskaleo* is not common in the New Testament, occurring only ten times. On only two occasions is it used in the perfect tense: here and in Acts 16:10—the Macedonian call. Elsewhere, whatever the tense employed, the indication is always of a point event, ie, a call occurring at that moment. The perfect tense, however, almost always refers to an event in the past that continues to affect the present. This is clearly illustrated in Acts 16:10 where the call that Luke and the others were discussing had, we are told, been received by Paul the previous night. This meaning of the tense, the confirmation of that usage in Acts 16:10 and, indeed, the very rapid way in which the expedition leaves, would all suggest that the Spirit's words are in fact confirming to the council of elders the authenticity of the call that he had *already given* and that Paul and Barnabas were keen to respond to.

Acts 16:10 is a further example, in a different context, of the mission team itself testing the particular guidance that Paul had received. Luke tells us that the decision to sail for Troas came after they had 'concluded' that the vision and its significance were authentic.

Both of these instances are also excellent examples of how this pattern of testing the vision can lead to a strong sense of group ownership of the project envisioned; note the corporate commissioning in Acts 13:3 and the conviction that 'God had called *us* to preach the gospel to them' (Acts 16:10).

A clear sense of God's leading is vital, then, and this should be considered in a mature and prayerful way by all those involved. No group should proceed with a church planting programme without reaching their Troas point.

Need Jesus was moved by need. His compassionate response to the sight of the large crowd on the shores of the Sea of Galilee (Mk 6:34) is typical not only of his own ministry but of everything that we know of our God's attitude towards a world of need. One of the great world mission affirmations of the Old Testament, found in Jonah 4:11, is a particularly telling challenge to today's UK church: 'But Nineveh has more than a hundred and twenty thousand people who cannot tell their right hand from their left ... should I not be concerned about that great city?' But whether the need is urban or rural, in the capital or the countryside, people's need to experience the arrival of the kingdom is quite properly a great spur to church planting.

David Barrett, perhaps the most informed individual on the state of global mission, suggests a division of the world population into three groups: worlds A, B and C.[1]

- World C (33 per cent) consists of all those who individually call themselves Christians.
- World B (44 per cent) stands for non-Christians who are in contact with Christians and who have at least some knowledge of Christ and the gospel.
- World A (23 per cent) stands for non-Christians who have never come into contact with Christians and have no knowledge of Christ and the gospel.

Given the enormous need for specifically targeted evangelism into the least reached communities, he goes on to challenge the prevailing allocation of Christian resources, presenting figures that should shock and probably shame:

- 99 per cent of the Christian world's income is spent on itself.
- Only 10 per cent of evangelistic activity is actually directed at non-Christians, and less than that percentage of missionary personnel is actually working directly in the most needy section of the world's population.

He concludes: 'A fundamental flaw in today's world mission is that most mission agencies are not targeting world A.'[2]

When considering where to plant, then, the question of need should be addressed. Some communities are more needy than others. Even though there might be keen members living in a particular community and even though other factors might be favourable, if there is already an evangelical church effectively reaching the group that is in view then can it be good stewardship to start a new church there when perhaps a nearby council housing estate has no witness or when there is an Asian community scattered around the area which is going unreached? The easy option is always to go for the community that is closest geographically and culturally. Result ... whole areas of our inner cities without worshipping and witnessing communities.

Colin Marchant, past President of the Baptist Union, who has spent his life in inner city ministry has stated that in some London boroughs there are fewer people meeting to worship in the name of Jesus than in any other non-Muslim mission field throughout the world. Simply because these communities don't fall within the physical and cultural backyard of our stronger suburban churches their residents live on without any realistic opportunity to hear the gospel in a meaningful way.

Need, then, is an uncomfortable criterion to reckon with but one that cannot be disregarded if we really aim to identify with Jesus in his approach to mission. It is interesting to note that faced with the relative needs of Capernaum and the surrounding villages at the successful beginning of his ministry, Jesus sets his face towards the unreached communities with the affirmation: 'That is why I have come' (Mk 1:38). Paul's personal testimony at the close of his letter to the Romans reflects this Christian concern for the most needy areas: 'It has always been my ambition to preach the gospel where Christ was not known' (Rom 15:20). It is evident from what he goes on to say that this criterion has taken precedent over his personal preferences: 'This is why I have often been hindered from coming to you' (Rom 15:22). Even then as he goes on to express his pleasure at finally being able to fulfil his 'longing' to see them (Rom 15:23); it is only because he will be able to do so en route to his next projected mission field in Spain (Rom 15:24).

If need is a criterion that must be taken seriously, how can it be assessed? To refer back to the article by David Barrett, he makes a statement that can, I believe, be helpful in an effort to establish a simple and useable means of assessing evangelistic need. He writes, 'No contact, no mission'.[3]

Mission need of a community, then, can be assessed in terms of the degree of contact that Christians have with non-Christians or 'unchurched individuals' resident in that community.

I have coined the phrase 'Christian contact count' to express this figure. The *Christian contact count* is defined as: Contacts

via resident Christians plus contacts through Church programmes expressed as a percentage of the total population of
the community in view.[4] A detailed account of how to conduct
this assessment is given in Appendix A.

Because 'need' is a relative term it is important to get a figure
against which to compare the Christian contact count of the
community which is under consideration for planting. For several
reasons it is recommended that this standard assessment be
made in the community in which the existing church is located.

First, carrying out the survey locally will give some experience
of collecting the necessary information in a familiar environment. Second, it will provide a standard of comparison that
church members are easily able to relate to when considering
the need of the community targeted for the plant.

It will also, of course, give an objective measure of the
effectiveness of the mission programmes of the existing church.
Many a local church and mission agency would benefit both
from the sobering impact of such an assessment and of having a
basis against which to judge the value of any changes in
outreach programmes.

There is, however, quite a danger here. It is possible that the
survey will reveal such a low level of mission penetration in the
immediate locality of the church that all thoughts of setting
aside resources for work outside the area will be shelved until
the home church performance has improved! A timely referral
back to the exemplary behaviour of the leadership of the
Antioch church would be in order if this possibility were
suggested. In fact, a balanced evangelistic programme should
always include involvement in both church growth and church
planting programmes.

Receptivity The fourth factor that should be considered by a
group considering a new church plant is that of the likely
receptivity to the gospel of the community that is being
targeted. Once again, it will not be possible to come to a
definite conclusion but if there are indicators of how quickly
the new church might establish itself then they are worth
noting down and bearing in mind when a decision is being made

about whether or not it is right to proceed with a particular plant.

A church that is slow in becoming established will draw upon the financial and personnel resources of the planting group for longer than one that gets off the ground more quickly. If the community in view is notoriously difficult to penetrate or has a high population turnover then the new fellowship might be destined for a life of chronic weakness. This may or may not be considered a disqualifying factor since it is precisely in the difficult areas that the need for courageous witness is greatest. But it is something that should be recognised, both by the planting team and sponsoring group, since otherwise unrealistically high expectations could lead to disillusionment or the withdrawal of support.

Similarly, the role of a plant at a certain stage in an ongoing programme of evangelistic expansion might require that rapid, resource-generating growth be achieved in order to fuel the development of the strategy. In such a case an estimate of the likely receptivity of a given target community would be of the greatest importance. Conversely, the likelihood of low receptivity and a slow take-off time will be accepted if the aim of the evangelistic programme were to establish a church planting movement within a culturally distinct people group, such as a particular ethnic community, which could then become the springboard for mission outreach from within the group.

Factors that should be borne in mind in making an estimate of receptivity can be both social and spiritual.

- The level of non-Christian religious activity. Competition for hearts and minds ebbs and flows in the history of a country but the influence of the New Age movement, the spread of Islam, and the startling rise in occultism has added to the competition from Mormons and Jehovah's Witnesses.
- The degree of cultural difference between the planting group and the target community. Culture and religious affiliation often go hand in hand, and certainly in the case of the ancient Eastern religions, socially embedded non-Christian ways of understanding the world and approaching life form serious

obstacles to Christian evangelism. The public acceptance of Christianity is always hampered when the church is perceived as belonging to an alien or even hostile social group. It should be noted, however, that this isn't relevant only in the case of cross-ethnic evangelism but of much trans-cultural outreach, such as among unchurched youth or so-called 'working class' communities.

- The spiritual history of a community. A history of unopposed demonic domination of the hearts and minds of any community will inevitably present a barrier to the reception of the gospel both in terms of active spiritual opposition and in terms of a generally negative attitude to Christian values and presence. The 'invasion' of Gentile territory by Jesus, recorded in Mark 4:35–5:20, is typical of the experience of many church planters who dare to repossess for the kingdom of God areas in which the devil has for many years had a free hand. From the storm on the lake, through the 'thunder and lightning' encounter with the demonised man on the beach, right up to the 'storm' of protest at his continued presence in their territory by the local residents, confrontation is the name of the game.

Biblical support is lacking for the significance being currently attributed to the activities of territorial spirits, and some mission practice grounded in this uncertain biblical and theological base is certainly open to question. The reality and the ferocity of demonic opposition to the expansion of the kingdom, however, has ample grounding both in Scripture and experience and should be taken most seriously when assessing the type and level of spiritual opposition to be encountered in a particular planting project.

- The level of social upheaval within a community. Man's extremity is God's opportunity. This saying has long expressed the general principle that whenever changes in circumstances break down the protective framework of beliefs and relationships that people build around themselves then they become particularly open to considering new belief and relationship patterns to restore the treasured sense of security. The so-called 'rites of passage'—birth, marriage, death, and so on—are often times when individuals are ready to reassess the basis upon which their life's beliefs and attitudes are predicated. Similarly, relocation, to a new area offers particular opportunities to present the gospel, a fact that underlies the rapid growth typical of church plants into new housing developments. The social and spiritual vacuum into which many refugee groups arrive when they find themselves washed up on our shores must present a similar opportunity for the gospel for churches prepared to employ resources beyond their own backyards.

- The receptivity of socially similar groups in other areas. It is well worth contacting denominational mission directors or church planting networks to gain insights into potential receptivity from plants carried out in similar communities elsewhere. Valuable lessons on how to proceed and what to expect can be learned from those who have faced a similar challenge.

Other factors will certainly tend to affect the likely rate of development of a self-supporting church: whether or not the community has a growth or decline mentality, whether or not able members of the community are likely to remain for any length of time in the area, whether or not there is support from other Christian groups in the area, and so on. These factors, although important, are not strictly speaking indicators of the inherent receptivity of the community, and they and others like them will be dealt with later in the chapter.

Presenting the results of the Stage 1 survey The purpose of the survey of possibility, vision, need and receptivity is to guide and ground the process of deciding whether or not a particular location is where a new church should be planted. Both the gathering of the data and the need to present it clearly will give first the leadership, and subsequently as many as possible of those who would be affected, the chance to sense both the rightness and reasonableness of a project and commit themselves to it with an informed conviction. The survey team will almost certainly have to make a presentation of their findings to a variety of audiences, large and small, and each should be approached with prayerfulness and due sensitivity to the purpose of the meeting. Presentation is a vital aspect of this process of discovering and embracing God's will as it gives the different groups a chance to focus on the issue and capture the vision.

No project should proceed without those involved having shared the vision and come to the conclusion that 'God [has] called us to preach the gospel to them' (Acts 16:10).

Stage 2. What are we planting?

The decision to go ahead with a church plant in a given area is only the first and in many ways the easiest step. The really challenging and crucially important issue is: What should this new church look like?

It is worth repeating the quote from Charles Brock already referred to in Chapter Two: 'The objective is more than planting a church, it is planting an indigenous church.' The unique benefit of new church planting as a means of evangelism is that it permits the development of a ministry programme that is genuinely sensitive to the target community.

The freedom that starting from scratch brings is not, however, a freedom to 'do your own thing'. The temptation for the core group to pursue its own preferences, previously restricted by the traditions of the mother church, should be resisted just as strongly as should any pressure from the sponsoring group to dictate the patterns of worship and witness of the new group. The freedom that new church planting brings is the freedom to become incarnate in and for the community that needs to be reached with the gospel. It is not that the needs of the community will write the theology of the church any more than Jesus allowed the aspirations of the Jews to shape his agenda for salvation. They must, however, shape the *form* of ministry adopted. Robert Warner, writing in the inaugural issue of *Planting Papers*, the journal of the Baptist network of church planters, BACUP, in an article entitled 'The Folly of Photocopying', sums it up well:

An indigenous church needs freedom. Freedom to discover what it means to serve Christ in a new cultural context. Freedom to become different from the sending church. Real church planting has no place for carbon copies.

'What are we planting?' is, then, a vital question to which the planting group must gain as thorough an answer as possible.

- What geographical factors are important for the target community?
- How is the community made up?
- What is the socio-economic profile of the main groups?
- What is the educational picture?
- Are there any distinctive needs or aspirations?
- Which political parties most actively represent the community?
- Who are the key figures, trendsetters, permission-givers?
- How, if at all, is the community changing?
- How do residents spend their time?
- Are there any possible meeting places for the new church?
- What are the prevailing attitudes towards church?
- What other groups are active in the community?
- How does news travel in the community?

The answers to these questions will give information that is vital to deciding key issues, such as those relating to the appropriate:

- Links—between the sponsoring group and the new group.
- Leadership—of the church plant.
- Lifestyle—of the new congregation.
- Location—of the meeting place(s).

These are questions that focus on the people God is calling the new group to reach. Any planning procedure that doesn't seriously address the question of who these people are, how do they live, and what are their particular needs, might well result in a church programme but will rarely if ever make effective mission impact. Appendix B offers a suggested procedure to carry out such a survey.

First, however, a brief consideration of each of the areas

Stage 2—WHAT TO PLANT?

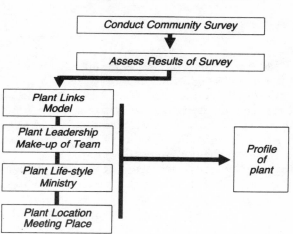

highlighted will give an indication of how such information can be useful to the core group as they prayerfully seek an appropriate profile for the projected plant.

'Where' questions

- Are there geographical factors that are important for the target community?
- Are there any possible meeting places for the new church?

'Where?' questions aim to paint a picture of the physical environment in which the people you want to reach have to live. Where do people live, where do they shop, where do they go for leisure activities, where are public amenities such as council offices, schools, churches and clinics situated, where do they work, where are the main roads, public transport facilities. All these are important questions to someone living in the community and so important to the church. They are best marked on a large-scale map along with photographs of focal points of the area and should be constantly kept in view while various possibilities of ministry are being considered.

These factors are, of course, especially relevant in considering the merits of possible meeting places for the new congregation in its ministry of public worship or witness. Visibility and accessibility are clearly important considerations, as are the user-friendliness of any building to be used. Places that are identified in the public mind with life and vitality are generally to be preferred although certain more traditional groups within the community may feel more comfortable in locations that speak of security and religion.

Practical considerations such as car parking space or the proximity of public transport can also be crucial and any information likely to be helpful in this respect should be marked on the map. A more detailed consideration of these issues will be given in a later chapter.

Beyond that, however, the layout of the area within which the community is resident will suggest problems and opportunities for ministry. Places where people meet and have time to talk can be noted as possible Christian contact points. Shopping centres and commonly used routes to shops, school, work, etc, will be potential sites for publicity. The location of particular groups of people such as the elderly, families with young children, immigrant groups, or of institutions such as hospitals or hostels will raise issues of specific ministries focused perhaps in cell groups at these locations. Physical obstacles to ease of movement or public access will need to be noted. Steep hills can be barriers to the elderly just as busy roads can be to children. A particularly scattered community may be faced with needs and limitations not faced in a more concentrated population centre. The homes of active Christians, especially those interested in the planting possibility, will be a further item of information that is most helpfully registered on the map.

'Who' questions

● How is the community made up?

The population of any given area can be divided up into different groups of people each of which has distinctive characteristics and needs. In order to offer patterns of service, fellowship, worship and Christian witness that are as effective as possible, it is of the greatest value to get a feel for the 'building material' out of which Jesus is planning to construct his new church.

Age distribution is important information. Consider the following table:

Age	Characteristics/attitudes	Possible significance for ministry
0–4	pre-school, mums and toddlers	childminding for working mums, creche facilities for services and other activities
5–14	school	resources for children's ministries on Sundays and weekdays, space, leadership, liaison with schools
15–24	experimenting with lifestyle, establishing norms for living, rejection of tradition, youth	creative, risky programmes
24–44	post-war, 'baby-boomer' attitudes, marriage/divorce, parents, career, ambition, distinctive male/female roles, crises	
45–64	pre-war attitudes, children leaving, job expectations, stable, more time, financial security	
65+	retirement, limited mobility, illness, loneliness, freedom, male/female imbalance, traditional, available	

Information on particular age groupings is directly available from the ten-yearly national census statistics for even quite small areas typical of those targeted for new church plants.

Any ethnic groups within the community will need to be identified. They might or might not have distinctive patterns of employment, social life, language, and so on, but in any event their presence will have to be acknowledged in the make-up of the leadership of the planting group if the new congregation is hoping to be responsive to their particular needs. Working women, the unemployed, students of 16+, institutionalised people, and others, are socially significant groups identified in the national census. One way or another, the leadership group will need to tune in to the opportunities and difficulties of ministry among such groups.

The different ministry requirements of each group should be taken seriously, especially when a new congregation with limited people and financial resources is being launched. It is unrealistic to aim to build a programme of ministry that will be equally attractive to every section of the community. A selective approach should be adopted in which particularly significant or needy groups not being reached by others become the focus of the church activities and ethos that will characterise the new work.

A particularly clear example of ministry targeting is found in the philosophy of the Willow Creek Community Church, situated in a wealthy suburb of Chicago. A paraphrase of part of the document that sets out their philosophy of ministry clearly illustrates the issue in hand.

The leaders believed that it was important to identify a target audience. Knowing who they wanted to reach allowed them to focus their efforts and energies. It was not enough just to state that the target audience was the unchurched individual, but rather to become more specific. The community surrounding the church encompasses many individuals who are employed in professional positions. Therefore professional men between the ages of 25 and 50 are the target audience for the Willow Creek Community Church Sunday service. Other age groups are reached through other ministries of the church but since men are more difficult to reach with the gospel message and are tougher in their demands on the church, the services are designed to speak and appeal to men. Women tend to be more open, forgiving and easier to please in church matters. Therefore if the service reaches men it will reach women as well. Additionally, men are traditionally the role model within the family. If the man in the household is not involved in the spiritual life of the family the spiritual growth of the family is curtailed.

As the church has grown to become, in only fifteen years, the second largest in the United States, the same principles of ministry targeting have been applied to a whole range of programmes maintained by the church. The result is a full-orbed ministry profile that impacts the local community in an extraordinarily effective way.

It is clear that foundational to such an approach is a readiness to let the needs and character of the target group determine the styles of worship and witness that the new church adopts. Since it will be the leadership of the new church that will largely determine the shape and style of its life then not only should the leaders live within the community, they should also reflect its age and ethnic balance.

'What' questions

- What is the socio-economic and educational profile of the main groups?
- What are the distinctive needs or aspirations of the community?

Housing, employment and educational background are important indicators of the lifestyle experienced by the community. Whether housing is owner-occupied or rented, whether there is a fast turnover of occupancy, whether it is difficult or easy to get accommodation in the area are all factors that will influence the potential growth rate and subsequent stability of a new congregation.

The prevailing economic climate will also exert a considerable influence over the character of the neighbourhood. Financial anxiety over mortgage repayments, both husband and wife working, and a commuter existence produce a stressed lifestyle that reduces the availability of members of the group for congregational responsibility and work and of unchurched folk to participate in church activities.

Low income, bad housing, poor employment prospects and unemployment generate a catalogue of social problems. A general lack of self-esteem, a spirit of hopelessness and decline are all too often characteristics of socially depressed communities which do not readily throw up local leadership potential or a stable core group for the new church. In such needy environments it is also all too tempting to concentrate the limited congregational resources on maintaining difficult social programmes that, valid though they might be, are unlikely to further the primary objective of establishing the new, indigenous Christian group.

The survey may, however, identify specific areas of social need that particularly gifted individuals within the church group can respond to, perhaps in conjunction with other Christian groups. But what is of greater value is for the new group to link in to the existing network of individuals and agencies who have the well-being of the community at heart. Contacts with all such agencies, from community police through social workers, local GPs, councillors and other voluntary agencies, should be a prime task within the Stage 2 process. Together with them a genuine Christian contribution can be made at the level of social need, while at the same time building credibility and acceptance within the community that can open valuable opportunities for developing the evangelistic thrust of the new church's programme.

A clear picture of lifestyles, attitudes and expectations will also allow the leadership to devise and promote evangelistic programmes that 'scratch where it itches' as the saying goes. Preaching and other presentations of the gospel will need to be made to sound authentic according to what are the accepted communication criteria of the particular community. Questions such as what are the most commonly read newspapers and most commonly watched TV programmes are good pointers to the type of 'communication package' that is to be preferred. There is no need for reticence here since Jesus himself, the incarnate Son of Man, stands as exemplar par excellence in the whole area of culturally appropriate communication.

'Change' questions

● How, if at all, is the community changing?

A church that is going to grow should always aim to keep one step ahead of the community in terms of changes taking place. If the social face of the community is changing through the immigration of more or less well-off groups with different lifestyles then the church needs to be aware of this so as to plan appropriate ministries to reach the new groups. The alternative is progressive marginalisation.

Any population movement that affects the availability of potential leaders for the future of the work is of great significance. If lack of affordable housing or suitable employment is causing younger people to leave the community to live elsewhere then this will have implications for certain aspects of any proposed ministry, particularly for any hope of church growth through 'biological growth'—the retaining of the children of believers. If an ethnic presence is growing or changing then a wise leadership will seek advice as to how best to keep abreast of that development by contacting the emerging community's local leaders and allying itself with the needs of the new group. Christians above all people have a manifesto to support the stranger in his isolation.

Spurgeon, the great Baptist church planter of the Victorian era, had an eye for the significance of population movements and social change. He used to urge that 'growing villages [such as Cheam!] near London, early be supplied with the gospel of Christ. Being on the spot the friends will be ready for greater things as the population increases.'[5]

So today areas earmarked for commercial and residential redevelopment should be recognised as areas of greater than average church planting significance and potential. Together with other short, medium and long-term council plans likely to effect the community, such information is readily available from local government. As in the case of contacts with political and social leaders, contact with civil servants having professional responsibility for the area can often yield both excellent information and good personal contacts and should, therefore, be sought and cultivated.

'Activity and attitude' questions

● How do residents spend their time?

The schedule of activities pursued by the various groups within the community will determine for each group when its members are most available for contact with members of the new church. Commuter journeys, sports clubs, the school playground or local pub can all take on the role of the 'village well', or community meeting places, and need to be identified.

Mission contact programmes should be organised to make the gospel and its representatives available to the people when the people are available to be reached! Paul's decision to begin the work at Philippi on the Sabbath, down by the river (Acts 16:13), is a good example of knowing your target group and responding intelligently to its availability. There was a time when the church could publish its timetable and people could be expected to fit in with it. Those days are gone. As any local businessman can tell you, you've got to be available when the customer is free and interested or you'll lose out to the opposition. And the church has never had so much opposition. Whether in the form of the ritual Sunday morning car boot sale, the evening soap opera, or the weekend outings to visit Asian relatives or country cottages, every community will have its own pattern of leisure activities and these need to be carefully and creatively studied with a view to avoiding unhelpful clashes and to obtaining ideas on how best to catch people with time to talk.

Patterns of employment can be equally as significant. Many people are effectively excluded from traditionally timetabled Christian activities by being tied into night-time or weekend working. If the churches were more aware of how normal people—and Christians are not normal!—spent their time a lot of resources wasted on ill-timed evangelistic activities could be saved. Once again, the selective targeting of a particular group or groups can help in making coherent decisions about programme scheduling and the development of outreach activities in which audience availability is taken seriously.

● What are the prevailing attitudes towards church?

In working out what its particular mission strategy was to be the Willow Creek Church carried out a simple piece of 'market research'. Members of the community were asked one question: 'Do you actively attend a local church?' If the response was yes, those conducting the survey thanked them for their time and left. If the answer was no, they asked them why.

Appendix B contains a simple survey with suggested questions that can help you discover what your target group thinks about God and the church. It should hardly need saying that a first-hand feel of where people are spiritually is absolutely basic to any serious attempt to formulate an evangelistic ministry that will address the questions that are really troubling people rather than those which the church believes are troubling them or ought to be troubling them.

● What other groups are active in the community?

The church isn't the only group interested in helping the community or harnessing/exploiting the goodwill or energy of its population. For reasons both good and bad, various groups will be seeking to promote themselves and gain recognition and support. Whether a particular group might be considered an enemy or an ally, the success or failure they enjoy can provide most helpful pointers to how best to develop the new church and should be carefully noted.

Very often good relationships established with other voluntary groups can become of the greatest help in gaining community acceptance and the use of community facilities over which the established groups exercise control.

'Way-in' questions

● Which political parties most actively represent the community?
● Who are the key figures, trend-setters, permission givers?

Contact with those perceived by the community as best able to represent their interests in matters of local and national concern should offer further opportunities to 'get into the mind' of the neighbourhood. Such people often hold the keys to networks of communication within the community that, if made available to the new church, can be of the greatest value in getting off the ground with a positive and high profile.

The goodwill and, if possible, the conversion of such people can be crucial to the future development of a new congregation. Few churches take this matter as seriously as its importance merits. Opportunities for the use of buildings, for media publicity, for the staging of large events, for permission to minister in educational and other institutions are just some of the many aspects of ministry development that can be helped or hindered by key people in the community. Occasionally, there will be disinterest or even hostility to the new venture but more often politeness or even commercial or political expediency will encourage a measure of interest and even co-operation.

Such individuals should, in fact, become strategic targets for prayer and witness, not because they are intrinsically more important to God than anyone else but because their conversion can be so much more significant in the building of the new church. Contact with councillors and other community leaders should also be sought without embarrassment since the gospel is not a private matter but, we believe, one that should influence every political and social agenda.

• How does news travel in the community?

One of the first challenges that the new church will face in making an impact in the community is that of letting the residents know that it is there. Finance usually limits the use of large-scale advertising which is in any event often of dubious value in projecting a positive and attractive image of the new church. Every use should be made of the informal networks of communication whereby information travels around the community. It's surprising how fast news travels when you talk to the right people!

Key individuals or groups of people are the transmitters of news and views. Once identified, a good public relations job needs to be done on them so that not only the news of the church's arrival becomes interesting news to pass on but also that it is accompanied by a positive commentary. It is more important that people are talking about the arrival of the new church than it is that they are receiving pieces of paper telling them about it. You get an echo when you open your mouth and project your voice in the right direction. In the same way, word of mouth publicity, when done in the right way, can spread news as effectively as any other publicity there is. Especially because the Christian good news is people with God in their lives, people are better communicators of the arrival of the new church than any amount of paper.

It's worth bearing in mind that conduct of the community survey itself will actually form the very first and possibly most eloquent publicity promotion that the church could mount. Careful preparation of those involved should reflect this recognition that the whole survey will also be, for better or worse, a public relations exercise.

Two final words of advice from others who have experience in surveying communities for mission:

> Do not rush the early stages of planning, networking, training interviewers, audit design, etc, in a mad panic to 'do a survey' and produce a report. It will take twice as long as you think anyway! And even then, when it comes to mission, you've only just begun.[6]

> While you will have collected a lot of data that will help you in establishing the new church, you need to remember that this is only information and above all else and through it all, you need to be listening to God the Holy Spirit and what he has to say in the whole process. When you do this you will begin on the road to successful church planting because God will be in charge and not data.[7]

For discussion and further study

1. Discuss the relative importance of the 'indicators' of need, vision, possibility and receptivity in determining the appropriateness of a particular planting proposal.
2. How valid is it to attempt to assess mission need using the type of mathematical procedure outlined in Appendix A?
3. Are the grounds for attempting to assess the receptivity of the target community primarily theological or pragmatic?
4. Make a case for conducting a community survey in an area identified for church planting.

Notes

1. David Barrett, *International Bulletin of Missionary Research*, (January 1991).
2. *Op cit*, p 24.
3. *Ibid*.
4. Charles Chaney, *Church Planting at the End of the Twentieth Century* (Tyndale, 1982), p 44 adopts a similar approach in attempting to identify an objective criterion that could be useful in making mission decisions based upon community need.
5. *Sword and Trowel* (1871), p 190, quoted from Mike Nicholls, *C.H. Spurgeon: Church Planter—Mission to the World*, (Baptist Historical Society, 1991).
6. *Mission Audits in Urban Priority Areas—resources to get you started* (BCGA, 1987).
7. Philip Bryant, *A Church Planting Workbook* (Baptist Union of Victoria, Australia).

CHAPTER EIGHT

PLANTING ACROSS CULTURAL BOUNDARIES

Stuart Christine

The task of spreading the gospel across cultural boundaries is one of the greatest challenges currently facing the UK church.

The challenge of cultural change

The way people behave, the expectations they have, their use of time at work and in leisure are matters which continue to change at an unprecedented rate. Circles of friends tend to increase in number and reduce in size, the different groups often having little overlap. The days when a neighbourhood was a community interlinked through marriage and shared employment or recreation have, for most, been replaced by a present in which you probably aren't sure of the names of your nextdoor neighbours, let alone whether or not they married. Within a given area, lifestyles will vary as never before according to generation, employment, family make-up or rather breakdown, ethnic background, and so on. Add to this cocktail of cultures the colours and distinctive flavourings of increasing internationalisation of the population and the result is a society whose complexity is enough to make your head spin.

The landscape of British society has altered. The wide expanses of largely monocultural blocks of population have become criss-crossed by the new boundaries belonging to a multiplication of subcultures, and the credibility and accept-ability of any group claiming to have the right to tell people how to live and what to think is challenged afresh at every border crossing! It's one thing to hear the apostle Paul proclaiming that 'God commands all men everywhere to repent ...' (Acts

17:30), but not all men are the same and it's increasingly difficult for the church to get access to 'where they're at'. The difficulties are compounded because the attitudes and lifestyle associated with the Christian church are perceived by many to have little relevance to the realities of their particular world where God, or at least the popular understanding of the Christian God, doesn't seem to fit or indeed to be necessary.

For the church, problems of communication and accessibility that were once associated with the challenge of foreign mission work have arrived on the doorstep. The fact that the need for cross-cultural mission is so often met with a 'return to sender—wrong address' attitude must be a matter of considerable concern, for unless the churches break out of the shrinking cultural ghettos in which too many are entrenched then the future can only be one of continued decline.

'Outreach' has been a commonly used term to describe evangelism. The challenge faced by many local churches today, however, requires more the idea of 'reaching over' cultural barriers or 'reaching across' cultural divides if contact with the neighbourhood is to be made. It is this reality that lies behind the statement with which the chapter began: The task of spreading the gospel across cultural boundaries is one of the greatest challenges currently facing the UK church.

The challenge is, however, one that the church of Jesus can take up with confidence. The experience of its earliest years of missionary expansion forms a record of precedents and pointers for positive cross-cultural evangelism and church planting.

Peter discovered the gospel need accept no boundaries. With Jesus he had crossed every social divide among his own people. He had witnessed Jesus breaking through the multiple barriers of gender, religion and race to introduce a Samaritian woman to God (Jn 4:1–42). He had seen Jesus refuse to allow the prejudice of a Samaritan village against him to dictate how he should respond to them (Lk 9:51–56). He had seen centuries of religious tradition set aside by a God who refused to exclude a Roman officer and his household (Acts 10:34,35). A good many Christian leaders and congregations today need to follow in Peter's footsteps and make that same uncomfortable but confidence-building journey.

Groundwork for growth across cultural boundaries

In a recent report on the religious scene in the capital, Colin Marchant wrote:

> In central London alone 400 places of worship, ranging from cathedral to basement room represent 8 major faiths as well as over 40 distinct Christian churches, denominations and groups. Athens is here![1]

The church has discovered, however, like the apostle Paul in Athens, that it's one thing to recognise and want to respond to the cultural and religious mishmash of a mixed-up world, it's quite another to do so in a way that is effective.

Most of our people are unused to deciphering the cultural codes that exclude the church from so much of what is going on 'out there'. However, some careful looking and listening and thinking can go a long way to disentangling what at first might seem like a hopelessly confusing social scene.

First of all, taking a look at the way you spend your own life will help. Most people find that their lives are built up around a number of different activities, for example, the work they have to do, whether at home, in paid employment or at school. The leisure activities they are able to pursue will form another such focus. Church involvement yet another. In each of these life centres there will be a circle of friends and acquaintances. It's interesting to note that the different groups of people often don't overlap that much.

The way you behave, the clothes you wear and the topics of conversation will tend to be different according to which group you're spending time with. Each social setting will tend to have its own norms of language and customs and even values. You feel at home there because of the way you were brought up or the education you had or the preferences you've developed. Whatever the underlying reason, you're familiar with those rules of behaviour and are more or less happy to go along with them. When people are very unhappy with the accepted life-style or attitudes of a group they usually manage, one way or another, to leave it and find a substitute group that can offer them similar benefits. The social climate of the UK is one that favours the multiplication of 'subcultures' with people having the opportunity to choose which subculture they want to belong to. Even though poverty and other factors such as illness can limit the range of options available to people, the underlying principle of life building in the UK is that people associate with groups with whom they feel 'at home'.

Most people do not feel 'at home' or comfortable in church. There are a variety of reasons for this but immediately the point to be recognised is that the feeling of 'not belonging' will mean that few people, even if they have a sense of spiritual need, will naturally go for the 'church option'. There are barriers to be overcome if an individual is going to feel able to relax and consider the message of the gospel in a positive way.

The number and the size of these barriers will depend a lot upon how much contact the person has had with the church and how different the people and lifestyle of the church are from those of the circles in which they normally move.

What is vital is that the church becomes more aware of just how real these barriers are for the large majority of the population of our land. You might help yourself to stand in an unchurched person's shoes by, for instance, going to visit a mosque or remembering how you felt on needing to attend a specialist hospital for some examinations with painful-sounding names that none of your friends knew much about. Most people will avoid such anxiety-creating experiences if they can. If your neighbours had a choice between going to your church or the dentist they would probably choose the dentist!

It's not just the fact that what goes on inside churches is unknown to a lot of people, although that, as we've seen, can be quite a barrier itself, the problem is that what does go on *really is strange*. The language used, the dress and the rituals, like singing all together, are strange and probably quite foreign to behaviour patterns in the other groups to which the unchurched person belongs. Culture shock is something experienced every time an unchurched person enters a church.

This behaviour barrier has well been referred to as the 'stained glass' barrier. It is a reality even for people who relate quite freely together in other areas of life. They might belong to the same sports club or work in the same office but once they cross the threshold of a church then they're moving into another world and the climate, language and customs all seem strange!

Now it is clear that the degree of strangeness an unchurched person might experience upon contact with the church and its message will vary according to his or her background. For instance, the teenage son of Christian parents might very well find the music and language of church anachronistic but he will at least be used to it from having accompanied his parents in earlier years. His situation will be different from that of the unchurched and unbelieving neighbours who otherwise belong to the same social group. They will be confronted not only with a religious way of understanding life, but also with all the religious trappings and jargon which make up the traditional packaging of the Christian message.

Worse off still is the Jamaican porter at the office whom our teenager's father has been persuading to visit the church. His discomfort is compounded by the colour of his skin and the whole way of talking and behaving that makes it extremely difficult to see the relevance of what is going on and being talked about for the community in which he lives.

The wife of the Indian owner of the local corner shop can barely understand the English, and in any case has her own religion that has formed the framework for every aspect of her life ever since she was born in Delhi fifty years ago. For her the experience of church is like that of a visit to another world.

These examples aim to show that there are distinct levels of cultural distance, or heights of cultural barrier, that may need to be crossed, depending upon the socio-cultural group that the non-Christian person belongs to. Dr Ralph Winter helpfully identified this reality and assigned the lables of E-0, E-1, E-2 and E-3, where the number indicates the degree of cultural difference that the evangelising church must reckon with.

E-0 evangelism describes the challenge of evangelising those already comfortable within the circle of the church. Our teenager would fit in here unless he was so involved with a youth subculture that the style of music, etc, represented a significant barrier to his 'hearing' the gospel.

E-1 evangelism refers to those who must cross the 'stained glass' barrier but who are otherwise able to relate reasonably well to the language and lifestyle of the social group attending the church (see the second example above).

E-2 evangelism, as the numbering suggests, recognises that there exists a further significant barrier to feeling 'at home'. This could be a different ethnic background, for example, the Jamaican porter, ill at ease in the middle-class white congregation.

E-3 evangelism would further include factors such as language and fundamental ethnic-religious differences. If the Indian lady referred to really only lived her life in a microcosm of India maintained in her own home, unable to communicate or relate to non-Indian society, then the church's task in reaching her with the gospel might best be described by this category.

Churches need to be both realistic and creative in considering how best Kingdom growth can be achieved in a multicultural environment. Bruce Patrick helpfully illustrates the options in his booklet *Reaching All the People Groups*.[2]

Growth through expansion

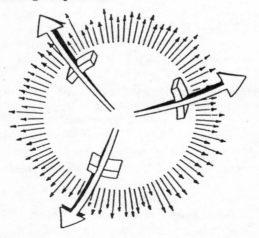

A local church can deliberately develop its lifestyle to be as 'user-friendly' as possible, keeping the 'stained glass' barrier low. Leaders representative of the different groups targeted by the church and the creative provision of programmes relevant to the different needs of the various groups will enable the church to develop beyond a narrow monoculturalism.

Growth through extension (E-1)

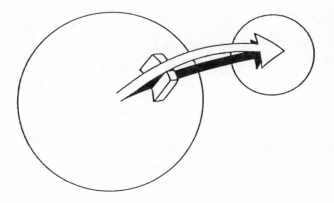

For a variety of reasons apart from those of geography, a church might feel that the opportunity for broadening the cultural appeal of the existing congregation is limited and that the best way to meet the needs of a particular section of the community would be to establish a new group to church plant. Where the existing church is particularly traditional or rigid in its lifestyle and ministry, this is almost certain to prove the most effective evangelistic strategy. Significant differences in culture between social groups or between generations can also strongly indicate this as the preferred way ahead even if on occasions the new 'church' meets in the same premises as the existing one.

Growth through bridging (E-2 and E-3)

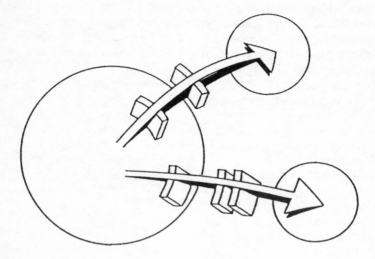

Where more substantial cultural differences are recognised then church planting is almost always the only sensible strategy to adopt. Multiple use of church premises is widely practised in E-2 and E-3 evangelism, particularly in crossing the barriers into other ethnic groups.

Whichever approach is adopted there can be no better guide to facing the challenge of mission across cultural barriers than the declaration of the Jerusalem Council: 'We should not make it difficult for the Gentiles who are turning to God' (Acts 15:19).

Recognising diversity within diversity

Paul learned from experience that different peoples react differently to the same words and acts. The miracle that brought such opportunities in Paphos (Acts 13:12) brought great confusion in Lystra (Acts 14:11ff) where the locals misinterpreted the healing because of their particular religious traditions. The 'Gentiles' were not and are not a single, monochrome group of people. Paul, no less than mission leaders today, had to learn to adapt his missions approach to each group in turn.

Sadly, it is the case that most British churchgoers of white Anglo origin are, in terms of cultural awareness, as undiscriminating as the majority of the population in general. Even among those who might vigorously advocate multicultural congregations as preferable to more culturally specific ones there is often little personal appreciation of the rich variety of cultural expression that currently characterises British national life. All black people 'look the same' and are expected to respond in the same way. The fact that Nigerians might not get along with Jamaicans, or Bangladeshis with Pakistanis, is for many whites a surprise and often a source of annoyance.

The church, however, must realise that the multiethnic missionfield that our land has become cannot be viewed in such simplistic terms. They are not all the same! Even among people of a single ethnic group there will be differences. An obvious example is the markedly distinct attitudes and expectations of first and second generation immigrants. These differences must be understood and taken into consideration when deciding what evangelistic approach should be adopted and, in particular, whether or not church planting is the preferred option.

Lon Chavez of Language Missions, Southern Baptist Convention, describes three subgroups that might be found within a given ethnic group. Peter Wagner describes four.[3]

1. 'Nuclear ethnics'—culturally isolated/segregated

This category of people are those who maintain the language and lifestyle of their country or ethnic origin. They are usually overseas born and older first generation immigrants. English people living abroad very often fall into this category, preferring to move in an exclusive expatriot circle rather than integrating with society at large. As far as the UK is concerned, however, where there has been a colonial history that bridges the ethno-linguistic barrier then it is possible that a measure of assimilation into the majority culture of white English-speaking congregations can be hoped for. Certainly, in the case of most new Commonwealth immigrants, however, this hope has not been fulfilled and the alienation of the immigrant Caribbean Christian community is a shameful page in the history of the British churches.

It is important to recognise that most people in this category are there unavoidably due to inherited language and culture and cannot easily integrate into society at large. This is particularly true of first generation Asian immigrants to Britain.

Such people are difficult to minister to through a majority culture church. They are best reached through a separate language congregation. They need, want and will attend such a church. The proliferation of ethnic churches made up of first generation immigrants is testimony to the truth of this.

2. 'Fellow traveller ethnics'—bicultural by choice

These people are usually bi- or multi-lingual and choose to function in more than one cultural lifestyle. Cross-cultural marriages often produce family units that fall in this category. Because both cultures are being affirmed out of choice by such people then ministry towards them should also recognise and reflect the dual culture. It might or might not be possible for a majority culture church to respond to such a need.

3. 'Marginal ethnics'—moving towards assimilation

Second and third generation immigrants or other socially motivated people committed to life within the UK will fall into this group. Links to the ethnic culture are tenuous and play no significant role in the acceptance of or progress in what are perceived to be the most important areas of life. They are best reached by a multicultural church.

4. 'Alienated ethnics'—effectively assimilated into the majority culture

People in this category have moved out of, become alienated from, their culture of origin. Skin colour might be the only indicator that this group has a cultural history significantly different from the majority of the population. In every other respect their lifestyle and 'worldview' will reflect that of society in general. These people do not need, and often do not want, separate facilities or churches. They can be evangelised by the caring majority culture church.

Questions about the formation of culturally specific churches

One of the great delights of the Christian gospel is to discover that within the family of God barriers of race and culture are overcome. Christians can 'put on the new self, which is being renewed in knowledge in the image of its Creator. Here there is no Greek or Jew, circumcised or uncircumcised, barbarian, Scythian, slave or free, but Christ is all, and is in all' (Col 3:11). In the kingdom of God, men and women are freed from the prejudices and fears that divide cultural groups within the kingdoms of this world, to share and serve, learn and worship together within the international body of Christ.

This cross-cultural freedom is, however, more than just a release from the sinful divisions of a world alienated from the character of its Creator. It is in fact an aspect of kingdom life that it is essential for a Christian to experience. The kingdom principle of 'mutuality' or interdependence among Christian peoples, set out in 1 Corinthians 12, commonly applied at the level of local church 'body life'. It is equally applicable at the level of international and intercultural relationships between Christians.

In 1 Corinthians 12:4–7 we read of one Head acting through the body by one Spirit for the common good. When God acts among different people groups he does so specifically to respond to the needs in a particular situation, of a particular people. However, the affirmation of this text is that while God's activity is specific, it is not private. It is always for the common good—not only for the benefit of the particular cultural group but for the good of the wider Christian family as well. Cross-cultural fellowship between Christians is essential if we are to learn more of the character and purposes of God.

Verses 14 to 21 speak of variety and interdependence between the different members of the body of Christ. Different ethnic groups have different strengths that need to be shared if the task of mission is to be accomplished. Few, for example, that have had contact with African Christian immigrants will fail to testify to the inspiration gained for bold witnessing and believing prayer.

Verses 22 to 26 speak of the need for mutual sharing in suffering and rejoicing. How little, even today, do the predominantly white congregations of our land appreciate of the pain and suffering of black Christians in our society. How many victories in suffering have failed to stimulate wider thanksgiving simply because Christians from different groups don't share their experiences of the grace of God. Without active involvement in the international and multicultural body of Christ, Christians cannot develop a maturity that is appropriate for life as God's people in the global village of today's Britain.

Wholehearted affirmation of the value and necessity of cross-cultural fellowship among Christians does not, however, invalidate the demands of cross-cultural mission towards the unchurched.

The same Paul who rejoices in the universality of the church of Christ quite unambiguously declares his mission policy to be one that is responsive to the particular cultural make-up of the group he is seeking to win into God's renewed humanity:

> To the Jews I became like a Jew, to win the Jews. ... To those not having the law I became like one not having the law so as to win those not having the law. ... I have become all things to all men so that by all possible means I might save some (1 Cor 9:20–22).

And there is ample evidence of his practical sensitivity to, and readiness to respond to cultural differences: his choice of the cross-cultural person, Timothy with his Greek father and Jewish mother (Acts 16:1–3); the speech in Athens (Acts 17:22ff); the readiness to make the Nazarite vow in Jerusalem (Acts 21:20ff), and so on. The priority of mission consistently determines the purpose and practice of the community of faith in the New Testament.

The early church sets the standard

The declaration of the Jerusalem Council, already referred to, set the standard for Christian mission policy. The temptation to impose a cultural uniformity upon the expanding network of churches was firmly rejected by the early church. In a similar way, the ecumenical movement in our own day has long since recognised that unity and fellowship does not require uniformity. This appreciation of how to respond to the divisions of tradition and belief within the Christian family provides a helpful analogy when addressing the issue of appropriate mission response to cultural divisions within society at large. It is wholly appropriate to affirm the value of different cultural expressions of church life in the multifaceted society in which we live. It is perhaps worthy of note that John's visions, recorded in Revelation, picture peoples and nations as recognisably distinct even in glory. If heaven is not a place of bland uniformity then we are out of tune with the purposes of God if we attempt to make the church on earth conform to a single cultural pattern. Recognition of cultural variety is not to confirm the sinfulness of cultural division and prejudice but rather to acknowledge and celebrate the rich variety and interdependence of God's creation.

To ignore the differing cultural frameworks within which people live and to expect 'all men everywhere' to respond to the same explanations, to be moved by the same challenges, or to feel at home in the same settings, is unrealistic. It is not acceptable to adopt a mission policy which in effect says, 'In order to join us you must become like us.' The proper challenge of the gospel is to receive Christ, not to receive culture. Certainly, every presentation of the gospel, whether in word or in lifestyle, will come wrapped in the culture of the communicator, but once received, and unpacked it is the gift of Christ that is retained, not the packaging. Just so long as the packaging is secure and protects the contents then the most important factor is that it should be attractive. It should encourage the receiver to accept and appreciate and retain the gift. At Christmas time parents will go to great lengths to find wrapping paper appropriate to their children's age or interests. At the first Christmas our heavenly Father went to the greatest lengths of all to ensure that humanity received the revelation of himself in a 'package' that could bridge the existential gap between God and man. Jesus is the greatest argument for the validity of cultural adaptability in communicating the gospel.

Areas of particular cultural sensitivity

Incarnation of the good news will mean patterns of witness and worship, teaching and service that will vary according to the culture of the group concerned.

Music is for most Christian traditions an important dimension of worship and witness. It is also very culturally sensitive. The style, the instrumentation, the lyrics will vary dramatically from generation to generation and between one social or ethnic group and another. Although it is possible for the Christian subculture to develop a commonly accepted approach to music that crosses many such barriers and facilitates fellowship in worship, the value of music in witness is largely determined by the extent to which the music style corresponds to the preference of the particular non-Christian group being targeted.

Learning about the faith and Christian life is another important feature of church life. In the learning process language and presentation will play a large part. Depending upon the educational background and experience of life, very different ways of communicating the same message will need to be adopted. The church already recognises this reality in regard to Christian education for children, through the provision of various types of Sunday school programmes prepared specifically for the different age groups. The Willow Creek Community Church in Illinois, USA, has determined that it is unrealistic to expect to both communicate with unchurched people and teach Christians in the same meeting and so devote the Sunday meetings to the unchurched and conduct the teaching programme for Christians midweek. Different social groups will also have different issues that are of particular importance to them and will need addressing. Black immigrants experiencing racial prejudice will be living in a different world and be looking for different patterns of teaching and help to Yuppies, or the elderly, and so on.

Other aspects of Christian community lifestyle will render the group more or less attractive and helpful as a vehicle for communicating to the unchurched.

The place of women and children in the activities of the group. The relaxed behaviour between men and women in many charismatic churches can be a cause of misunderstanding and even offence for many Asian visitors used to different rules governing the relations between the sexes. Codes of behaviour expected of children can equally be an effective bar to single parents or other social groups unused to imposing the degree of control often expected in many more traditional churches.

The sort of religious ritual involved in meetings. Christian attitudes to religious ceremony, while seen as over the top by many young whites, are perceived as lax by some groups brought up within Eastern religious traditions. For some, the presence of the divine is evoked through the lavish or other-worldly, while for others through simplicity or 'down-to-earthness'. Ancient symbols are a help to some and a 'turn-off' to others.

The length and timing of Christian meetings. Black churches are famous for working to time schedules that defy the Western preoccupation for clockwatching. Inherited attitudes to time-keeping will make punctuality an expression of Christian character to one and a reflection of diminished humanity and legalism to another.

The expectations of leadership or community life received from non-UK experience mean that some seek a paternalistic or even authoritarian framework for their Christian discipleship while others look more naturally for a non-directive community approach to decision making and pastoral support. It is notice-able that some first generation Afro-Caribbean congregations flourish under a white leadership style that might be reminiscent of church life as experienced by the congregation in their younger days in the Caribbean, while second generation black youth will tend to relate more readily to black-led groups that more strongly affirm their ethnic identity within an oppressive white majority culture.

These and other aspects of cultural distinctiveness and

sensitivity must not be ignored if the challenge to make disciples of all peoples is to be seriously addressed by the UK churches in our day. To be effective in providing our multicultural country with opportunities to know and worship God there must be a readiness to establish, more than ever before in our history, varieties of Christian groups able to tune in to the cultural frequency of the different groups within our society. To quote Bruce Patrick once again: 'Where culture is the context then congregations are the key.'

Particular strengths of 'in-culture' congregations

Perhaps one of the most compelling arguments for the planting of culturally specific congregations as a response to the reality of cultural diversity is to be found in the very aim of evangelism itself, namely that of integrating an individual into the new *community* of the kingdom.

All community living is characterised by common culture. Although some aspects of that culture will grow directly out of the religious beliefs that the members share, many others will come from the wider non-Christian society from which the members are drawn. For an individual from a different group to have to conform to the secular as well as the religious culture of a church is therefore to require him to surmount a double barrier. Even when this difficult task is achieved, the prospects for ongoing mission among the 'foreign group' are in no way improved since each successive convert must make the same double decision, namely to embrace Christ and to embrace the foreign cultural lifestyle of the community of Christ.

In contrast to this pattern of fishing converts out of one cultural pool into another, one at a time, church planting within the target group will ensure that the new converts are enabled to form a new Christian community that will embody the codes of behaviour and belief that may be described as 'kingdom culture' but invest them with the cultural shape and colour of their own particular group. This will mean that the more difficult task of cross-cultural mission, necessary for the original founding of the new church, is substituted by the easier and more effective ongoing 'in-culture' mission conducted from within the newly established, indigenous church. Cross-cultural church planting is therefore the most effective form of cross-cultural evangelism since it not only wins converts from the target community but also establishes within the community a witnessing group able to minister with an authenticity and sensitivity that is difficult for an outside agency to sustain.

A congregation that is 'homegrown', indigenous to a particular socio-cultural group, will also be tuned in to the realities and possibilities of that group in a way that an 'outsider' church or agency can never hope to be. Although a 'foreign' church group might pick up snatches of the messages of need and opportunity being transmitted from the community, much will be missed and some even of what is picked up may be misunderstood. *Potential for growth* is far more readily identified from within a cultural group than from the outside. The natural tendency for an outsider is to expect that the same possibilities exist, the same rules apply in the new group as his experience has shown that they do in his own group.

I recently came across a striking example of this in regard to a local church project to develop an Asian Christian ministry within its locality. Having obtained the service of an Asian evangelist and accommodated him within the area, the work began to take shape. After about a year, the local church was somewhat taken aback to hear that the evangelist had planned an evangelistic convention aimed at reaching several hundred! After the initial shock, the leaders were delighted with the success of the venture but conceded in private that their expectations of the man's ministry were far more modest, being limited to the formation of a number of housegroups for interested Asian families, and that after some three or four years' work!

A personal experience of the difference in expectation that can characterise different cultural groups happened recently when I was invited to preach at a local Ghanaian fellowship. In the vestry, prior to the service, the minister was asking about my ministry before joining Oasis and Spurgeon's College. Upon being told that I had spent some eleven years in Brazil in a church planting ministry he enthusiastically exclaimed that I must have planted a dozen or twenty or more churches in that period. He was clearly not at all impressed with the half a dozen I felt that I could claim!

Inappropriate estimates of the possibilities of growth, whether they err on the side of modesty or excess, will inevitably lead to inappropriate planning and programmes. They are most readily avoided by ensuring that the leadership of the mission group includes those 'indigenous' to the community being targeted.

Programmes that are likely to prove effective in penetrating the community and reaching its members are equally most likely to be identified by those who, by virtue of their origins, can feel 'where the people are itching' and understand how the community ticks. Programmes that are ineffective in one group can be recognised as being powerful vehicles of mission in another. Children's work for example, has been largely dismissed as a means of reaching adults in our majority white culture. Within some Afro-Caribbean groups, however, the more positive community attitude to children means that traditional Sunday school work can still represent an effective tool of mission to the whole family.

Preaching style and content will vary markedly according to the concerns and the ways of communication that characterise the group. The language of Zion, old and new, that legitimates Christian ceremony for many believers, is incomprehensible to the average unchurched individual. The streetwise style of the youth evangelist can be an offence to the churchgoer steeped in the liturgy and poetry of Christian tradition.

Patterns of pastoral care are very culture dependent. What one group would consider an expression of love and support another may find an intrusion of privacy. Particularly on the occasion of the so-called rites of passage—birth, marriage, death, and so on—the need for cultural awareness is of the greatest importance as expectations can vary considerably from group to group. The open expression of grieving in bereavement that would be frowned upon in white Anglo society, Christian as well as non-Christian, may be expected and needed for someone from an African background.

Whether the area is that of caring or sharing, of evangelising or of discipling, the culture factor is one that can be ignored only at the cost of ministry effectiveness.

The fact that there are in excess of 23,000 different Christian denominations active around the world has far more to do with the issues of cultural preference touched upon above than with personality clashes and doctrinal differences. That 98 per cent of churches within these groupings are in effect monocultural is further evidence that most people find it easier to worship and serve and reach out from within a community that reflects their personal cultural background. The real threat to the integrity of the gospel comes not from recognising the value of culturally specific congregations—this is in fact the prevailing reality within Christendom—but from doing so to the exclusion of the intercongregational fellowshipping across cultural boundaries that is so necessary and so enriching for the churches and so compelling a testimony to the power and purpose of God to bring all things together under Christ as Head.

Qualities of a cross-cultural church planter

Where indigenous leadership to establish a new congregation is not available then the church is faced with one of its most demanding tasks, that of discovering and supporting church planters that can operate across cultural barriers. The experience of foreign missions is that people able to work effectively in this area are not easy to come by.

In addition to the qualities appropriate to the leader of a planting team set out in the next chapter, three qualities merit particular attention: personal integrity, servant leadership, community sensitivity.

Personal integrity

The ability of the cross-cultural missionary to present the gospel in a credible and acceptable way among the target community will be limited by a number of factors.

Beyond being a representative of a new religion, the missionary will also be perceived as a representative of the particular cultural group from which he or she comes. Associations and prejudices related to people of that cultural background will either enhance or more normally call into question the credibility of the message proclaimed. Where there exists a language barrier then the capacity for effective verbal communication will be further reduced. Given these limitations upon the normal channels of communication, the quality of life displayed by the missionary and other members of the planting team becomes of particular importance.

Quality of conduct in family, social and business affairs will all come under scrutiny and be judged according to the norms prevailing within the target group. The fact that the 'foreign devils', an endearing Chinese description of Westerners, will stand out as being strangers to the community, will serve to keep the team constantly under critical examination. In these conditions the personal integrity of each member of the team assumes the highest importance. Both as individuals and as a religious community the gospel will be modelled in conduct more easily than it might be communicated by word. The saying 'What you are speaks so loudly that I cannot hear what you are saying' would be a suitable epitaph to many a venture in cross-cultural mission that failed through not recognising the fundamental importance of Christian character within the mission team. Conversely, it is true that integrity and authenticity are very transferable concepts and ones that are generally affirmed as commendable, so serving as a counter to the negative attitudes deriving from the cultural gap between gospel representatives and the members of the community.

Servant leadership

The inherent limitations of understanding, social acceptability and capacity for communication with which the cross-cultural evangelist has to wrestle require that as soon as possible and as far as possible the actual task of evangelism is transferred away from the 'foreigner' to converts from within the target community. Writing in a booklet of guidance for pioneer cross-cultural mission workers, George Patterson states, 'The most effective evangelist is a new convert. The most effective witness comes from those who are culturally close to the people of the community.'[4]

What is true of the role of the outsider in the task of personal evangelism is equally true in the process of building the new believers together into a new indigenous congregation that will be able to develop and reproduce itself within its own cultural group. David Burnett writes that 'a deep trust in the young converts and an indigenous leadership should be encouraged from the very beginning.'[5]

A commitment to delegation and an ability to work through others are therefore key features in the desired gifting profile. Not all who have the ability to lead display the readiness to transfer decision making and status away from themselves to emerging leaders. In a cross-cultural setting this is an essential aspect of the planter's role. The apostolic model of Paul is a classic example of how local leadership is both discerned and affirmed at the earliest possible moment (Acts 14:23). 'Midwife Ministries' would be an appropriate title for a group specialising in this type of mission activity.

Community sensitivity

Paul's personal background was a help to him in understanding and addressing the challenge of commending Christ across cultural boundaries. As a Pharisee trained in Jerusalem he had credentials in the eyes of the Jewish community. As a native of the Hellenistic city of Tarsus he could relate to the cultural sensitivities of communities dominated by Greek culture, as his use of illustrations from the games, etc, was to show, and as a Roman citizen he had status before the prevailing political authorities. He was himself a 'cross-cultural person' and had no difficulty in building multicultural teams in order to best meet the needs of the different groups that he was aiming to reach.

A leader likely to develop an acceptable ministry among a different cultural group will need to demonstrate particular sensitivity toward the target community. The sensitivity that leads to acceptability will have at least three dimensions:

Awareness + Appreciativeness + Adaptability = Acceptability

These attributes will reveal themselves both in terms of behaviour and communication. They will enable the principle of incarnation to be transferred into practice in the attempt to 'become all things to all men that by all means possible might save some' (1 Cor 9:22). Hesselgrave highlights the principle of incarnation at work throughout the record of God's mission to the world:

> Not only does the Scripture reveal a salvific core, it also reveals that the salvific core was adapted to various audiences—not to their prejudice and taste in order to make the message palatable, but to their world view and knowledge in order to make it understandable.[6]

He goes on to cite Paul's different approaches to different audiences:

- To monotheists in the synagogues of Damascus (Acts 9:20–22).
- To polytheists in Lystra (Acts 14:15–17).
- To the pantheistically inclined Athenians (Acts 17:22–33).

The cross-cultural missionary and church planter is someone who will have both a secure grasp of the essentials of the faith and a sensitive creativity that can discern the implications of those essentials in the context of the new culture.

If the incarnation may be considered a measure of God's commitment to the 'how' of communication then so also must the effective church planter be prepared to face the target community and wrestle with the challenge of what it means to be the herald of the gospel and the church of Christ in that particular cultural setting.

Cross-cultural planting and the local church

Pathways to planting

It is a proper role of leadership to help a group determine direction. However, it is difficult to envisage possibilities that go beyond the limits of personal experience and many churches live imprisoned within the small horizons of their leaders' parochiality. The Acts 13 account of the Antioch church's bold response to the Spirit's call into cross-cultural mission is significant particularly, I believe, because of the make-up of the leadership team, that the Spirit has ensured was recorded for us. A Cypriot, a Moroccan or perhaps Ethiopian, a Syrian, a Lybian, an Israeli constituted a team whose windows were open to the world which then, as now, God is committed to win. The multiethnic mix is a model for churches keen to be sensitive to the possibilities of mission among other people groups. The sharing of mission perspectives with other local ethnic churches would offer a further way of opening windows to broaden vision and allow in the wind of the Spirit.

Possibilities for partnership

At a recent meeting of black church planters in London a matter of concern that was widely expressed was the difficulty experienced by many emerging groups in gaining access to adequate buildings at an affordable cost. Increasingly, white churches are discovering that a first step into aiding the movement of cross-cultural mission can be through making their own premises available at helpful times to ethnic church groups. Westbourne Park Baptist Church in Paddington currently has several groups meeting in its buildings, including a Philippino, a Brazilian, and a Nigerian group. It also maintains a ministry to Muslims through the agency of a partnership with another mission group. The degree of interaction between such groups may not go much beyond an administrative one, relating to the maintenance of the premises, but the cause of the kingdom in a multiethnic area is forwarded.

Partnership between a number of churches both Anglican and Baptist, Spurgeon's College and the Baptist Union Home Mission department led to the development of an innovative experiment in cross-cultural mission among Asians in south-west London. Through the employment of a former Baptist Missionary Society missionary, Jean Westlake, an international ministry team has been built up, currently with Dutch, Korean, Bangladeshi and Pakistani members. Asian congregations catering for different language groups are being established in fellowship with the various local churches that have been supporting the venture. It is worthy of note that in multi-congregational ventures, the closer the degree of co-operation between the different groups the more important it becomes that the co-ordinator is someone of cross-cultural ability and experience.

Patterns of planting

The patterns of planting mentioned so far have been based upon the recognised need for a culturally specific congregation whose emergence has been facilitated through some measure of partnership. Examples of such co-operative associations are becoming more common, with the partners representing different ethnic, socio-economic or age characteristics.

The emergence of youth congregations and those specifically catering for the elderly are becoming increasingly common, although in these instances the tendency will be for the members of the age group congregation to actually form a constituent part of the main congregation. This is far less common in the case of groups which are ethnically distinct. There is a real need for the modelling of such a multiethnic church in the UK along the lines of perhaps the Northshore Baptist Church, Chicago, in which the several ethnic congregations are all considered to belong to the one fellowship and the different leaderships jointly constitute the leadership of the whole church. Needless to say, leadership of an apostolic and cross-cultural nature would be a prerequisite for any attempt to develop such a multiethnic community.

Cross-cultural planting and the denominational group

The cultural and ecclesiological inertia of the main church groupings in the UK has led to the emergence of an increasing number of culturally specific and unassociated churches that owe their origin to the vision of individuals rather than to any denominational cross-cultural mission policy. Among these new congregations, however, as indeed increasingly within the mainline denominational groupings, there is a growing recognition of the need for patterns of association which can offer the benefits of cross-cultural fellowship without involving the cultural takeover of one group by another.

It is depressingly apparent, however, that the higher up the tree of ecclesiastical government one climbs the more monocultural the agendas and personal outlooks of leaders tend to become. The long arm of a far more monochrome past still tends to dictate the issues and activities generated at executive level, with the challenges of the far more colourful present being hived off as the concern of various special interest groups, doing their own thing on the fringes of mainline policy-making bodies.

The continued preoccupation with maintenance rather than mission, with the survival of the church rather than the salvation of unchurched perpetuates the process of cultural marginalisation that is sidelining the vast majority of Christian communities from the multicultural realities that will characterise the development of British national life into the foreseeable future.

A similar blinkeredness to contemporary cultural realities in the UK also determines the policies of many traditional foreign mission agencies. Precisely the bodies that have most experience of cross-cultural mission are found unable or unwilling to recognise that global mission is about all the peoples of the world, not all the countries of the world, and that all the peoples of the world are now drifting unreached past the doors of churches throughout the land who feel at a loss to know how to respond. For lack of a readiness to adopt more flexible policies with regard to the placement of cross-culturally able personnel in conjunction with the home mission departments of the various denominations, opportunities for establishing churches among peoples whose homelands are virtually closed to foreign missionaries are lost.

Agencies such as Interserve undoubtedly show the way ahead through the implementation of a policy of internationalisation of the mission agency in partnership with its associated church groups overseas.

Pathways that invite cross-cultural and international partnership in the mission task of targeting peoples, not places, must be opened up if the churches of the UK are to remain true to their fine heritage of cross-cultural missionary concern. Both at local and national church levels the need and the opportunities abound. What is lacking is vision. What could it mean in your part of the country, in your church, to take as a basis for mission policy the words of the Lord, 'Turn to me and be saved, all you ends of the earth' (Is 45:22)?

For discussion and further study

1. Discuss the extent to which the mission challenge facing the British churches today might be described as the challenge of cross-cultural evangelism.
2. Identify as many factors as you can that have contributed to the cultural diversification of British society during the course of this century.
3. Formulate a definition of 'a people group' that you could use to introduce the concept to members of your own church.
4. How many 'people groups' can you identify in the area surrounding your church? Discuss the extent to which each group might find the current mission and ministry programmes of your church more or less helpful.

Notes

1. *London Calling—A survey of a mission field for London Baptists* (1990).
2. Bruce Patrick, *Reaching All the People Groups* (Baptist Union of New Zealand, 1990), p 4.
3. Cited in Patrick *op cit*, p 7.
4. G. Patterson, '20 Principles of Church Growth and Reproduction for Pioneer Cross-Cultural Disciplers' (An unpublished paper).
5. Monica Hill (ed), *How to Plant Churches* (MARC Europe, 1984), ch 4.
6. David Burnett, *Cultural Factors and Indigenisation* (WEC), p 51. David Hesselgrave, *Planting Churches Cross-Culturally* (Baker Book House, 1980), p 207.

CHAPTER NINE

WHO TO PLANT? – LEADERSHIP AND TEAM WORK

Stuart Christine

The importance of leadership

Jesus set in motion the church planting movement, and he gave it a flying start through the careful selection of leadership. Early in his ministry, after a night of prayer, he called out from among those who had begun to follow him, a dozen men, 'that they might be with him and that he might send them out to preach and to have authority to drive out demons' (Lk 6:12; Mk 3:14, 15): disciples, teachable and utterly committed to their Master, but also apostles able to pioneer kingdom work after his own example; men to continue his own mission agenda; special people who could be inspired and envisioned by the Spirit and whom the Spirit could use to inspire and envision others; men whose lives would become, like their Master's, seeds of new kingdom communities, scattering and implanting themselves, giving birth to a network of new life right across the face of the earth. It is a measure of just how important Jesus considered their role to be that he went to such extraordinary lengths to prepare these men and put in place key figures such as Peter and Paul.

The task of founding and forming new locally relevant worshipping and witnessing Christian communities is still the prime mission task of the churches. The task remains unchanged, as does its essential requirement—called and gifted leadership.

Wherever in the world I have experienced church planting or talked with those engaged in church planting this one clear message from the ministry of Jesus has been reaffirmed.

From the States:

As I will reiterate time and again, the leader is the principal key to a successful church planting endeavour (Peter Wagner).[1]

Everything rises or falls on leadership (Elmer Towns).[2]

From Australia:

It has been shown that the success of a new church is very largely dependent on the Church Planter (Philip Bryant).[3]

From New Zealand:

The leader is the single most important human factor for success (Graham Lee).[4]

From Brazil—the second of seven strategy guidelines for doubling the number of Baptist churches in a five-year period reads:

To use the theological training institutions in the forma tion of workers specializing in the planting of new churches.

From Zaire—Pastor Konde Kivuna, planter of fourteen churches in eleven years in the capital, Kinshasa, states that the first step in establishing a cell aiming to become a church is to: 'name a spiritual leader for each cell, a dynamic lay leader.'[5]

Is this international experience also true of the UK situation? That was a more than academic question for me in January 1989. I had an invitation to respond to. Did my experience of starting new churches in Brazil equip me for the task of developing a course for church planters at Spurgeon's College?

That leadership was a key factor in the Brazilian context I had learned through experience. The confirmation by UK planters that this was their perception here also encouraged me to accept the validity of my South American background and take up the appointment.

A recent survey of Baptist church planting has confirmed the personal opinions of those with whom I had spoken.[6] Roger Sutton and Adrian Argyle found that for a significant proportion of newly planted churches they surveyed, the aspect of the experience that had proved least satisfactory was the quality of leadership. In a separate study of six failed plants in the West Midlands area, presented at the same consultation, the prime cause of failure was identified as inadequate leadership. It is interesting to note that John Wimber cites similar results in a study of the failure of twenty-two Vineyard fellowships in the States.[7]

It is surprising how reluctant many good Christian folk are to accept either the voice of the Master through the Scriptures or the voice of the Spirit through the churches. Bill Wagner—no relation to Peter Wagner as far as I am aware—prefaces a recent book on church growth in the 'dark continent' with a list of ten church growth principles that he has discerned in the course of his long experience of Baptist work in Western Europe. The second of these refers to the role of leadership: 'Much to my disappointment (since it is sad that the "earthen vessel" should play such an important part), I have discovered that the leader is the key to practically all church growth.'[8]

The Scriptures clearly acknowledge variety in the leadership gifting required for each aspect of the task that the church body is called upon to undertake. It is a feature both of fallen and of restored humanity that corporate life involves such variety and is surely no cause for 'disappointment' or 'sadness'. Rather, it is something to be acknowledged and acted upon.

In this respect the saying is true that the sons of darkness are often wiser than the sons of light. Entrepreneurial skill has long been recognised, sought after and highly compensated by commercial firms keen to break into new markets. In a recent review of articles on the theme of 'Creating and managing new ventures' the expansion strategy of Detriot Edison, an American electric utility, was assessed. The formation of task forces to develop new ventures was based upon two essentials:

> First, there should be a clear leader, with clear responsibility for the output of the task force and the authority to assemble a functioning organisation. ... Second, the task force members must be given some release time from current assignments to function properly and be recognized for their work.[9]

The importance of team work

This last reference is helpful because it places the leader clearly in the context of a team or task force. There should be no misunderstanding at this point. Biblical precedent and contemporary experience show that church planting demands that the leader is endowed with certain distinctive qualities that are by the very nature of the task of vital importance, but he or she cannot be omnicompetent. Nor, indeed, would it necessarily be helpful if numbers of such spiritual supermen and women were available. The goal of church planting is the birth of a new community of believers described in Scripture as a body. Church planting is about body building. It is a task that requires the recognition, affirmation and cultivation of gifts of every type from each of the members that the Spirit draws into the body. The effective body builder is precisely someone who is able to exercise his own particular leadership gift within the context of a growing complex of gifts, recognising the God-given value and necessity of each.

It is true that super-competent individuals can readily gather a following. Such groups, however, can easily remain precisely that, a dependent group of followers. The objective of the church planter is not a following but a church, an interdependent body of believers, 'joined and held together by every supporting ligament, growing and building itself up in love, as each part does its work' (Eph 4:16). Church planting is no place for leaders with a lone ranger mentality. From start to finish church planting is team work.

Both Jesus and Paul modelled the team ministry approach to mission. The twelve disciple-apostles, as the duality of their title suggests, were gathered by Jesus both to learn for future leadership and also to share in present service. Paul likewise developed a pattern of team ministry whereby as he travelled members were brought into his team where they laboured and learned before moving on to become leaders in their own right.

The list of those who are mentioned as Paul's co-workers is impressive:

Team Members

Barnabas	Acts 4:36 et al	Epaphroditus	Phil 2:25 et al
John Mark	Acts 12:12 et al	Syntyche	Phil 4:2
Silas	Acts 15:22 et al	Euodia	Phil 4:2
Timothy	Acts 16:1 et al	Clement	Phil 4:3
Aquila	Acts 18:2 et al	Epaphroditus	Phil 2:25 et al
Priscilla	Acts 18:2 et al	Epaphras	Col 1:17 et al
Sosthenes	Acts 18:17	Jesus Justus	Col 4:11 et al
Aristarchus	Acts 19:29 et al	Demas	Col 4:14 et al
Gaius	Acts 19:29 et al	Luke	Col 4:14 et al
Secundus	Acts 20:4 et al	Phygellus	2 Tim 1:15
Trophimus	Acts 20:4 et al	Hermogenes	2 Tim 1:15
Tychicus	Acts 20:4 et al	Onesiphorus	2 Tim 1:16 et al
Sopater	Acts 20:4	Crescens	2 Tim 4:10
Urbanus	Rom 16:9	Carpus	2 Tim 4:13
Stephanus	1 Cor 1:16 et al	Claudia	2 Tim 4:21
Achaicus	1 Cor 16:17	Eubulus	2 Tim 4:21
Fortunatus	1 Cor 16:17	Linus	2 Tim 4:21
Silvanus	2 Cor 1:19 et al	Pudens	2 Tim 4:21
Titus	2 Cor 2:13 et al	Artemas	Tit 3:12

In a most helpful chapter of their outstanding book on New Testament models of church planting,[10] Schenk and Stutzman cite this list of Paul's mission partners and go on to highlight a number of reasons why a team is important for church planting:

1. A team working in harmony models Christian community life. It is the new church in embryo.
2. A multi-cultural environment is more readily penetrated by a team representative of the different people groups.
3. A team provides a model and a means of sharing authority and responsibility.
4. A team approach allows God to gather the human resources necessary to respond to the size of the task.
5. The work that can be achieved by team working is greater than if individual team members were to work separately.
6. Members of a team are able to support and encourage one

another in what is one of the most pressured forms of Christian service.
7. The team provides a training ground for future leaders.

The practical implications of what has been said about the importance of team work for planting will be worked out later in Chapter 10, the chapter dealing with the preparation of the core group. It is, however, important to establish the principle at this stage that because of the body nature of the church, team work should be seen as both a proper method and appropriate goal of the church planter's activity.

The profile of a planter

It is, of course, the task that will determine the qualities that a prospective planter should possess. These will need to be owned at least in sufficient measure for them to be projected into the life and thinking of the core group. There they may be supplemented and complemented by the gifts of the rest of the team.

The planter's remit may be defined as follows: *The founding and forming of a new, locally relevant worshipping and witnessing Christian community*.

A detailed examination of the requirements of each part of this task will highlight those particular aspects of gifting, spirituality and personality that should characterise the effective leader.

Remit: The founding ...
Requirement:

- Called and envisioned by God. Church planting is God's work.
- An ability to inspire others to capture the vision.
- An ability to draw up action plans to achieve vision goals.
- Resourcefulness and organisational ability to make things happen.
- Hardworking and resilient. Foundations are hard work, often with little to show on the surface.

• Prayerful—foundations must follow the Architect's design.

These qualities should have been evidenced in a track record of being able to turn ideas into realities that have proved to be blessed by God in their usefulness to the kingdom. The sense of specific calling to a church planting ministry should be supported by the testimony of those who have first-hand experience of the candidate's character, spiritual maturity and gifting, and weighed by those with experience in the demands of new church founding ministry.

The planting experiences of Peter and Paul clearly illustrate the vital importance of divine calling in facing with confidence the challenges of establishing new Christian churches. Traditional values (Acts 10:28), patterns of ministry (Acts 13:1; 15:35,36), lifestyle and personal security (1 Cor 4:10–13) had all required radical remodelling. The assurance of God's personal commissioning (Acts 13:2; 18:9,10) served like an anchor securing their commitment when storms of misunderstanding and persecution threatened to wreck the potential of their ministry (2 Tim 1:6,7).

Remit: and the forming . . .

Requirement:

• A clear theological understanding of the nature and the purpose of the church.
• A wisdom in knowing when to take each step in giving teaching and in developing structures that will promote the continued growth of the work.
• A commitment and ability to develop the gifting of others without feeling threatened.
• Adaptability to vary leadership style as the group grows. General indicators of sizes at which change is needed if growth is not to plateau out are 12, 60 and 200.

Evidence of capacity in this area will be seen in the maturity of an individual's behaviour in previously held leadership positions. Easy and positive relationships with fellow team workers and an ability to understand the dynamics and issues involved in a given situation linked to good problem solving skills are good indicators of suitable gifting.

Remit: of a new ...
Requirement:

- A real commitment to reach the unchurched. Church planting is about bringing new people into the kingdom.
- A streetwise spirituality that can handle the problems of the newly converted.
- An ability to maintain an outward-looking and united congregation as numbers grow, effectively integrating new members.
- The sort of personality that sees the lacks and difficulties associated with a new work as challenges, not problems.
- A spiritually, emotionally and morally secure person, or couple, able to withstand the spiritual attacks, emotional pressures and moral temptations so commonly experienced by those engaged in wresting new ground from Satan's dominion. An Ephesians 6 person!

Romans 1:16 and 1 John 4:4 express the mature confidence that should have been noted in the prospective planter's attitude to and involvement in mission. The difference between evangelistic aspirations and actual experience can be great, however, so evidence of solid achievement is a must.

Remit: locally relevant ...
Requirement:

- A real interest in and commitment to reach the local community, not just unsaved people in general.
- An ability to see and hear what is going on in the neighbourhood.
- A creative spirituality that discovers ways of interpreting the word and the will of God in the language of the locals.

A 'churchy' person whose friends are all Christians and whose life is lived within the frontiers of Zion is unlikely to make a credible or sensitive missionary. Lifestyle, language style and dress style will all be indicators of how streetwise an individual is. Traditionalism is the enemy of culturally responsive church planting. A strong performer in this area is likely to be known for fresh ways of doing routine things or of presenting well worn themes.

Remit: worshipping ...

Requirement:

- A genuine lover of God. An example of devotion and commitment.
- A joyful and generous spirit.
- A delight in corporate expressions of worship and fellowship.
- An appreciation of the varied possibilities of contemporary worship, the importance of music and congregational participation.

The manner in which an individual leads a congregation in worship can reveal a lot about his attitude to mission. Boring, unattractive or incomprehensible worship is part of the stereotype of Christianity that contemporary society has rejected. A leader likely to be effective in stimulating the emergence of a new Christian community is unlikely to be at ease with worship patterns that are a barrier to reaching the unchurched. Rather, one would expect a strong affirmation of attractive participatory worship in which the Spirit can meet with and unite the growing body of God's people.

Remit: and witnessing ...

Requirement:

- A commitment to numerical growth.
- An understanding of church growth principles.
- The ability to inspire people with a confidence in the gospel.
- The capacity to lead a team in the formulation and implementation of a mission strategy.
- A genuinely mission rather than maintenance mentality.

The extent of an individual's commitment to witnessing as a priority will be evident from the activities that he has been involved in. Effectiveness in personal evangelism should not, however, be confused with the ability to be an effective mission leader. A church planter need not have a special gifting as an evangelist. But what must be present is a heart commitment to reaching the unsaved, together with a demonstrable ability to inspire and mobilise others to work for that goal.

Remit: Christian community.

Requirement:

- A likeable, Christlike person who inspires confidence in others to both accept leadership and to emulate discipleship.
- An ability to relate personally with a leadership team in such a way as to model the attitudes and behaviour that should characterise the life of the church as a whole.
- An ability to manage a growing group through sharing responsibility, maintaining good channels of communication, and expanding the leadership base.
- A commitment to the church as God's principal mission agency.

Such people are those who have shown themselves in the past to be natural leaders whom Christian people have been glad to follow. A warm heart and genuine concern for the well-being of the individual within the group will not have gone unnoticed in the conduct of past leadership responsibilities.

Responsibility

Not only in terms of *remit* but also in terms of *responsibility* the leader of the planting team, the church planter, faces a demanding task. In carrying out this task the planter has responsibility to God, to the emerging church, to the target community, to the sponsoring group and to his family.

All five responsibilities are real and make particular demands which the church planter must be able to keep in healthy balance if the work is to make solid and steady progress.

- In relation to God—the planter must at all times live with a genuine sense of utter dependence upon the Spirit and yet not be so heavenly minded as to be no earthly good.
- In relation to the emerging church and to the target community there must be a radical commitment to evangelism and yet without neglecting the work of 'body building'.
- In relation to the sponsoring group there must be responsiveness to their expectations and fellowship yet without compromising the fundamental commitment to grow a new congregation free to fully identify with the ethos of the particular community to which God has called it.
- In relation to family and friends—the need to maintain a work schedule that could occupy forty-eight hours a day and yet without treating home as a boarding house, or physical and emotional health as optional extras.

Maturity is probably the word that most adequately describes the qualities needed to handle the tensions and limitations that these competing responsibilities impose day by day. Self-awareness and a sense of priorities are particularly important aspects of the maturity that should be looked for.

A case study in selection

John Mark and Timothy are the individuals involved. John formed part of the first church planting venture sponsored by the Antioch church but was subsequently deselected by Paul and replaced by Timothy for the second. What can be learned from the record of this selection process?

As the following analysis will show, these two candidates for team membership differed in significant ways. One thing they had in common, however, was youthfulness, and it is worth pausing to consider this issue before continuing.

Peter Wagner recounts his own journey of understanding about the most appropriate age of prospective planters. He writes:

One thing I thought I knew was that the best church planters would probably be experienced pastors who had served several parishes and who had accumulated the wisdom and maturity to do it well. Wrong! Not that some fitting this description wouldn't make good church planters because they do. However, experienced pastors do not turn out to be the most likely talent pool. Younger people who still have more options and more flexibility are considerably more likely to do well.[11]

In contrast to this, George Patterson, speaking from his experience in Honduras urges:

Avoid 'Preacher Boys' ... to start a new work, train mature men. Beware of the bright single youth who can't wait to preach. He will usually let you down; he does not command respect from the community. He has no roots; his 'congregations' are not stable. ...[12]

It is evident from the reasons given for preferring younger or older men respectively that both are recognising criteria for selection that we have highlighted above, but perhaps due to the differing cultural contexts of their planting ministries Wagner has given greater emphasis to 'adaptability' where as Patterson has preferred 'social maturity'.

Certainly, the tension between these two desirable qualities has been one that we have sensed in the development of the church planting training course at Spurgeon's College. Given the greater degree of cultural diversity in the UK, our leaning has been more towards Wagner's position. The context of Patterson's work in Honduras would have been religiously more positive and culturally less complex, making the value of adaptability somewhat less critical than we believe to be the case in Western Europe or the States. It is certainly true, however, that 'risk factor' does increase with lack of personal maturity as the case of John Mark probably illustrates, and so where Timothy-type leadership is affirmed then suitable 'Pauls' should be found to give apostolic support and oversight. (Excellent guidelines for potential 'Pauls' can be found in a manual by Logan and Rast, available through the Charles Fuller Institute, entitled, *A Supervisor's Manual for New Church Development*.[13])

John Mark

Paul's refusal to countenance John as a continuing member of his team underlines the point made at the beginning of this chapter about the careful vetting and preparation of candidates for church planting mission leadership.

John was apparently the young member of the Jerusalem church mentioned in Acts 12:12 and cousin of Barnabas (Col 4:10), which could explain his presence in Antioch when the first missionary expedition was mounted (Acts 13:1–5). At first glance it might seem most commendable that the young man was ready to accompany the two apostles 'as their helper' (Acts 13:5). On what grounds, however, did he find this place in the team? There is no suggestion that he had shared in the sense of call and act of church commissioning that formed the basis of Paul and Barnabas' credentials. Rather, on the contrary, the manner in which he is referred to almost as an afterthought at the end of verse 5 has an uneasy feel about it. Was it perhaps more for family reasons, because Barnabas was his uncle, that he was given a role? In any case, he doesn't last long! After a first experience of the realities of pioneer missioning in Cyprus and the confrontation with the sorcerer Bar-Jesus he takes the earliest opportunity to return home (Acts 13:15).

A reunion apparently takes place in Jerusalem on the occasion of the special council meeting at which Paul and Barnabas were present. Returning with them to Antioch once again, the question of his suitability for a team place becomes a bone of contention just as soon as the new church planting journey is proposed (Acts 15:36–40).

Whatever the questions of personality involved, the incident does indicate something of the criteria that Paul used for the selection of his team. Acts 15:38 in particular merits careful study: 'Paul did not think it wise' that he should accompany them. The force of the word employed, *axiou*, 'wise', found seven times in the New Testament, is well illustrated in its usage in Acts 28:22. On that occasion the Jewish leaders in Rome who gathered to meet with Paul had no first-hand report of wrong-doing on his part but, as people everywhere were speaking against the Christian sect they thought it wise to hear for themselves. The implication is clear that they sense the responsibility that they bear in making this judgement about Paul. They recognise that they must act with care as a lot might hinge upon their decision.

Paul's response to the suggestion that John be reappointed to the team is equally coloured by a recognition of the weightiness of the issue. Paul doesn't write John off as a Christian, but believes that at that stage of his Christian life and maturity John Mark has not shown himself ready for the important and pressured work of pioneer mission. It is a matter of spiritual wisdom that he is not accepted. Later in life, Paul is happy to work with him and indeed describes him in affectionate terms as being 'helpful to me in my ministry' (2 Tim 4:11), and exhorts the Colossian church to receive him well (Col 4:10). If Mark was in fact the author of the second Gospel then he was certainly destined for significant Christian service, but for the present wisdom dictated caution.

The reason for this caution is also significant. John's departure for home is described as 'desertion' (Acts 15:38). Again, a word study of the language employed is revealing. The fourteen New Testament uses make it clear that what is being described is a crucial decision, made when the chips are down, to stay with or break with a particular course of action in which you're already involved. John had weighed his convictions against the risks and decides to play safe. Paul's judgement was that it wasn't wise to place either the well-being of his team or the work in which he was engaged in the position of having to depend upon such a man; especially so as the task in hand was known to be beset with spiritual and physical pressures.

It is worth noting also the way in which Luke describes the consequence of his departure: John 'had not continued with them in *the work*' (Acts 15:38). He had not remained committed to the specific work of mission that the team had been called by the Holy Spirit and released by the church to do. Paul recognised that the nature of the work was such that only those who were truly called and equipped could safely be entrusted with it. The confrontation at Paphos was typical of the opposition to be encountered. Their experiences in founding the

churches at Pisidian Antioch, Iconium, Lystra and Derbe had
shown that all too clearly. Church planting was no joy ride and
there was no room for passengers.

Timothy

Only six verses after reading of the rejection of John Mark we
have been introduced to another young man Timothy, of whom
we are told that 'Paul wanted to take him along on the journey'
(Acts 16:3). What is it about Timothy that commended him to
Paul's exacting standards of qualification for church planting
team membership?

First, like John no doubt, he was well grounded in the
Scriptures. Both his Jewish mother, Eunice, and grandmother,
Lois had seen to that (2 Tim 1:5).

Second, there is, however, the commendation of the local
churches that was so conspicuously absent in the record of
John's candidature: 'The brothers at Lystra and Aconium spoke
well of him' (Acts 16:2).

Third, he lived at Lystra where he would have seen Paul
stoned to within an inch of his life. Perhaps he had been among
the group that had gathered round his battered body and helped
him back into the city (Acts 14:19,20). He knew at first hand the
opposition that church planters were likely to face and had
stood firm. Here was someone that Paul was to be able to send
alone to revisit the newly established church at Thessalonica
only a matter of months after they had barely escaped the mob
there (1 Thess 3:2).

Fourth, he knew the cost of conversion. He knew what it had
meant to him and his mother not to have his father support their
Jewish religious conviction. The fact that he had not been
circumcised as a baby (Acts 16:3) was evidence of that. He'd
experienced the sting of religious misunderstanding and persecution a second time and twice over upon embracing Christianity
from within Judaism in a town whose local religion was centred
upon the Greek divinities (Acts 14:11–13).

Finally, and perhaps of particular significance, he could
play a specific and much needed role in the team. Timothy was
a cross-cultural person. His mixed religious and cultural

background would serve the team well as an ambassador to the Gentiles. Paul had learned from his first experience of the region that there was potential for conversion among the Hellenist community but that there was also potential for cross-cultural misunderstanding (Acts 14:13–15). A worker who could straddle the cultural divide, and gain credibility with both Jewish and Gentile communities, was an asset indeed. Timothy's background made him a gift from God for this role and he showed that where anything might form a barrier to his acceptance he was prepared to pay the price (Acts 16:3).

Timothy, then, in contrast to John Mark, joined the team with *commendation*, *conviction* and a *specific contribution* to make. Paul wanted to have him along, and the fulfilment of these three criteria form a sound basis for forming church planting teams today.

Some cautionary tales from the twentieth century

Not only in the case of John Mark, but throughout his ministry, Paul saw the work suffer through inadequate leaders. His letters are shot through with exhortations about the need for care in this matter and in the closing verses of his final letter to Timothy there is a moving section in which he appeals to his disciple to 'come to me quickly', as so many to whom leadership had been entrusted had failed to fulfil their promise (2 Tim 4:9–18).

Examples from my own experience come readily to mind and illustrate that the need for constant vigilance and careful discernment has in no way diminished. It is worth sharing several instances as they highlight shortcomings in a planter's profile that are all too often overlooked.

• The new town was growing and this, together with the emergence of a lively Pentecostal church, gave two good indicators that the community was good soil for planting in. A prime site and unexpectedly generous gift to enable building work to commence added to a general sense of expectancy that the new work would prosper. It didn't, it struggled. Shortcomings in the moral life of the leader's wife were undermining the credibility in the gospel and the new church that he was faithfully working to build up.

In the early days of any church plant, the leader and his family are very closely identified in the eyes of the community with the new congregation itself. As someone recently put it to me, a salesman who drives a beat-up old Ford will not make a convincing salesman for a Rolls Royce. The personal and family life of the leader must be an attractive commendation of the gospel that is being offered to the community.

- It had been difficult to find any accommodation for Antonio and his family, and as I helped them move in I had sympathy for his wife's less than enthusiastic attitude. It wasn't just the house, however, the town itself of some 10,000 could well have been described as a place unlikely to need a church since it was so hot that Satan wouldn't set foot in there! Quite the contrary was true, of course, and the fact that this established community had proved such unfertile soil for the gospel over almost 200 years had led us to look long and hard at Antonio before inviting him to act as pioneer for the new work. Antonio fulfilled our hopes, but his wife to whom we had paid little attention beyond assuring ourselves of her good standing in the church where they had been working, couldn't stick it. Her commitment to the venture didn't go deep enough and when the hardships bore in on them her resolve withered like the corn grown from the seed in stony ground. Like John Mark she took the earliest opportunity to leave and a promising start and a lot of resources were lost.

Church planting is frontline work and not for everyone. It is absolutely essential that where the planter is married then the whole family should be committed to the work.

- The mother church was desperate to find a leader for the emerging group out in the burgeoning suburb of their rapidly expanding town. The young man they appointed had not long completed theological training and presented himself as keen to get into ministry. After only four months spent, it seemed, largely in acquiring a desk a director would have been proud of and visiting and making a card index of the small congregation, he complained of having nothing to do and shortly afterwards accepted an invitation from another hard-pressed but more established church elsewhere.

He had nothing to do because he was an administrator, a maintenance man and in a church plant there is nothing to maintain or administer. He simply didn't have eyes for mission. It is surprising how many churches actually make this mistake when appointing leadership. This is particularly true when the new church is being formed upon a house group that has been in existence for some time. The temptation is to think that the same leadership that served what was perhaps essentially a fellowship group is appropriate for a group committed to mission. The leadership team will certainly need to include someone with pastoral gifting but altogether different gifts of vision and growth-oriented thinking will be required if the group is going to move beyond being a self-help club for Christians to becoming a vigorous centre of evangelism in the unchurched community.

• On two occasions we were confronted with planting in communities that had a distinctive cultural colouring. In one, the new town was comprised largely of young families from the south of Brazil. In the other, a significant number of the residents were associated with the university around which the housing development was situated. In neither instance did we get the leadership issue right. Contact with a Bible school in south Brazil yielded a personable young man able to relate extremely well to the families moving in but who simply didn't put in the hard work necessary to build up the contacts and exploit the opportunities for witness and service. At Spurgeon's we have found that the reference obtained from the secular employer is one of the best indicators of how hardworking and responsible an individual is.

The only candidate for the university suburb was a man in his late seventies with little education. Here the cultural mismatch was clearly a contraindication. As is often the case, however, churches are faced with 'Hobson's choice' and we decided to go ahead on the basis that careful selection of other team members could compensate for his weaknesses. To some extent this was successful although only at the cost of a lot of supervisory involvement from myself, and even then the new work tended not to attract the original target group of university folk. There can be real difficulties in finding plant leaders of a suitable age, ethnic or social background. Although the temptation to ignore this criterion of cultural correspondence is great, experience shows that the wider the cultural divide between the sponsoring group and the target community the more significant this factor becomes.

● A final example is one that in these days of increasing ecumenical openness is one that is particularly relevant. Mr Ferraz was an able preacher, a mature Christian of impeccable moral stature, and had just moved into the centre of the target area. He seemed like a Godsend to the newly launched team. The problem was, however, as it soon became evident, that he didn't share the ministry philosophy of the rest of the nuclear group. It was only with some difficulty that he was eased out of an involvement that was threatening to cause division and so an early demise for the new congregation.

Different patterns of leadership

Within the general profile pointers that have been outlined above there is clearly room for variety. Team make-up, the target community and the type of planting model being followed are all factors that may vary the blend of attributes required.

Perhaps the most distinct variation from the 'local church planter' whose gifting is defined largely by the demands of growing a single congregation is that of the individual envisioned and gifted for a more extensive 'apostolic' type of ministry. A strong sense of vision, a capacity to see and think on a wider strategic level, wisdom, sensitivity and empathy in dealing with local plant leaders, and the ability to relate easily to a variety of different situations at the same time would all be characteristics of particular importance.

Bruce Patrick identifies three approaches to planting that demand apostolic gifting.[14]

First, the multiplication of culturally different congregations within a single centre.

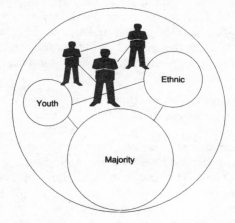

Second, radial church model, increasingly common, especially among Anglicans planting within parish boundaries.

Third, the networking model exemplified by Pioneer or Ichthus.

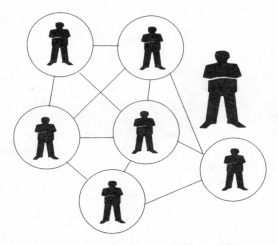

To these three examples it is significant from a mainline denominational standpoint to mention the development of a fourth, that of 'area missioners'. These are individuals commissioned specifically to exercise a wider apostolic style of ministry within the context of denominational structures, identifying potential planting opportunities and acting in liaison with local and national church bodies to facilitate the focusing of resources and emergence of a new work. The Methodist Church is beginning to experiment in this area in the person of Rob Frost, who co-ordinates their 'Seed team' approach to planting, using teams of young people.[15] It is the Baptist Union, however, that is demonstrating most clearly the value of such ministries within traditional structures, with a dozen appointments so far, likely to double by the end of the decade.

One further style of church planting leadership is that exemplified by men such as George Patterson in Honduras, Edwin Erickson in Ethiopia and Chris Marantika in Indonesia. The approach adopted by each of these men has been to utilise mission training programmes to fuel church planting movements.

- In a five-year period from April 1984 the membership of the Baptist Evangelical Association of Ethiopia rose from 1,422 to 8,009 largely due to a programme of mission training by extension whose explicit goal was the establishing of new churches.[16]
- Patterson's work in establishing a lay training programme for potential planters is based upon the principles of TEE, with a further 'E' added to produce Theological Education by Extension and Evangelism. Its great strength lies in its goal of training those who are also able to train other planters, resulting in the development of a planting *movement* that in Patterson's own experience led to the founding of some 200 churches during his ministry with the Conservative Baptists out of the Honduras Bible Institute in Olanchito. Donald McGavran's assessment of the TEEE concept as 'pure gold',[17] and his advocacy of the principle as one that 'ought to be used in all six continents'[18] is a timely corrective to any temptation to discount the relevance of 'foreign missions' experience for the UK situation.
- Certainly, the general philosophy of the 'Church Planting and Evangelism Course' sponsored by the Oasis Trust at Spurgeon's College shares the same belief in the potential of combining mission training with mission practice that Spurgeon himself employed so fruitfully in the late nineteenth century. It remains to be seen whether the Oasis/Spurgeon's experience will develop to the extent of the programme based on the Evangelical Theological Seminary of Indonesia, led by Chris Marantika, in which a graduation requirement is the founding of a church with at least thirty members!

What is significant for the question of gifting for leadership in this area is, of course, that an aptitude for training is appropriate. Paul's own example and his exhortation to Timothy readily spring to mind (2 Tim 2:2).

How to grow tomorrow's planters today

Where are tomorrow's church planters going to come from? In a thought-provoking article on strategic management, 'New Ventures and Small Business', Professor A. C. Cooper of the Krannert Graduate School of Management, Indiana,[19] identifies three influences upon the emergence of entrepreneurs that are relevant to our consideration of the church's problem.

1. The individual's personal background.
2. The organisation in which the individual has been working.
3. Factors which make the climate more or less favourable to new ventures.

The categories are valid and it is worthwhile examining them from a Christian perspective.

1. The personal gifting—is God still calling and gifting church planters?

This was well illustrated for me back in 1988 when attending a general committee meeting of the Baptist Missionary Society with which my wife Georgie and I served. The Society had recently accepted an invitation from the French Baptist Federation to look for missionaries to assist them in church planting in France. On the day in question two couples, previously interviewed and approved by the candidate selection committee, were being proposed for appointment and a representative of the Devon and Cornwall Associations of Baptist Churches rose to request the opportunity to second the recommendation. He told how eighteen months previously a group had met and resolved to promote the missionary challenge by publishing a leaflet featuring the photographs of serving missionaries from the area and concluding with an outline face captioned, 'Who will go for us to France?' There followed an appeal to pray for candidates to come forward, echoing Jesus' words in Luke 10:2: 'The harvest is plentiful, but the workers are few. Ask the Lord of the harvest, therefore, to send out workers into his harvest field.' Within nine months, the two couples that were being proposed had offered for service.

Where groups are taking seriously the command of the Lord to pray for pioneers, pioneers are being called. It is anomalous that while pioneer missionaries for overseas church planting continue to be prayed out, the glaring need of our own land goes largely unresponded to. The words of James 4:2–3 that the church did not have because it did not ask, and when it did ask, asked for its own benefit, are well applied to the current attitude towards leadership procurement already outlined above.

2. *The experience that potential planters have from their own church organisations*

The graph below shows the record of Baptist church planting in London from 1865 to 1985.

Of interest to the issue in hand is the observation that hardly any of those likely to be in management positions in churches in

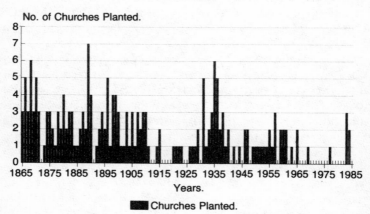

Church Planting in the L.B.A.
1865–1985

Source: L.B.A. Handbooks.

1990 would have had any experience of being part of a church that had planted or of having known of any such. Among all mainline denominations there is a serious lack of know how in regard to establishing new works. For many, church planting isn't on the agenda simply because it has never been on the agenda of any church with which they have been associated.

In contrast, it would be almost impossible to be a member of one of the new or ethnic churches without being aware that starting new congregations is a normal part of the work of a church. It is one of the benefits of such interchurch activities as Spring Harvest, and the deliberate policy of interchurch co-operation pursued by groups such as the Ichthus Fellowship, that a cross-fertilisation of experience is stimulating a rapidly growing awareness of the possibilities of planting among the larger church groupings. The creation of forums for sharing vision and experience, such as the Baptist Church Planters' Network, and the opportunities offered by interdenominational church planting training days initiated by Bob Hopkins of the Anglican network, all help to restore 'church planter' to the list of possible 'callings'.

One further practical consequence of the general lack of church planting experience and recognition of giftedness is that the pool of suitably envisioned and capable individuals in any one fellowship will be rapidly diminished should that church actually engage in the planting process. Although a church may find itself able to sustain two or even three plants in a five- or six-year period, the drain upon potential leadership talent will soon become apparent. As in human childbearing, continued, frequent reproduction can be weakening. More significantly, however, it should be recognised that whereas the talent pool of a mother church might be diminishing, that of the newly established daughters will be growing rapidly. It is in fact in the newly planted churches, particularly in their early years of life, that the greatest repository of vision and expertise is to be found. A strategic consideration of churches committed to an ongoing programme of evangelism through church planting should be, therefore, not only to engage in a sustainable rate of planting themselves, but also to invest in grandchildren by making resources available to recently produced daughter churches to encourage them to get into the 'family way'!

3. External factors that make church planting a realistic option for suitably gifted individuals

For a whole range of reasons outlined in Chapter 2, church planting is back on the agenda of Christian groups across the country. The probable continued decline in 'national Christianity', together with continued and rapid societal change, are likely to promote a growing desire for a fresh sense of spiritual security and expression, particularly as the year 2000 approaches. Against this backdrop, church planting is a ministry whose value has once again grasped the imagination of a new generation of Christian men and women committed to serving the Lord. Whereas fifteen years ago the first church planter I had ever met was upon beginning missionary service in Brazil, it is true today that the two most buoyant job markets on the British church scene are for youth ministers and church planters. As the growing rate of enquiries from across the denominational spectrum for places on the Spurgeon's course indicates, an increasing number of individuals, suitable and unsuitable, are likely to be attracted to this ministry in the years ahead. This fact is a cause for both excitement and caution and underscores the importance of learning quickly about the credentials of an effective church planter.

For discussion and further study

1. To what extent can the importance attached to leadership in church planting projects be justified in the light of biblical teaching?
2. How valid is it to compare the qualities required by an individual starting a new business with those required by the leader of a new church plant?
3. Draw up a set of criteria for screening applicants wishing to join a team being formed to plant a new congregation in a suburb some five miles from the parent church.

4. Identify six key qualities of those engaged in new church planting leadership, justifying each both from Scripture and experience.

Notes

1. Peter Wagner, *Church Planting for a Greater Harvest* (Regal Books, 1991), p 51.
2. Elmer Towns, *Getting a Church Started* (Church Growth Institute: Lynchburg, VA, 1985), p 124.
3. Philip Bryant, *Church Planting Workbook* (Baptist Union of Victoria, PO Box 377, Hawthorn, Australia), p 20.
4. Graham Lee, '10 Church Planting Keys', in Bruce Patrick, *A Clear Call to Mission in New Zealand* (Baptist Union of New Zealand, 1990).
5. *Church Growth through Church Planting* (The International Centre of Evangelism, BP 4577, Kinshasa 2, Zaire), p 95.
6. Roger Sutton, Altrincham Baptist Church and Adrian Argyle, Leyland Baptist Church; presented at the 1990 Baptist Union Consultation on Church Planting.
7. Article by John Wimber, 'The Church Planter', reproduced by Bruce Patrick for the New Zealand Baptist Union.
8. William L. Wagner, (ed), *Eight Growing Baptist Churches in Western Europe* (Brentwood Christian Press: Georgia 31904, USA, 1989).
9. *Long Range Planning—Entrepreneurship—the Creating and Managing of New Ventures* (Pergamon Press, 1989), p 20.
10. Schenk and Stutzman, Creating Communities of the Kingdom (Herald Press: Ontario, 1988).
11. Wagner, *op cit*, pp 16, 17.
12. George Patterson, *Church Planting through Obedience-Oriented Teaching* (William Carey Library, 1989), p 53.
13. Logan and Rast, *A Supervisor's Manual for New Church Development* (Charles Fuller Institute, PO Box 91990, Pasadena, CA 91109, USA, 1990).
14. Bruce Patrick, *Multiplication of Congregations* (Baptist Union of New Zealand, 1989), pp 6–9.

15. Article in *Planting Papers*, no 1 (February 1991): pp 6, 7;
    reproduced in *The Link*, the journal of the International
    Network of Church Planters, vol 2, no 3 (1991).
16. Edwin Erickson, article in *Global Church Growth*, vol 26,
    no 4 (1989): p 8.
17. Preface by Donald McGavran in G. Patterson, *Church
    Planting through Obedience-Oriented Teaching* (William
    Carey Library, 1981), p v.
18. *Ibid*.
19. In *Long Range Planning*, *op cit*, pp 97–103.

CHAPTER TEN

GUIDELINES FOR THE PLANTING TEAM

Stuart Christine

The objective of the church planting team is to form a community rooted in God and reaching out to the world.

Rooted in God

The first ground to be prepared in the task of planting a new kingdom community is that of the hearts and minds of the planting team. From first to last, from blueprint to materials, from labourers to functioning end product, the building of 'living temples' is the work of God.

The planting purpose, the planting plan, the planting people and the planting power can and should be determined by God. He it is who has *purposed* to build a kingdom, each individual in it saved from the consequences of his rebellion and ignorance to become his people. He it is who has determined the *plan*, that it should be through the agency of this kingdom community, multiplying throughout the world, that the good news of his purposes be proclaimed. He it is who calls and equips each member of the kingdom, forming a *people* willing and able to embrace his purposes and become part of his plan. He it is who provides the *power* that enables his people to live out the policies of the kingdom of God throughout the kingdoms of this world and be assured that he will build his church and that not even the gates of hell will prevail against it. 'For yours is the kingdom and the power and the glory ... (Mt 6:13).

The implications of this divine ownership of the planting process should be carefully thought through by the planting team, therefore, and allowed to determine guidelines for every aspect of their role as co-partners with God. 1 Corinthians 3:5–15 reflects some of Paul and Apollos' experience and understanding of this issue.

God's purpose

The church planting team is to be driven above all by the love of God to see people saved from a life without hope and without God in the world to that eternal life with him which is found in the family of faith. This is God's purpose in all history and must be the purpose of the new congregation. And if it is to be the purpose of the new congregation it must be the declared and unambiguous motivation and commitment of the planting team. The new church will reflect the attitudes and priorities of the founding group to an extent that will determine its lifestyle and usefulness to God for years to come. In this crucial commitment to evangelism, therefore, there can be no compromise!

Practical implications can immediately be highlighted:

- The *motivation* for the plant should be evangelistic, ie, the reason that the new church is being projected is out of a desire to reach the target community more effectively. Other reasons must be secondary to this mission emphasis. A church that is bursting at the seams might well be prompted to consider planting out, but let it be from a desire to make more space for the unchurched to be reached, not more space for the churched to worship in comfort.[1]

Personality clashes, differences of preference in worship style, local convenience are all motives that focus inwards and will not form the basis of a fellowship committed to God's mission agenda. Ventures that are born out of a desire to pool the resources of failing works, or as expressions of ecumenical fellowship, are similarly flawed. Mission is the motor that will drive the work forward. Monuments to other motivations scatter the ecclesiastical landscape of all denominations, and should not be added to.

- The *leadership* of the planting team must be directed by those with mission vision and gifting. Especially if the nucleus for a plant is based upon a house fellowship already meeting in the target area, then care must be taken not to perpetuate a leadership style that was previously aimed at servicing a prayer, study and fellowship group for Christians. It is important that a balance of gifting be represented in the team leadership, but the driving authority must be focused in an individual committed to body building through evangelism.

• Neither must *the development of a strong group identity*, so vital for vigorous common vision and action, be allowed to become an end in itself. The prelaunch fellowship bonding programme can produce a Christian club mentality if the leadership does not maintain the mission profile.

God's plan

Commitment to God's strategy of mission through the multiplication of witnessing Christian communities must not only be the ground of the planting project but also its goal. The establishment of a new church alone is *not* an adequate objective for the planting team. What should be in view is the establishment of a congregation that will have both the vision and the capacity for itself *reproducing*.

This goal will have implications for the formulation of the *ministry philosophy* of the new church. 'Giving out' will need to be built into the ethos of the new group as well as 'going out'. Care will need to be taken to avoid the development of a dependent spirit, whereby an expectation is promoted that as the new 'baby' the Christian world owes them a living. Self-centred adults grow from spoilt children. The church at Corinth seems to have suffered from a range of problems symptomatic of excessive spiritual navel-gazing and, judging from Paul's exhortations in 2 Corinthians 8 and 9, an inadequate attitude towards giving was one of them. The model of the churches in Macedonia (2 Cor 8:1, is an excellent one for any new group to emulate, recalled again by Paul in his letter to the Philippi church (Phil 4:14–16).

Our experience in Mato Grosso, Brazil, has taught us the value of instilling a generous mission-focused attitude early into the heart of a newly planted fellowship. In the first 6 years of its life, the fledgling Baptist church initiated one new congregation in a housing development some 3 miles away, one in a town 100 miles away, and further sent a team to build new church premises for a congregation over 1,000 miles distant in the neighbouring country of Paraguay!

A church that will be available to God for mission will need to learn the truth of the promise of the Lord:

> 'Give, and it will be given to you. A good measure, pressed down, shaken together and running over, will be poured into your lap. For with the measure you use, it will be measured to you' (Lk 6:38).

A generous spirit born of a confidence in the giving God and commitment to his plan of mission through multiplication is a plank that should be well nailed into the ministry platform of the new church.

God's people

> ... the apostles Barnabas and Paul ... rushed into the crowd, shouting: ... We too are only men, human like you. We are bringing you good news ... (Acts 14:14,15).

> Paul then stood up ... and said: 'Men of Athens ... God ... commands all people everywhere to repent (Acts 17:22,30).

> We are therefore Christ's ambassadors, as though God were making his appeal through us (2 Cor 5:20).

Whether addressing the crowds in Lystra, the Areopagus in Athens or the church in Corinth, Paul reveals a conviction necessary to all who would engage in new church planting, namely that they understand themselves to be, though 'only human', envoys, mouthpieces and representatives of the living God.

The link between call and mission vision is well established in the history of God's people. Patriarchs, prophets, apostles, all alike are men and women fired by an experience of personal call by the voice of God. The disciples of Jesus, no less, were called out (Mk 3:13–15) to become those who could go 'ahead of him to every town and place where he was about to go' (Lk 10:1,2). The church planting team must share the conviction that they are not only people with a mission but also people with a commission, a call and divine charter authorising them to engage in the business of establishing an extension to God's network of kingdom communities.

The founding vision of the leadership of the team must become the fellowship vision of every member. This capacity to communicate the sense of divine calling and direction, literally 'to enthuse' the whole team with the vision for the new work, is an essential gift of an effective church planter. Not only in the period of initial team building but also as the new congregation grows care must be taken to ensure that all new members are imbued with it.

All the members of the team must have shared in the same vision and calling, and be pulling in the same direction if the new work is going to move ahead. Although ecumenical openness is to be welcomed, there must be a common mind among the core team members on the central features of the ministry philosophy of the new church. Where significant differences exist over matters such as the charismatic gifts, membership, church government, or the mission purpose of the group, then the greatest caution is necessary. Ignoring such differences, many new ventures have been launched with a built-in time bomb, destined to explode into disunity when the need to develop more clearly defined structures for the congregation's life becomes necessary.

There is also a tendency for new ventures to attract folk that have problems with their current churches. Especially in the case of those with strong personalities, the new group offers an opportunity for them to enjoy influence and to expound their pet ideas. Genuine unity and mutual respect and trust is vital in the process of building the leadership team of any new group and this may mean, as it did for Paul, selecting some and deselecting others.

One recently successful plant in the north of England expressed its approach to this potentially thorny issue in these words:

We tackled the issue of who should form the initial core of the new church along the lines of *picking a Team*. We said that residence in the area was not in itself conclusive, though a strong argument for inclusion. A number of people who lived in the catchment area were sent letters from the leadership telling them that we felt their place was still at the mother church. Most of these people were either potential boat-rockers or were relative new-comers who for some reason were felt to be in need of a longer stay at HQ. We asked four people (3 Sunday school staff and a keyboard player) from outside the area to help in the new work. This approach met with only one mild protest. We stated that mother church regulars would not be welcome on day-trips to the plant—on the analogy that it would be like taking your mother-in-law on your honeymoon! . . . *We heartily recommend this rather authoritarian approach.*

God's guidance for Gideon (Judg 7:1–8) is a helpful model for justifying this serious concern to ensure *compatibility* and *conviction* among the church planting team.

God's power

The authority of the Lord of the church guarantees the growth and fruitfulness of the church. It is through Jesus that the power for planting will come:

> I am the vine; you are the branches. If a man remains in me and I in him, he will bear much fruit; apart from me you can do nothing (Jn 15:5).

Dependency on God, prayerfulness and expectancy are therefore attitudes that must be cultivated in the fellowship life of every new offshoot of the kingdom. However the links between the new congregation and the parent body are set up, they must not threaten the development of these qualities. The promise of fruitfulness is to the one who remains linked to and dependent upon Jesus, not linked to and dependent upon another Christian group. The proper relationship between kingdom communities, like between branches on a vine, is one of *interdependency* with each other, while they share a common dependency upon the Lord who is the vine.

Factors affecting this sense of dependency are particularly those related to the decision-making processes established for governing the new congregation. It is imperative that from the outset the planting team sense both the need and possibility of receiving the direct guidance of the Lord through his Spirit. Whatever checks and balances, or system of federal government might be devised for the plant in relation to the parent body, nothing must be allowed to inhibit the growth of a conviction that the Spirit is guiding the new group. This conviction will promote the faith in the same Spirit to provide the power to enable the guidance to be worked through. It might well be that the parent body will be among the agencies that the Spirit will stimulate to co-operate with the new group in facing some particular issue, but what is crucial is that the fledgling fellowship understand that God is ministering to their needs. This will build a fellowship-consciousness that God is with them, a consciousness without which the embryonic church will neither aspire to nor achieve life as a local expression of the body of Christ.

When Jesus began his public ministry, affirming that the kingdom of God had drawn near and that therefore men were to take action, there was an authority and power at work in him that galvanised men's imaginations and inspired them to give up everything to commit themselves to this decisive work of God, (Mk 1:15–20). This same sense that the kingdom has drawn near to the planting team, underwriting and enabling their kingdom-building task, must possess the membership of the new group. The well known passage in Zechariah 4:1–10 proved determinative for a particular new church plant that I was involved with. 'Mighty mountains' (v 7) there were a plenty, both material and spiritual, but the lively conviction that the Spirit of the Lord Almighty was with us all formed a firm foundation for facing the challenges and checks of planting that can seem so daunting, especially in the 'day of small things' (v 10).

Rooted in God—but reaching out to the world

The reason for God's calling the new church into life was because existing agencies of the kingdom were not proving able to meet the needs of all the people in the targeted area. Mission need and mission vision combined with mission possibility to mobilise God's people into this new and distinct mission initiative. A particular people, area or community is the focus of the Spirit's activity and great care must be taken to ensure that nothing is allowed to compromise the establishment of a relevant and effective ministry among these people.

Practical implications readily flow from this basic principle.

- Leaders must live within the target community in order to sense 'where the people are at', and determine relevant ways of expressing the gospel among them. Commuter missionaries are a contradiction in terms and mission initiatives that allow them have long since been discredited.

- The leadership team of the new church must include within it some 'creative thinkers' if it is to be successful in formulating patterns of church life and mission that are sensitive and responsive to the particular characteristics of the target community.

- Decision-making procedures that are drawn up should ensure that ministry priorities and philosophy are determined by local conditions and not by the patterns prevailing in the parent body. No church has the right to presume from its past experience or preferences what shape God will want its 'child' to take or what ministries to develop. Each new congregation has the demanding job of standing within its particular mission field and seeking what it means to authentically represent the kingdom of God in that setting. Central agendas should not be allowed to compromise this freedom to respond to local realities.

- All those seeking to be involved in the planting team, and in particular all the leadership of that team, should be actively involved in the community survey work. This will provide a common experience of the situation in the target community upon which the discussions and prayers for the development of the philosophy of ministry can be based. A programme of target community familiarisation should also be made an entry requirement of any Christians who might subsequently wish to join the new church from 'out of the area'.

The purpose of all these suggestions is to safeguard clarity of focus of the second lens of the 'vision glasses' through which the planting team will look to find its way ahead. The clearest view of the planting pathway will be obtained when both the God 'lens' and the world 'lens' are carefully prepared and built together into the new congregation's mindset.

Developing a philosophy of ministry/mission

What is a philosophy of ministry?

The term *philosophy of ministry* refers to the intentional design and format a church establishes to best carry out its unique mission under God.[2]

A philosophy of ministry answers two simple but critical questions that every embryonic church must repeatedly ask itself during its gestation period:

- *Who* has God called us and equipped us to reach?
- *How* will we most effectively reach those to whom God has called us?

Some principles that will guide the formulation of the philosophy of ministry have already been laid down in the preceding sections of this chapter. The specifics of each new church's approach to their task must, however, be worked out in response to their particular situation and calling.

An example might be helpful at this point. The Willow Creek Community Church was founded back in the mid-seventies, and in the period up to 1991 has grown to become the second largest congregation in the USA.

The literature introducing the church begins by making a general statement of the purpose for which the church exists:

Purpose

Exaltation: to offer the body of believers the opportunity to worship and glorify God together.

Edification: to help believers build a foundation of biblical understanding, establish a devotional life, discover their spiritual gifts, and to encourage believers to become participating members in the body of Christ.

Evangelism: to reach people who are facing a Christless eternity. Members of the body are encouraged to seek out the unchurched as the Holy Spirit has sought them out, and to look for opportunities to share Christ's love.

Social Action: to act as a conscience to the world by demonstrating the love and righteousness of God in both word and deed.

This general statement of purpose, which most evangelical churches could affirm, is then followed by a more specific statement of their philosophy of ministry, ie, the particular principles that will guide them to the fulfilment of their declared purpose.

Philosophy

Willow Creek Community Church is founded on the following basic principles:

1. *Every believer has the responsibility of being a witness in their faith and walk with Christ.*

While only a small group of believers may have the spiritual gift of evangelism and feel called to go out into the world and preach the gospel, it is the responsibility of every believer to reach out to individuals who are within their circle of influence and share with them the fact that a relationship with Jesus Christ is a life-changing experience.

The effectiveness of the church in reaching the unchurched is dramatically increased when we are able to moblize the 95% of the believers who are not gifted evangelists. We are able to mobilize these believers when we assist them in their evangelism efforts. Willow Creek Community Church supplements the believers' evangelism efforts by providing a service designed to communicate the message of Christ to their friends with relevance, creativity and with a contemporary style.

2. *The needs of the seeker differ from those of a believer.*

Individuals who have not accepted Jesus Christ as their Saviour do not understand Christian terminology. They are often reluctant to attend a church service, and when they do attend, they come with little or no knowledge of basic Christian principles. It is imperative that they are ministered to on a level that they can understand. Willow Creek Community Church provides a service that has been designed specifically to meet the needs of the seeker.

Recognizing that the need of the believer must be met as well, Willow Creek Community Church provides a service designed specifically for the believing community. This service provides for corporate worship in creative ways, the sharing of communion and the opportunity to be challenged by the expository preaching of the Word.

3. *Believers must respect the individual's process of a faith decision and the journey one must travel to maturity in Christ.*

Theologically, it is recognized that there is a moment in time when an individual is birthed into the family of God through a commitment to the person and work of Jesus Christ. Practically, however, this event occurs after a process of examining, considering, evaluating and weighing the costs of the Christian faith. The point of conversion is not the end of the process, but rather the line between the journey to faith and the process of maturity in that new faith. As a result, Willow Creek Community Church actually chooses to be process-oriented, rather than event driven.

4. *Every believer is a minister, gifted by God for the benefit of the body.*

Recognizing that every believer is gifted by God to be a vital part of the equipping and maturing of the body of Christ, Willow Creek Community Church attempts to mobilize the body in service and ministry. This is accomplished by challenging people to put on the mantle of leadership and service through the discovery, development and implementation of their spiritual gift(s).

A careful reading of the Willow Creek document is helpful in understanding what sort of issues should be covered in a 'philosophy of ministry'.

First, certain declarations are made about what it means for someone to be a member of the church. Certain expectations are set out:

- Every member is called to be a witness to the unchurched, though not every member has the gift of evangelism.

- Every member has a need to worship and grow in the faith.
- Every member is gifted by God and has a vital role in the church.

Second, certain convictions about unchurched people are expressed;

- They have little knowledge of the faith.
- They don't feel at home with 'churchy' language or customs.
- Their needs cannot be met in a service designed for believers.
- Their spiritual journey to faith will take time.

Third, certain convictions about what will represent an appropriate ministry response to these factors are set out:

- The church is to encourage and develop, every member witnessing.
- The church is to supplement personal witnessing by specially prepared, culturally appropriate evangelising events.
- The church's evangelistic programmes are to anticipate an extended process of conversion.
- The church is to offer corporate worship and expository Bible teaching in a contemporary style.
- The church is committed to a policy of gift identification and development through service, for all members.

A clear picture has been painted for us of the church: It is to be a mission-oriented, Bible-based, highly participative community conducting all its activities in a contemporary style. Everything that the church plans to do, or is doing, will reflect these guiding principles. They establish the ethos of the church.

- Prospective members will have a clear idea of what membership will entail for them if they join the church.
- Leaders will have a set of principles which can be applied to the development and evaluation of all the ministry programmes of the church.

The result is a common approach to mutually agreed goals—a good basic formula for an harmonious, purposeful and effective church.

Once the basic philosophy of ministry has been clarified then the leadership group must go on to work out what *strategy* will enable the purpose of the church to be fulfilled, given the ethos that has been agreed upon.

Strategy

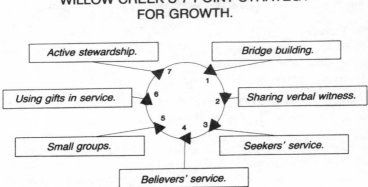

WILLOW CREEK'S 7 POINT STRATEGY FOR GROWTH.

Active stewardship.

Bridge building.

Using gifts in service.

Sharing verbal witness.

Small groups.

Seekers' service.

Believers' service.

The cycle of discipleship continues as the newly established believer takes up the bridge-building process with their own friends.

Clearly, then, if each stage in the cycle is completed then the mission ethos of the church will be satisfied, ie, it is a strategy which has the potential to achieve the primary goal of the church. If each stage is also carried through in a biblically based, culturally sensitive way that involves the co-operation and ownership of all the church then the resulting ministry life of the church should conform to the particular ethos that has been decided upon.

Another clearly set out strategy of ministry, focusing not only on the need to grow a vigorous church but also one that will be geared to reproduce itself through church planting (unlike the Willow Creek model) is presented by David Hesselgrave in his book, *Planting Churches Cross-Culturally*. An analysis of the record of the Pauline church planting ministry forms the basis of a ten-point 'Master Plan of Evangelism' which he entitles, 'the Pauline Cycle'.[3]

1. Missionaries commissioned.
2. Audience contacted.
3. Gospel communicated.
4. Hearers converted.
5. Believers congregated.
6. Faith confirmed.
7. Leadership consecrated.
8. Believers commended.
9. Relationships continued.
10. Sending churches convened.

While acknowledging that the ten-point approach might appear contrived, he makes the very valid point that:

> If any of us as the modern counterparts of Paul, Peter, Thomas, or Timothy, were to go to a designated city to evangelize and establish a church, would we not carry out these very same steps? And would we not carry them out in this order, more or less?[4]

It is not surprising that the Willow Creek strategy is contained within the 'Pauline cycle' in steps 2 to 7. The additional steps are a direct consequence of church planting being both the starting point and goal of the Hesselgrave model.

Whatever the precise description of strategy that the planting team adopts, it is to the question of what *ministry programmes* should be set up in order to make each stage of the strategy work in the particular setting of the church that the group will now need to turn their attention.

Ministry programme planning

Once established, the strategy forms an easy to understand pathway along which the church knows it can move in order to reach its particular goal. How it must organise itself and what resources it will need to take each step along this pathway is the

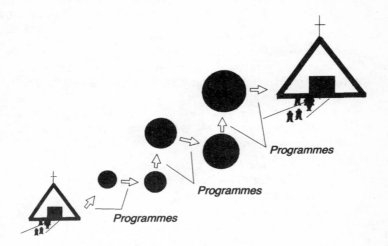

PROGRAMMES PLANNED TO ACHIEVE
EACH STRATEGIC STEP.

next important stage in developing the ministry package of the
new church.

Between each stage the group must determine one or more
programmes of church activity that will enable the particular
step to be taken, and identify the people who will be responsible
for making each programme work.

The Willow Creek example of ministry programme planning

As a first example of how to go about this process we can look
again at the Willow Creek Church and how they approached
the development of a suitable programme for step 3 of their
strategic plan—the 'seeker service'.

In addressing the question of what a 'seeker service' should
look like and who it should be targeted at, the Willow Creek
leadership first of all did some 'market research' to find out
what they could do about the attitudes to church among the
unchurched living in their target community and whom they
would be wanting to attend such services.

Five basic reasons for indifference to church emerged in their situation:

1. Churches are always asking for money.
2. Church services are boring and lifeless.
3. Church services are predictable and repetitive.
4. Sermons are irrelevant to daily life as it is lived in the real world.
5. The pastor makes people feel guilty and ignorant, so they leave church feeling worse than when they entered the doors.

They also identified, from a social survey of the area, a picture of the typical household from which their 'seeker service' congregation would be drawn.

The results of this analysis led them to adopt a 'seeker service' aimed at professional men between the ages of twenty-five and fifty, conducted at a time most convenient to the unchurched person, in an auditorium free from religious symbols and offering amenities that were familiar and of a standard comparable to that which the audience would experience in their professional and home lives. The attention given to the 'seeker' was to be courteous, warm and yet respectful of the right for the 'seeker' to retain his anonymity, attending without being pressurised. Every aspect of the programme presented was to acknowledge the spiritual position of the unchurched, reflect contemporary culture and display the highest quality possible.

At a recent visit to the church I was impressed, along with 15,000 others each weekend, by the extent to which these features of the programme are in fact being delivered. The programme is mounted and monitored each week by a team of members who understand this to be their specific ministry within the life of the church.

The Hesselgrave approach to ministry programme planning

Hesselgrave carries through his study of Paul's methodology in Acts as a means of identifying some general principles governing the development of ministry programmes aimed at achieving each stage of his ten-point strategic plan. An example of his approach can be cited with reference to the 'audience contact' stage.

After establishing the biblically affirmed commitment of God to all peoples and recognising that people are divided into distinctive cultural groups, he goes on to expose three commonly held misconceptions regarding the process of 'making contact' with unchurched people, namely that:

- The community owes the missionary a hearing.
- That it makes no difference how you communicate.
- That it makes no difference with whom you communicate.

A four-tiered programme is then suggested to guide the contacting process:

1. Gain the good will of community leaders.
2. Reach any unchurched Christians.
3. Target spiritually prepared peoples.
4. Get as wide a hearing as possible for the gospel.

A planting team can readily address the challenge of the 'contacting process' once the task is broken down in such a way.

- Lists of community leaders can be drawn up and visitors appointed.
- Suitable publicity should be organised to alert any 'hidden disciples' to this new opportunity of joining with a Christian community.
- Survey forms need to be examined to identify the most responsive groups among the population.
- High profile events or social action programmes can be identified that will alert and attract the community in general to the arrival of the new church.

But beware . . .

Some particular words of counsel and caution should be noted by the planting team working on a ministry programme.

Does it fit? No activity should be planned or undertaken which does not form a coherent part of one of the ministry programmes needed to achieve the strategic goals of the congregation. Everyone must know precisely why everything is being done, especially when resources are limited.

Questions that should be asked of any proposed ministry programme are:

- Who is this programme aimed at?
- What is the purpose of this programme?
- How does it tie in with the overall purpose statement of the church?
- Does it reflect the values of the church as set out in the ministry philosophy of the church?
- What resources will it require to operate?
- Who will lead and assist in running it?
- What will be its measurable results?

Do we have the people to run it? No ministry programme should be sanctioned unless there is a gifted leader who has a vision for it and is available to head it up. It is far better to wait and do what is done well, according to God's timetable, than to try to sustain an unrealistic level of ministry activity, which if done poorly will be ineffective and drain the energy and morale of the membership.

Training programmes will need to be built into the ministry package of the new church from the outset both in order to help furnish immediate staffing needs and in anticipation of the growth in leadership demand that will occur as the fellowship increases in size. A key feature of growing causes is that they plan in anticipation of growth.

Workers borrowed from the parent body can be a blessing that becomes a curse. Group identity and ministry continuity can both be put in jeopardy through the involvement of workers who do not share the commitment level and ethos of the planting group. Certain service tasks, such as in music and Sunday school teaching, can be appropriate avenues of assistance, but even then the 'contract' should be for a clearly defined period after which evaluation will be understood to take place. *Is now the right time to launch it?* Ministry programmes that are believed to be legitimate and possible are prioritised in terms of the timing of their introduction. When you can't do everything at once, which is invariably the case in church planting, then there needs to be a clear understanding of which activities are most important in order to develop and keep up momentum in the growth of the work.

Timetables and evaluation

Once a schedule of activities has been drawn up that is within the resourcing capability of the new group, perhaps with the help of the parent church, then a timetable can be established to put the process into operation and thought given to how the effectiveness of the anticipated programme will be evaluated after a certain period.

Without the establishment of a timetable for implementation and evaluation, ministry programmes of churches very easily degenerate into a collection of uncontrolled and unrelated activities, understood as the 'personal property' of individuals or groups. In doing so they not only lose their effectiveness both as vehicles for mission and as vehicles for gift development and the growth of Christians involved in them, but also become a block to the redeployment of church resources into more effective programmes.

Questions that could form the basis of ministry programme evaluation on an annual basis could include the following:

- Is the programme still targeting the people it was set up to minister to?
- Is the programme operating within the purposes and ministry philosophy of the church?
- Has the programme been achieving its goals?
- How many new contacts has the programme made for the church?
- How could the programme be improved?
- What are the future needs of the programme?
- What are its measurable goals for the coming year?[5]

Checklist for ministry planning

Don't forget:

- Clearly identify your target community.
- Learn all you can about it by using community surveys.

- Agree on a general strategy which, if successful, will enable the plant to become the church that God has called it to be in that setting.
- For each stage of the strategy, identify a ministry pro- gramme(s) that can be expected to work in your specific community.
- Ensure that each programme reflects the ministry philosophy agreed upon.
- Identify the leadership functions associated with each min- istry and draw up job descriptions for each one.
- Identify the members of the planting team who are able and willing to carry out those functions.
- Set a timetable for the implementation of the programmes.
- Agree on a process of ongoing evaluation of the programmes' effectiveness.

Developing the 'body life' of the whole planting team

Although a good deal of the hard thinking associated with the defining and refining of the ministry vision of the new church will be carried out by the leadership of the planting group, it should never be forgotten that the 'seed' that God has chosen to plant is not comprised only of leaders but of all the members of the embryonic body. All are called, all have a vital role to play and all must develop their sense of belonging to one another.

It has been my personal experience that this unity, expressed in mutual trust, esteem and shared vision, is the most important dynamic in the process of plant development.

How good and pleasant it is when brothers live together in unity! . . . For there the Lord bestows his blessing, even life for evermore! (Ps 133:1,3).

The role of leadership is unquestionably paramount in a church planting venture, but it must be leadership that serves the larger group and identifies fully with it. As has already been stated, church planting is about 'body building' and great care must be taken by the leadership that the planning process never excludes the rest of the membership but is rather taken forward in an interactive way, with constant sharing and praying, serving to strengthen bonds of mutual respect and common ownership as the vision builds and the body shapes up for its birthday.

Roger Logan and Jeff Rast highlight the importance of just these issues, suggesting that church planters check that they are assured on the following points:

- Interpersonal relationships are developing well on the team.
- We are cultivating a spirit of unity, openness, honesty, and mutual encouragement and edification.
- Each team-mate is aware of his/her key areas of contribution to the team and has worked with me to develop his/her own general job description.
- We all realise that we are entering into spiritual warfare and that Satan will try to stop our project at all costs. We know that some of the most serious attacks will be aimed at destroying our unity.
- The spouses of those on the team are entirely supportive of the new project and serve as active participants.[6]

Creating an effective 'body-building' programme

It takes a suitable *environment* a helpful *programme* and *time* to build a strong sense of purposeful fellowship.

Environment

During a recent visit to Glasgow, I commented to a friend on the large number of buildings with the British Petroleum logo attached to them. On discovering that he, too, worked for the company in the area of new oil-fields development, I asked in which of the buildings he was based. To my surprise he replied that he was currently working out of a rented suite of rooms separate from the large administrative complexes. He explained:

In new fields development, it has been found that the most effective way of producing a development plan tailored to the particular needs of the new prospect, is to hive the planning team off, away from the existing offices, so as to allow them to develop a strong sense of group identity wholly focused upon the particular challenges of the new venture.

Whether its new oil-fields or new mission fields, the principle is a good one.

Regular meetings of the planting team in the run-up to the public launch of the new congregation are an essential part of the gestation period for bringing a new church to birth. If the location of these meetings can be within the target community itself, so much the better as a means of re-enforcing the missionary purpose of the fellowship gatherings.

Programme

Probably no better blueprint for this body-building process can be found than the record of the early meetings of the gathering together of the new Christians in Acts 2:42–47.

Learning together   With team members coming from a variety of different backgrounds it is important to establish a common basis of shared understanding on what are the biblical principles upon which a church operates. George Patterson bases his choice of topics for such preparatory studies upon a definition of the church as 'a fellowship of believers committed to obeying the Lord Jesus Christ'.[7] From that statement he identifies seven basic areas of obedience that are commanded by the Lord Jesus and that should therefore be thoroughly understood and agreed upon by any founding church group.

1. Faith and repentance from sin
2. Baptism
3. Love
4. The Lord's Supper (Communion)
5. Prayer
6. Giving
7. Witnessing (including disciple making).

Such a series of group studies will clarify the group's thinking on how and why they should develop their life together in a certain way. It will also build confidence in the fact that they can hear God's word guiding them as a group separate from the main body of the church or churches from which they are drawn.

Praying together It is vital that the planting group learn to open their hearts together and articulate their common concerns before God. The experience of praying together and discovering that God is actually paying attention to the cries of the embryo church creates both a common ground of spiritual experience as prayers are answered and, like shared Bible study, builds confidence that God really is involved with them in the planting work. Verse 43 of Acts 2 links the release and appreciation of God's power to this commitment to prayer. According to David Finnell, Director of the International Network of Church Planters, 'Probably the weakest link in the armour of the average church planter is his prayer life.'[8]

The importance of the establishment of corporate prayer as the pivot of all congregational life cannot be overstated. Prayer focuses the congregation's attention on God, and whether that is for wisdom in planning, protection against spiritual powers or for any aspect of power for growth and faithfulness, it is to God that the congregation must learn to look. Acts 4:23–31 is a perfect example of how a church trained to pray is able to respond to difficulty with a naturalness and trust that God is able to answer powerfully in order to see them through the trouble.

Fellowshipping together Since the aim of the meetings is to encourage the development of a lively sense of 'belonging' then it will be helpful to find a warm, relaxed setting where refreshments can be made available. One of the lasting impressions of the opening year of the most recent church plant that I was involved in was of how much time we all spent eating together. Large quantities of crockery and cutlery were among the very first items purchased by the new group! It is interesting to note that the value of these fellowship meals became so appreciated by the emerging congregation that a large and well equipped kitchen was one of the features of the buildings subsequently constructed to serve the ministry. Plenty of time needs to be allowed simply for building relationships. The ultimate success or failure of the congregation to develop effective 'mutual ministry' patterns of caring, supporting, co-operating and en- couraging will depend greatly upon how well this way of 'being the church' can be established as the norm during the early months. Neither should the emphasis upon the financial impli- cations of congregational commitment, so clearly brought out in Acts 2:45, be played down in this formative period, especially since the levels of financial support needed to maintain the momentum of congregational growth are likely to be con- siderably greater than those common among the membership of the parent church.

Remember that new members joining the fellowship will take their cue about standards of behaviour from those they find being practised when they arrive. The leadership and all the planting group must set those standards high right from the beginning because, as any leader knows to his pain, it is most difficult to raise them once a pattern has been set.

Worshipping together   Joyful worship should characterise the congregational life of an emerging church. Although many groups will continue to meet with the parent church for Sunday worship, opportunities for mid-week or weekend praise and testimony meetings must certainly be created.

Music is important to worship and the leadership of the group will need to ensure that wherever possible adequate musical support is built into the nucleus of the planting group. The worship style adopted will be a critical aspect of the philosophy of ministry and there must be common accord on this issue from the outset. Wherever the traditions of the denominational group permit, it is important in these early months to establish the value of celebrating the Lord's Supper. The cost of disciple- ship and the mission focus of the sacrament will help counter any tendency towards the development of a cosy Christian club mentality.

Growing together   During the run-up to the launch the mem- bership of the planting group will tend to change as some decide that it is not for them and others are drawn in. It is good that this should happen before the public services are begun. There needs to be mutual trust and a sense of responsibility and accountability among the group. Instability in attendance or commitment once public meetings have begun is very unsettling to members of the group and visitors alike.

Time

All of the processes outlined above take time. How much time will depend upon how much 'common wisdom' there is about church planting in the group and how well integrated the members were to start with. Corners should not be cut, however, and for most groups in a UK setting a period of between four and eight months or even longer might be necessary. It is important, though, that the momentum of the planting process isn't lost. Timing as much as time is a key issue in the early stages, both before and after the public launch.

Relationships with the parent church

Although this topic has been dealt with more fully in Chapter 6, the chapter specifically devoted to the role of the parenting body, it is helpful to highlight some issues here, from the standpoint of the planting team.

Communication

One of the biggest dangers associated with the links between the 'parent' and 'child' is the development of different under-standings of how things ought to be done, where authority lies and the direction things are going. Steps to avoid such mis-understanding arising should include:

- The early public recognition by the parent body of those who represent the leadership of the embryo congregation.
- The formation of a church planting steering group to serve as the recognised forum for joint consultation on all issues relating to the planting project and answerable to the leader-ships of both the established and new congregations.
- The regular reporting of progress to both groups via the 'official channels' of church newsletters or a special 'planting paper', and agenda items in business/fellowship meetings.

Co-operation

The call to plant is one that the whole church should embrace even though some will be more directly involved with the process than others. The planting team should do all it can to encourage this to take place through informal contacts within the ongoing life of the parent church to stimulate interest and prayer support.

Specific co-operation might be sought in certain areas of ministry, and when this is the case then the reasons for any approach to the parent body for resources, be they material or personnel, should be carefully thought through, explained and made through the agreed channels. This will help avoid any sense of confusion or 'poaching' of gifted individuals from this or that ministry of the existing church. In particular there needs to be close liaison over the issue of who will and who won't be forming part of the group going out to establish the new work.

In all of these areas the planting team should bear in mind the impact of their project upon the life of the parent body, recognising that they will have a ministry towards it as well as vice versa.

Commissioning

Considerable importance should be given to the 'setting aside' of the whole planting group shortly before the public launch of the new congregation. From the point of view of the planting group it will add legitimacy to their departure, while for the sending group their identification with and support of the ongoing ministry of the leaving group will be affirmed. Both groups, whether going or staying, will benefit from the 'ceremonial' expression of commitment before God to the work into which he has called them.

Continuing contact

Whether the model of planting adopted envisages a federative pattern of interdependence or a more independent relationship between the two congregations, the newly established congregation should recognise that it will have a unique opportunity to minister to the parent body. This will, however, need to be both affirmed, and worked at, by the new church leadership especially in the first year of life. It is surprising how quickly ties with the sending church can wither and die unless they are nurtured and justified as an important part of the new plant's ministry. Particularly if the possibility for co-operation in the production of 'grandchildren' is envisaged then it is vital that the family ties be cultivated and appreciated by both parties.

For discussion and further study

1. Prepare a presentation aimed at persuading the leadership of your current church to define and adopt a philosophy of ministry.
2. Discuss the differences between a mission strategy, a philosophy of mission and a mission programme.
3. To what extent can the practices of goal setting and evaluation be justified biblically?
4. Identify ten important factors to be borne in mind when considering how to prepare a group soon to be commissioned as the core of a new congregation.

Notes

1. George Lings' analysis of changing patterns of motivation in Anglican church planting over the period 1967–1990 is worth noting. See *Planting New Churches* (Eagle, 1991), p 165.
2. Frank Ward, 'Your Church's Philosophy of Ministry', *Growing Churches* (October–December 1991): a Publication of the Sunday School Board of the Southern Baptist Convention.
3. David Hesselgrave, *Planting Churches Cross-Culturally* (Baker Book House, 1980), pp 58ff.
4. *Ibid*, p 61.
5. See Philip Bryant, *Church Planting Workbook* (Baptist Union of Victoria: Hawthorn, Australia, 1991).
6. Robert Logan and Jeff Rast, *Church Planter's Checklist* (Fuller Institute, 1987), p 15.

7. George Patterson, *Church Planting through Obedience-Oriented Teaching* (William Carey Library: Pasadena, 1981), p 1.
8. David Finnell, 'Power Planting', *The Link*, Vol 1, No 3 (1990).

Part Three
Launching Out

CHAPTER ELEVEN

BUILDING THE CHURCH AND FINDING A BUILDING

Martin Robinson

Those who have even a small amount of knowledge of contemporary missions will know from missionaries' reports how diverse are the types of buildings used by the church around the world. From crystal cathedrals in California to the spreading panoply of an ancient tree in Tanzania, from huge edifices designed to seat many thousands in countries as far apart as Brazil and Korea to the modest tin tabernacles of the Welsh valleys or the dusty streets of Soweto outside Johannesburg, the church of Jesus Christ meets in the most diverse and surprising of settings.

Even when the church does have purpose-built facilities, such buildings have very little in common. Ecclesiastical architecture seems to owe more to local tastes of design and tradition than to any universal theme. From the onion domes of churches in Eastern Europe to the simple white-painted wood of churches in rural America, church buildings reflect local needs and conditions to an almost bewildering degree.

Nor is such diversity a recent trend. It is sometimes noted that the first Christians did not have any buildings of their own until the time of Constantine, as if the very act of introducing buildings somehow compromised the witness of the church. Such a sweeping claim does not represent the whole story. The very first Christians met in the Temple in Jerusalem, in local synagogues, as well as in homes. While it is true that the churches referred to in the New Testament usually met in homes, we need to remember that the homes in which they met were often rather substantial ones, some of which were larger than many of the church buildings that we use today. In fact, all kinds of accommodation was pressed into service—from catacombs in Rome to caves in Asia Minor.

Our own land has had two clear traditions of church building. One was characterised by the very simple low-roofed structures associated with the Celtic missionaries. That same tradition of church building can be seen today in many of the older parish churches of Scotland and Wales. These simple stone buildings would at one time have been built of wood. Today, this building style is often characterised by the single open bell placed just above the roof at one end of the building. The emphasis of Celtic tradition was on a simplicity that was both beautiful and functional.

The second tradition was one which was begun by the Roman missionaries but which reached its finest expression in the medieval Norman and Gothic styles. Again, the first churches built by the missionaries from Canterbury were of wood but these quickly gave way to much larger and more permanent structures. Such buildings were not primarily concerned with functionality, but grandeur. The dominance of this tradition has been so great that the kind of church building produced by it has almost come to define what those who do not attend church imagine a 'proper' church building to be like. Even later architectural styles, such as the neoclassicism of the seventeenth century, copied the intention of this tradition in terms of placing a major emphasis on splendour rather than on function. Nonconformity has tended to borrow from both these traditions, some favouring the functionality of the older Celtic tradition, others the prestigous example of the English norm of church building.

The message of our buildings

No matter which tradition is followed, all buildings, both secular and sacred, inevitably make an important statement to the community that surrounds them. Moreover, we can also learn a great deal about the values of those who erected particular buildings from the buildings themselves. The size of our present city centre office and commercial buildings tends to mask the original grandeur of the great cathedral buildings. Yet even today, cathedrals such as Salisbury and Ely dominate the skyline from miles away. When they were first built the effect was even more stunning.

Even in the context of the Houses of Parliament, Westminster Abbey is still a remarkable building today. Imagine, though, what it must have looked like to a traveller floating up the Thames in medieval times. Much of the surrounding land was somewhat marshy, the typical houses of the majority of the population consisted of mud and wattle. Rising out of the marshes rose a building which dwarfed all other structures that were anywhere in the vicinity. Buildings such as these trumpeted the grandeur and permanence of the faith that built them. The goal of medieval society was to ensure that every community had access to a place of worship. So many churches were built in some parts of England that it was hardly possible to stand anywhere in the countryside without being able to see the spire of at least one church! The church spire itself, standing as it did significantly higher than any other building in the town or village, made an important statement about the place of the church in society.

Buildings continue to make important statements about where power and influence lies in our society. It is not just for functional reasons that banks and other financial institutions dominate the skyline in most of our cities. Some banks have been fairly explicit in making a connection between the physical profile of their head office buildings and the profile of the bank in the mind of their actual and potential customers. Not far behind the banks come those buildings erected by local and central government which also serve to make statements (not always flattering ones—witness the existence of tower block housing) about the relative importance of government as an institution in our society. Other examples from business and from education could be given of the way in which buildings serve to communicate a message long before we ever venture inside them.

It is not very likely that church buildings in our city centres will ever again compete in size and grandeur with the power of major financial institutions, nor am I arguing that they should. Nevertheless, the profile of church buildings has changed considerably during this century, reflecting all kinds of changes that have taken place in the life of the church in our communities. Inner city and city centre churches, especially those with large Victorian preaching barns for buildings, have often redeveloped their buildings in such a way that their profile has been significantly reduced. Many new buildings have been erected using radically different building styles, most of which have tried to reflect the concern of such congregations to have a dimension of community service demonstrated through their architecture. The growing strength of the evangelical and charismatic wing of the church has often been reflected in the emergence of a style of church building which has conveyed something of the values of such congregations, a desire to reflect informality and a contemporary, rather warm and welcoming feel. Buildings are important even for those churches whose very theology claims that buildings are unimportant!

Until relatively recently, the major denominations always assumed that a church planting project would involve the provision of a building. The concept of a new church and a new building were inextricably linked. Perhaps this explains to some extent why so little church planting has been attempted by the larger denominations as compared with the activities of the smaller and newer denominations. Finances have not permitted the unthinking erection of new buildings. Economics may also have increased pressures for many of the ventures that were entered into to be ecumenical projects. Certainly, an extremely good case had to be made out before permission and finance were granted for projects which were single denomination in origin. Moreover, some of the buildings that have been erected by the major denominations, whether on their own or ecumenically, have been far too small to meet the needs of the population that they were intended to serve.

The realisation that churches can be planted without first providing the funds for a building has opened up all kinds of possibilities for the major denominations. For smaller denominations, the concept of church planting without the provision of buildings was not just a good idea but an absolute neccessity if any planting was to take place at all. Yet even in the case of the smaller denominations, the linkage between church plant and church building has been a strong one. The black-led churches often started in homes and other small rooms but were quick to make the transition to the many inner city churches that had small and often elderly white congregations. At first they came as tenants; in some cases their rental contribution came as a great relief to the congregation that actually owned the building. In many cases, it was not too many years before the more vibrant black-led groups were able to buy the buildings that they had formerly used as tenants.

White-led Pentecostal groups have also tended to look for redundant churches as part of the process of establishing new congregations. The pages of the *Elim Evangel* and other Pentecostal papers contain many pictures of new churches being started in churches and chapels that once belonged to other groups. I well remember a photograph in the *Elim Evangel* of one such building, with a huge banner proudly displaying the words, 'Under New Management'!

Despite the strength of the connection between building and planting, in recent years, a number of factors have served to weaken this link and so open up a wider range of possibilities in the minds of church planters. Not the least of these factors has been the fact that there is a limit to the number of redundant churches that are available in the areas where church planters have wished to plant. The building of completely new buildings has become increasingly expensive as land and property values have risen dramatically over the last twenty years. (The one possible exception to this dimension of church planting is where dying churches are being renewed and the extent of the renewal is so great that a new church is in effect being planted. Groups such as Ichthus and Oasis have been involved in this kind of renewal/planting, mostly in inner city areas.)

This absence of available buildings has coincided with the emergence of a strong evangelical/charismatic emphasis which has sought to make a definite distinction between the church as a building and the church as the people of God. The true New

Testament church is clearly the active, obedient people of God, and the building purely a convenient place for the people of God to meet. Of course, such a theme is not new. Many nineteenth-century congregations, wishing to make the same point, placed a plaque on their buildings on which were inscribed such phrases as 'Christian Meeting House', thus stating that this was not the church, only a place where the church met.

Nowhere has this emphasis been more keenly felt than in the curiously named 'house church' movement, now increasingly known as the new church networks. In fact, many of the house churches did not meet in homes for anything but a very short period of time, and some never did at all. But their theology, combined with the absence of suitable church buildings, has enabled them to be innovative in terms of the kinds of buildings that they have used. The flexibility not just of the house churches but of the whole evangelical/charismatic tradition of which they are a part has played a vital role in opening up all kinds of other options in the minds of church groups wishing to engage in church planting.

To build or not to build?

Although the link between erecting a building and planting a church may have been broken in the mindset of Christians, ironically, it has not been broken in the minds of those whom newly planted churches wish to reach. Therefore, the issue of the building that we do or do not use is critical in terms of those people with whom we wish to make contact. From a purely practical point of view, most church plants will not be able to have a building from day one. In most cases, the congregation will need to be created before a purpose-built building can be considered. Such a change from the days when a building was provided in order to attract a congregation marks the transition from a largely pastoral concern in which the function of the church was to meet the pastoral needs of a people who could be expected to be largely Christian to a missionary emphasis where the task of the church is to make converts and to build the church as the people of God. Therefore, the congregation newly created would take a major responsibility for the provision of their own building needs. Such a change is welcome. Nevertheless, the fact remains that in the minds of those whom we are attempting to reach with the gospel message church buildings carry two contradictory and crucially important messages.

The first of these messages is that of alienation. Put very simply, a church building does not look like any other building that most people are ever likely to use, with the possible unfortunate exception of a court of law! Those who only darken the doors of a church for the purposes of hatching, matching or dispatching are often not encouraged by what they see, and yet paradoxically the very sense of strangeness speaks to them of otherworldliness, of holiness and of God. Even if they do not feel comfortable here, it nevertheless forms the expectation of many that this is what a church should look like.

More critical than the issue of form and appearance is the question of permanence and trustworthiness. Even if a church does not have its own building, a signal of its intention to have a building one day is critical to the way in which the unchurched in the community will respond. The acquisition of a building clearly brings other advantages in terms of the kinds of community events that can be staged and even in terms of removing the need to set up and take down large amounts of equipment before and after every service, which is inevitable in hired premises. A permanent building has the potential to increase the profile and presence of a church in the community.

However, despite the long-term advantages of owning a building, we must remember that the ownership of a building conveys contradictory messages to the unchurched community. There are some disadvantages in owning a building. A church building, no matter how modern, can represent a significant barrier for people to cross. The use of the right community premises offers a half-way house to those for whom coming to church is a huge cultural step. One church of which I am aware began in a pub.[1] The reason for this choice was solely the fact that there were no other community buildings available.

Interestingly, many of the unchurched people who attended did not use the pub during the week, but the very fact that the church had been willing to use a pub conveyed to them that this might be a place where they would feel comfortable. Hopefully, people may well have used the community buildings for other events and so may feel that to some extent the church is coming to meet them on their territory. At the very least, a community building does not represent the same kind of threat that a church building might offer.

The use of such community buildings often has an interesting impact on Christians themselves. The break with the traditional feel of a church building often allows groups and individuals to worship in ways that they would not have considered possible previously. Even churches which are not new plants but which have had to vacate their premises for a time in order to allow major rennovation, bear witness to the impact that a more informal environment has had on their worship life during that time. Some congregations that I have met trace their subsequent renewal and growth to the time spent in rented accommodation.

Moreover, church buildings are not only expensive to build in the first place, they are also very expensive to maintain. It is often the case that a community building can be rented for far less than it would cost to heat, light and maintain one's own building. During the early stages of the life of a church it is much more important to put money into ministry and programmes than it is to put those limited resources into buildings.

A number of Anglican church plants have been able to have the best of both worlds with regard to buildings. They have rented community buildings in the parish for extra morning congregations and yet been able to draw folk back to the parish church for evening worship.[2] They have, therefore, enjoyed both the neutrality and cost effectiveness of rented buildings while also maintaining a sense of safety and permanence for people by virtue of the relationship to the parish church.

Interestingly, not all of the parish plants that I have seen have resulted in the winning of first time converts. Some have used their new church plants as overspill congregations, with the real growth continuing to come through the pastoral opportunities at the mother church. Only when people have been won to Christ have they then felt comfortable about going and worshipping in the congregations that meet in community facilities. Such situations simply serve to further illustrate the complexity of this issue in the face of the contradictory messages that buildings convey to those that we are trying to reach!

If, finally, a church does decide to build its own facility then there is a tendency for the size of building that they plan to erect to define the size of congregation they are likely to become. Although it is true that the use of strategies such as multiple worship services means that such an outcome is not inevitable, nevertheless, it is surprising how often the size of a building acts as a physical expression of the vision of those in the church.

What kind of building?

What kind of rented buildings are the best when starting a new congregation? The sheer variety of facilities rented by churches is staggering. In the last century, the Salvation Army used an ice house in Hull, which had formerly been used as a fish packing factory! Today, churches rent town halls, leisure centres, community centres, schools, nursery and play group facilities, pubs, cinemas, scout huts and even warehouses! There is virtually no limit to the kind of building that churches can adapt for the cause of the gospel.

As you might suspect, there is no ideal venue. What will work in one area might not work in another. Probably the most common community building that churches use is the local school. Sometimes this works well, but a school is not always as helpful a meeting place as many seem to think it might be and I am certainly aware of a number of congregations that began in schools and later moved out because the arrangement just did not work.[3]

Problems with local schools include the following:

1. Not all local authorities are keen to rent to outside agencies and so the rental agreements can be both expensive and restrictive.

2. Almost all rental agreements will depend for their successful implementation on the local caretaker. The goodwill of the headmaster can help but will not be as crucial as the goodwill of the caretaker. Almost the only type of school where one can be relatively sure of a good response is a church school, where church and school work well together and the church concerned is happy with the proposed project.

3. Schools are often rather functional places and do not necessarily have the kind of ambience that is helpful in creating a place of worship. The school atmosphere can be rather intimidating for some, especially if school days were not happy days!

4. Contrary to what we might suppose, not all schools enjoy the kind of close links with the community that qualify the school as a genuine community building. Very often, the staff do not live close to the school, and even the pupils can be drawn from a much wider area than that served by the local church. In some urban areas, the school can be a focus of hostility between authority and local people.

5. Perhaps the most common problem of all is that schools are often large places surrounded by significant areas of playground and even playing fields. The effect of this is to isolate groups using the premises and so prevent them making any kind of impact on the community. To put it more simply, a school is so large that few people will even notice you are there! Even large noticeboards at every one of the entrances make little impact beside the large entrance gates.

Certainly, some schools will be exceptions to all of the above, and using them works very well. However, as has already been mentioned, it is frequently the case that although schools are often the first place that many groups consider using, other buildings might serve them better. In any case, there is no substitute for prayer in seeking God's guidance for the right place. One church I know did find an ideal school. It was a Church of England school and the local vicar was very keen for it to be used. However, the church group in question felt that God was leading them to another building which superficially did not look as suitable. Moreover, when they enquired about the other building they were told that two other Christian groups had been refused before and it was not available for regular Sunday hire. So convinced were they that they had heard God correctly on this matter that they began a week of prayer and fasting, asking that God would cause the 'no' to become a 'yes'. Within a week, the building became available to them and subsequent events have demonstrated that it has been much more suitable in terms of impact on the community than the school would have been.

In making the above suggestions, we are assuming that a choice of community buildings is available. In fact, this is not always the case. One of the phenomenas of the late 1970s and the 1980s, has been the creation of large private housing developments where there are no local community facilities at all. In some exteme cases, not only are there no local shops and community centres, but there are no local schools and not even any local pubs. What does a church do if it wants to locate in such an environment?

In such circumstances, one of the reasons why there are so few local facilities is that land costs are extremely high, so high that very few churches, if any, could afford to buy sufficient land to build anything of any significance.

Such situations are all the more frustating when, as in some cases, the development takes place in expanded villages where ten to twenty years ago small village chapels did exist but were closed down and sold for a fraction of their present site value. The church has not always been very good at predicting or even thinking about where development will take place in the future.

In these situations, and possibly even in others, it is important for the church to be increasingly imaginative in the kinds of buildings that are utilised. It may be necessary to engage in creative relationships with businessmen to identify buildings that have commercial usage in the week but can double up as a worship area on a weekend. Perhaps another solution is to utilise homes with large extensions for mid-week meetings, and introduce the concept of an area church to which people can commute for weekend celebrations. Whatever solution any particular church opts for, it is likely that an increasing diversity of solutions will feature in the coming decade.

Insides matter too!

So far we have commented largely on the overall message that a building conveys. This overall message has to do with the type of building. But we have to remember that buildings have interiors as well as exteriors and that the interior of a building can be vastly different from its exterior.

To date, many new, purpose-built church buildings, especially those in the broadly charismatic/evangelical tradition, have had a somewhat utilitarian feel to their interior. This does not mean that they are spartan, far from it. The house church leader Dave Tomlinson describes them as feeling rather like an executive office suite.[4] Certainly, the emphasis is on warmth and informality, reflecting the values that we try to build into our modern homes. It is not unusual for newer buildings as diverse as cinemas, theatres, department stores, offices, conference centres, and even whole shopping centres to exude something of the same design style. Dave Tomlinson raises the issue of the more ancient aesthetic styles and asks what has happened to them in our newer church buildings?

It is a good question and asking it might provide a clue as to how to overcome the essential contradiction that we noted early on in this chapter between the feeling that older and more traditional forms of building alienate people and yet form part of their expectation of what a worship sanctuary, as opposed to an auditorium, might look like.

The language used to describe these different architectural concerns carries a theological content. The rather functional nature of an auditorium, no matter how tastefully presented, suggests that the purpose of such a construction is to focus attention on the platform, with the attenders constituting an audience. This does not mean that there cannot be audience participation, but the emphasis is on the functionality of the building. That part of the evangelical tradition which has little sacramental emphasis in its worship tends to view its buildings in this way. The use of the term 'sanctuary', on the other hand, tends to suggest that the worship area has more than just a functional purpose. The more sacramental traditions tend to see the worship place as actually playing a part in the worship itself. In such a tradition the use of colour and beauty helps to direct the worshipper towards an encounter with God.

Whatever tradition we feel more comfortable with in terms of purpose-built church buildings, these basic insights are tremendously important when using rented accommodation. The careful use of colour and symbolism can help to overcome the element of suspicion that is engendered when a group is not using a 'proper' building.

Such thinking is very difficult for those of us from a non-sacramental tradition, who tend to see buildings from a utilitarian perspective. It is also hard for Philistines such as myself, whose concept of design in churches often extends no further than a vase of flowers on a table near the front! Despite the difficulty, it is worth the effort. We may also be surprised at the gifts that we unearth in our congregation, or indeed in our prospective congregation, as we begin to publicise our need for people with such insights.

What follows is by no means a comprehensive list of elements to consider but hopefully will serve to spark your own creativity.

1. Light Where does the light come from in the building and how does that affect the feel of the building? Apart from the very obvious fact that it is not good for people to have the sun shining in their eyes while they are trying to concentrate on someone speaking, it in any case enhances the focus of the building if natural light shines in from behind the congregation. Maybe there is insufficient natural light in the building that you want to use. It is vital that those who are leading from the front have light focused on them so it may be necessary to think about the purchase of some portable lighting.

2. Sound Aside from the fact that it is essential for the music group and other leaders to have good quality amplification available, the issue of accoustics is important. In some buildings, natural sound seems to travel better in one direction than another. There is no way to discover this except by trial and error. It is therefore crucial to have some dress rehearsals to

find out what works and what does not. For practical reasons it
may not be possible to take advantage of the best accoustics in
the building and that will make it hard for people at the back or
at the sides to hear clearly. This needs to be taken into account
in the placing of the speaker system. Some halls work well for
speaking but deaden all public singing. Some are the reverse. It
is crucial to seek a balance between hard and soft surfaces so
that a good overall sound balance is obtained. The introduction
of small amounts of carpeting for the aisles and the platform
area, which can be rolled away before and after the meeting,
can help to reduce echo in a room with many hard floor
surfaces. It is more difficult to introduce hard surfaces into a
room which has none at all. You can make side screens but
usually the problem is the roof area. Sometimes you will need
to use microphones to pick up congregational singing and
amplify it slightly.

3. *Focus.* What is the natural focus of the room and is it the
one that you want? It is possible to change the focus of a room,
not only with the layout of chairs but with the careful use of
lighting, banners and other decorative features. Try to ensure
that there is only one focal point for the room and that
you do not confuse people by having several focal points or
other significant distractions. That will help people to feel
comfortable in the room.

4. *Colour.* What are the predominant colours in the room?
Are these the colours that you want and if not how can you
introduce those colours that will enhance a sense of worship? In
general terms it is important to use a consistent colour scheme
that will help to give a sense of light and space to the room.
Dark colours, or indeed the absence of all colour, can be
depressive and oppressive. Colour is part of God's wonderful
creation and gift to us!

5. *Layout.* How do you want to arrange your chairs? Usually
seating arrangements which are long and thin produce a very
formal response, whereas seating which is wider and less deep,
particularly if it is slightly semi-circular, will produce a
more informal response. Seating arranged in a circle implies
that a significant degree of response is expected. It is a highly

confrontational seating arrangement for those who do not know each other well. It is good to give some thought to the quality of seating that is being used. Many school buildings use chairs that are just slightly smaller than those normally used by adults. If these are the only seats available you may need to think of bringing in your own seating. How comfortable are the chairs even if they are full adult size? Many plastic bucket-type seats are only comfortable for twenty minutes or so. If this is the case then the length of time that people are forced to sit down needs to be carefully thought through in the design of the service order.

6. *Symbols.*   The use of very simple symbols, such as a large cross, can help enormously to give a sense of 'church'. Candles, banners and Communion elements are other potent symbolic items. It is surprising how careful thought can transform ordinary pieces of furniture into items that help to induce a sense of worship. One example would be the use of an embroidered cloth to place over a table to turn it into a focus of attention. Even a functional trestle table can look attractive with the use of a cloth of the right colour and the addition of some simple designs on the front.

Planning and praying over a building together, with sub-sequent action, can result in even the most ordinary room, familiar to many in the community in the context of other uses, being transformed into a cathedral of colour and praise. These kinds of efforts will convey a powerful message to those who attend for the first time.

For discussion and further study

1. What message does your present church building com-municate to your community? What message would you like to communicate?
2. What buildings are available in the target area that you have for church planting? Are there any that you have overlooked?
3. Who in your fellowship or church has gifts in the areas of art and design to help you with interior design?

Notes

1. The church in question is the Baptist Church in Mexborough in Yorkshire, referred to in Chapter 12 of this book.
2. The concept of 'strawberry runner' church planting was first pioneered by St Mary's, Chester le Street, and is referred to in Chapter 5 of this book.
3. Zion Baptist Church, Creech St Michael, Taunton.
4. *Faith in the Future*, Channel Three, 18 August 1991.

CHAPTER TWELVE
YOU ONLY LAUNCH ONCE!
Martin Robinson

You only launch once so get it right! While this may seem a very obvious point, it is astonishing how often it is ignored. The enthusiasm of many groups to simply get on with the job is such that there is a tendency to launch the new work without taking full advantage of the impact that a public launch can have. The evidence of church planting on both sides of the Atlantic suggests that a well planned launch can result in at least the doubling of the original group as a direct result of this one activity. I do not refer here to the attendance of the first public meeting—that may be much greater than twice that of the original core group—rather, I mean the total of those people who will become committed core members as a direct result of the launch activity. The potential for growth at this point is so great that it is well worth expending considerable effort to get it right.

It is almost always the case that groups anticipating their launch date seriously underestimate the time that needs to be allowed to plan effectively for a successful launch. Why do Christians so consistently make this mistake? Perhaps it is because we are so used to running services at our existing churches week by week that we have the idea that launching a new work is only a matter of doing the same thing in a different location. It isn't! What we are trying to create is a whole new worshipping community, with its own culture, mix of gifts, strengths, weaknesses, and above all an ability to 'read' how to communicate the gospel in the unique context in whch God has placed the group in question. The actual launch doesn't create all of this but it does bring this whole process to a critical point of focus in such a way that we need to be sure we have got many of these ingredients right. Therefore, it cannot be said too many times: don't launch too soon, give yourself plenty of time to plan. A group is very rarely harmed by taking longer to launch. Indeed, if you are pushing ahead with the launch because you want to hold the group together then you most certainly are not ready to launch! Far more potential churches have been harmed by launching too soon than by launching too late.[1]

When I have made this point in a teaching situation, there comes the almost inevitable follow-up question: 'How long, then, should we allow to plan a launch programme?' As you might imagine, it is almost impossible to give a definitive answer. Groups will vary in terms of the amount of time that they can give to the project, in terms of the resources available to them and in the degree to which they have set ambitious goals. A further critical factor is the length of time that those in the group have known each other before the church planting project commenced. Those who have known each other because they have been members of a single sending church and who can therefore assume a great deal about a shared philosophy of ministry will clearly need less time than those who have come from a variety of backgrounds. However, most groups will probably need at least nine months from the time that they set their launch date to the launch date itself. Certainly, some groups will take longer than this, and some can push ahead with such verve and energy that they can have a good launch programme in less time than this. But for the majority, it is almost always the case that you should add three months on to the time frame that you had already considered.

Launching a new work is almost always more complex than you think, so much so that if you have never yet used a formal planning process then this is the time to consider doing so. The PERT planning model, described in Chapter Four is very well suited to the complexity of co-ordinating a new church launch. What follows in this chapter is a discussion of the ingredients that you should consider, leading up to the actual launch. It assumes that you have already located your target community, your building, and have established the core group that will be involved with the launch. What comes next?

Seeking the permission of the community

There is always a danger that the planting of a new church will be seen by the community in question as an unwanted intrusion. Quite apart from what the existing Christian groups in the area might think, it may well be that those in the community will have difficulty in understanding why it is that a new church is really necessary. Their impression may well be that there are plenty of existing churches at the moment.

As Christians, we can be guilty of an arrogance that assumes that we know what is best for a given community. Such arrogance can be disguised as a zeal to obey the call of God, but while we can easily fool ourselves, it is not always so easy to fool the community that we seek to serve. It is very rare for groups considering a church plant to ask the community whether or not they see the need for a new church. Why is it so rare for this to happen? Is it that we are afraid of what the answer might be?

A group that was planning to launch a new Baptist church on an estate in Mexborough in Yorkshire decided that they would ask their target community if they thought that a new church was needed. They were pleasantly surprised by the results. They visited 1,400 homes and found that 567 people thought that the area did need a new church. Three hundred said they would go if a new church was opened.[2] Clearly, that kind of positive affirmation from the community helped enormously in everything else that the church wanted to do from then on. At the very least, some kind of community survey which indicates what the community is thinking will be instructive for those who are planning a launch. It will give the group a feel for the issues that concern the community and can act as a valuable resource in terms of shaping the actual launch plans.

Even if it is not considered to be feasible or strictly necessary for the launch group to ask the permission of the community through the more formal process of a survey, it is important to find other more informal channels for establishing that permission. The community needs to be able to feel that in some way what is being planned is 'a good thing' and not simply the arrival of yet another group of people who, in their minds at least, are scarcely distinguishable from the Mormons or Jehovah's Witnesses.

In terms of relating to the community, the core group needs to be able to answer the central question: 'Why do you want to start another church?' Even if it is not asked explicitly, it will be at the back of people's minds. Sometimes the answer will be obvious—there is no church on this large new estate, there is no church working with a particular age group, there is no church with an informal approach to worship. On other occasions, we might not like to reveal the real reason which might be more like, there is no church of our denomination, there is no church that we consider to be lively enough. But whatever the reason behind our intent, we do need to find ways of sharing it because the response of the community to the validity or otherwise of our motivation will be crucial to everything else that we do.

Selecting the launch date

The selection of an actual launch date for a church plant is not quite as straightforward as we might suppose. Roy Pointer, in his book *How Do Churches Grow?*, makes the observation that '. . . most societies also mark the passing of the seasons with religious ceremony indicating spiritual sensitivity.'[3] As the medieval church in Europe attempted to evangelise pagan Europe, it recognised this and responded to this deep religious impulse through the festivals of harvest, Christmas, Easter, and Whitsun, each of which stands in a different season of the year. As Roy Pointer also notes, these festivals, '. . . continue to offer opportunities for evangelism among people who become "religiou" just because of the time of year!'[4]

The importance of these festivals varies a great deal throughout our country. There are still some areas where the harvest festival has the greatest impact on the community. For most communities, Whitsun has lost almost all significance and therefore it is the festivals of Christmas and Easter that have the greatest impact. Some research suggests that as many as 40 per cent of adults in the United Kingdom will attend a service of worship over the Christmas period and that as many as 33 per cent will do so over the Easter period. Interestingly, whenever I present these figures to clergy they usually respond with great scepticism. The reason that they do so is because they are adding up in their own minds those who attend their own church over these festival times and are also doing a quick calculation of the other churches' attendances. They then come to the conclusion that nothing like that number could possibly attend church over the period in question.

We can often underestimate what actually goes on in our community. When people tell researchers that they have attended a service of worship over these festival times, they do not mean that they all turned up at the Easter Day service or the midnight Communion service. What they mean is that they attended something at some time over that period, and not necessarily in church. It might have been a carol service at the local school, in an old people's home or even in the local pub. The church does not enjoy a monopoly over the celebration of Christian festivals in our nation!

It is even more vital to understand that not only do we not always realise what is happening in our community, we are also not always aware of the potential strength of the religious impulse in our community. A local Council of Churches that I know first organised an open-air carol service on Christmas Eve some twenty years ago. The service consisted of carol singing, readings and prayers, with a few informal greetings. The total length of the event was just half an hour. Those who attended were offered no shelter and had to stand. The service has continued each year since then. When I ask people how many they think attend this event, they think of their local Council of Churches and say optimistically, 'Around 400?' In fact, that would have been too optimistic for the first year. Today, however, the figure would be closer to 5,000. Very large numbers of people who normally never attend church at any other time of the year are present at this event. As a matter of fact, I know of many Christians in the area who don't attend because they prefer their carols in a warm church with a mince pie to follow! What this event, and others like it that I also know of, demonstrates is that the religious impulse that

Christian festivals tap into is not as insignificant as we sometimes suppose

It is good to take account of the festivals when planning our launch date. For most communities, Christmas and Easter are going to be the times of greatest potential response and it is therefore wise to think of launch dates that take account of those times. The two strongest possibilities are, therefore, to launch a few weeks before Christmas or close to Easter. To some extent, the date needs to be influenced by your plans for follow-up activities. This aspect is discussed in more detail in the next chapter.

Pre-launch activities

The process of gaining community permission and of helping our own understanding of the community can be enhanced by holding a number of pre-launch activities which all help to build towards the launch itself. We can take advantage of the growth in religious sentiment surrounding the various Christian festival times by holding services of worship as 'one off' special events. For example, Christmas worship events can be as diverse as a simple service by candle-light, worship with a performance of the nativity, a community carol service, or a Christingle. Whatever we opt for, it needs to be newsworthy in some way. I know of one church who had obtained a donkey for their Easter March of Witness and were trying to obtain a camel for their nativity play. I don't know if they succeeded, but if they did, they would have had no difficulty being featured in the local press!

It is not essential for the pre-launch activities to take the form of services. The range of possibilities is limited only by our imagination and ability to organise them. Activities that I have heard of include street theatre, concerts both indoor and in the local park, coffee mornings, special seminars for parents on child rearing, lunch-time seminars, afternoon teas, and social events, some of which centre on other significant dates, such as firework displays on 5th November or Mother's Day specials. The precise choice will depend on the opportunities open to you in your community. Don't feel that you have to run each of these events all by yourself in order to feel that they are authentic. There is a wider range of Christian specialist organisations working in the general field of evangelism than ever before. The *UK Christian Handbook* is a valuable resource for locating organisations. The only proviso is that you should not expect others to do all the work for you, but should rather see yourself in partnership with those you call upon for assistance.

When you are planning pre-launch activities, remember that a small number of well chosen events will be more effective than a large number of events chosen at random. Keep in mind that the purpose of these events is to build an effective line of communication between the church planting group and the community you are trying to reach. Note which events work the best—you may wish to build repeats of these into your post-launch activities (see Chapter 13).

Whenever you hold a pre-launch event it is critical that you find ways of registering who has attended and then think through the best way to follow up these contacts. At the very least, you will be building a contact list of people who can be invited to other events and to the launch itself. You may also find that a personal visit will help you to discover those in the community who are receptive to the Christian message even before you launch.[5] A further value in these events is that you will build a knowledge of people in the community with skills that you might be able to draw on as you draw closer to the actual launch. At this stage, it is very much the case that 'whoever is not against you is for you'! (Mk 9:38–41).

Press and publicity

The world of communication becomes more sophisticated by the day. The advent of the computer and of satellite communication means that the flow of information available to us increases all the time. In consequence, the means by which advertisers seek to hold our attention also become ever more ingenious. Strangely, and perhaps reassuringly, there still is no more effective way of interesting people in a given message than the personal invitation, received from one we know and trust. You yourself will be aware that if someone you do not know gives you a piece of literature to read, you probably will not read it, even if it is quite short. Your interest level will be low and you will more than likely decide that you do not have the time to read it. On the other hand, if someone you do know sends you a book to read, with a strong recommendation that you should read it, then even though the time required to read it is much greater, there is a very good possibility that you will make the time to do so.

Whatever else you do when publicising the launch of your new church, you must ensure that the core group give as many personal invitations to those they know as possible. It can be a help to set a target fairly early on for the number of personal invitations that your group will give out. Only you will know how many contacts your people could reasonably expect to have, but it is good to aim for a factor of six times as many invites as you have people in your core group. Once you have established your target, keep a list of the names and addresses of the people your group is going to invite, together with an indication of who is going to invite each one. Let people know how the list is growing week by week.

Although a personal invitation requires verbal communication, it can help your people if you print an invitation card of some kind to give to people. A card such as this must be tastefully and professionally produced. If you don't have someone with access to such skills, use one of the cards produced by organisations such as the Christian Publicity Organisation (CPO) of Worthing. An invitation card not only assists people to speak to others about the launch, but a card with the date and time on will help the person who has received the invitation to remember when the launch event takes place.

Effective as the personal invitation is, this does not mean that we should not engage in any other kind of publicity. The old advertising maxim that 90 per cent of all advertising is a waste of money but nobody knows which 90 per cent, holds true. Additional publicity serves two functions. First, it serves to reinforce any personal invitations that are given by helping to generate a sense of profile and excitement about the event. Second, it will be a means of reaching many that we do not know about and yet who are receptive because of something that God is doing in their lives.

The launch of a new church is still something that is newsworthy, although we may need to think of some extra dimension to feature in our general publicity. Many Christians are suspicious or afraid of the press. Experience would suggest that we should regard the local press as our friends. From their point of view, they need to find a good deal of local news to fill many columns of print each week, or each day, as the case may be. The entry on to the market of the many free newspapers can also help us to get the event covered. The more local the paper, the better from our point of view. Most local papers in large cities have district editions which again are looking for stories that have high local interest.

The press will be more interested if you can point to an aspect of the story which suggests that the opening of this new church helps the community in some important respect. It may be that one of the leaders or members of the church is newsworthy. You may feel uncomfortable about featuring an individual in this way, and a certain amount of honest heartsearching is sometimes necessary before you can agree on the approach that you might want to suggest to the press. It can help enormously if you know a Christian who has professional experience of journalism or marketing and who can therefore help to sharpen your story. If you know that a particular paper is going to run a story on the launch, then you might want to consider reinforcing the story with some advertising in the same edition of the paper.

Despite the poor reputation of the press in society in general, any story carried by a secular newspaper will have greater impact than we can generate through our own publicity. Nevertheless, experience tells us that running a regular community newsletter is also effective in communicating with those whom we seek to reach. A number of churches I know tried to put out occasional pieces of publicity before their launch, only to find, that they failed to bring anyone to any event by this means. This ran so contrary to my own experience in putting out regular community newsletters that I looked a little harder at these pieces of publicity to see if I could discover why they had not worked. My conclusions are not fully researched but I suspect that what had gone wrong in these cases is that although the material that was distributed was very well presented in each case, it either was not distributed regularly enough or there was an insufficient recognition factor that linked the publicity. Both of these factors are key elements in the potential effectiveness of community newsletters.

In the run-up to a launch it is essential that if a community newsletter is attempted then it needs to go out at least once a month, but more importantly, over a long enough period for a sense of long-term presence in the community to be established. Some groups make the mistake of making the visual presentation of each edition radically different in the hope that each one will look fresh and so encourage people to read it. In fact, the reverse is true. There needs to be a strong similarity in masthead and layout to encourage a recognition factor. The casual reader can easily assume that a number of visually different papers are each produced by different groups!

Posters are not particularly effective on their own but can help to reinforce the message being generated by the other avenues of communication being used. A good number of shopkeepers will put up an A4-sized poster and some may be willing to display an A3-sized poster. The more shops that display posters the better, but don't limit your options to shops. There may be other places where community newsboards exist. Community centres, health care centres, schools, colleges, and even neighbourhood housing offices may all be willing to display posters if permission is sought. If you want their future co-operation, make sure that you visit the day after the event to take the poster down, communicate how it all went and thank them for their help.

Door-to-door visitation before the event to issue a personal invitation to attend is very time consuming but is likely to generate a good response if added to all of the other means of communication. If you attempt a visitation approach, make sure that you have an attractive card (of A5 size at most), invitation to leave behind. A more detailed account of running door-to-door visitation can be found in a Grove booklet in their evangelism series written by Martin Robinson.[6]

Finally, use other organisations in the community as part of your publicity strategy. Every community will have a whole variety of community organisations, from social and sports clubs, through to mother and toddler groups and neighbourhood watch groups. Some of these groups may already have strong links with existing churches, others may have no interest in what you are doing whatsoever. However, don't assume that community groups will have no interest. Find out what groups exist, what their aims are and what kind of people belong, and try to meet their leaders. Some of these groups might like to put up an information booth at the opening service, others such as choral groups or handbell choirs might be involved in some of the pre-launch activities. At the very least, some of these groups may be willing to hand out some invitation cards of the type that you would be putting out on a door-to-door visitation programme.

Putting all of these activities together, your overall goal should be to ensure that by one means or another everyone in the community is aware of your launch service and that a good number of people will be aware of it by more than one means. You cannot really put out too much publicity!

Mobilise your members

By now it should be clear why we said earlier that most groups do not allow enough time for planning their launch! It should also be clear that it is critical for a successful launch that everyone in the core group should be mobilised as part of the total effort. A first step is clearly to identify the gifts of everyone in the core group so that tasks can be assigned on the basis of the gifts available. Just as crucial, such a gift identification exercise will also reveal at an early stage what gifts are missing from the core group. Some important gifts will possibly not be present in the core group and the absence of these gifts will significantly affect the way in which the launch exercise is conducted. It may be necessary simply to live with this reality or it may be possible to import people with those needed gifts from other churches for a short time. Clearly, a great deal will depend on the precise relationship with other churches.

If the church planting core group is an entirely independent group, unrelated to any other, then the question of how to obtain other key workers does become difficult, though not impossible. Relationships between the denominations are increasingly warm and it may be that visionary congregations even of another denomination will be willing to lend people on a short-term or even a longer-term basis. One or two congregations I know who are strongly committed to church planting have recruited members of their own congregation to go and work with groups from other denominations on a permanent basis. Such generosity was almost unheard of until recent times.

Even apart from the question of the need for people with specific gifts, it may be helpful to recruit some short-term volunteers simply to provide extra person power to help with the sheer volume of work that develops in the few months just prior to the launch and immediately afterwards. Certainly, it becomes much easier to engage in the potentially productive activity of door-to-door visitation if extra workers are available. However, it is vital that any importation of workers should not be a substitute for fully mobilising the members you do have. There is no quicker way of demotivating borrowed workers than to use them for tasks that the core group is perfectly capable of doing but is insufficiently committed to undertake!

The programme for the day itself

There is a natural tension between wanting the opening day to be special and planning a service so unlike anything that will normally take place that you wonder if you are in danger of unintentionally misleading people as to the kind of church they really will be attending. In many ways it is more important to be true to who you really are than to put on a highly professional, but in the end inauthentic, occasion. This does not mean that you should not do anything special. There is nothing wrong with inviting some talented musicians, singers or even a drama group from outside. It is only important that the special ingredients are not so numerous or so dominant that they effectively commandeer the event.

If you invite others to perform a special piece of music, or some other item, make sure that you have already seen the people in question perform something similar. This is especially the case with drama. It is not so much a question of competence as fit. Do not take the recommendation of others, see for yourself, and even then take time to carefully explain what it is that you are trying to accomplish.

Take a good deal of time to think about the overall programme. There is a tendency for it to become crowded with special items and for those who are taking part to take more time than you had intended. If you do not keep a strict eye on programming you will end up with an event that is an hour longer than you had planned. It is not a question of aiming for a short service but of keeping closer to your own norm and to some extent meeting the expectations of those you have invited. Your guests will have come with a fairly clear idea of how long the event is likely to last and may have other commitments following the service. It will not help your cause if you have to cut your sermon to two minutes in order to stay on time or find that some people start leaving the service while you are speaking because you have lost control of the timing.

The combination of special event, unfamiliar surroundings, a large crowd of people, the potential for technical problems with sound and lighting equipment, and a host of unforseen difficulties means that it is very wise to have a rehearsal of parts of the service at least a week before. This is particularly crucial to ensure that the various parts flow well. Not only is it good from a timing point of view to avoid large gaps between items as musicians or readers or actors sort themselves out; it also helps to convey the impression that you know what you are doing if there is a natural and smooth flow as the service progresses. The whole point of a worship service is that the participants should be directing the attention of the congregation to the Lord and not to themselves as they trip over microphone cables, deafen people with feedback screams and generally threaten life and limb by clambering over equipment, simply to speak from the front.

Hard as it may be for preachers to accept, there is a strong possibility that what most people will remember about the day is the music. In our culture, music communicates to an increasingly important extent and in a way that words do not. In some ways, the choice of hymns and other music will be much more critical than your choice of text. Here we face a real dilemma. Most churches have changed their tradition of hymnody more quickly in the last ten years than in the previous hundred. However, the population at large, who have not been in any church over the last ten years, have not caught up with this change. A quick glance at television satire will tell you that the unchurched population suspects that churches have recently been invaded by trendy vicars armed with guitars and tambourines. Others have a view of some churches as places where there is a great deal of handclapping and other activities that would make them feel uncomfortable.

Those who have had to help non-churchgoers choose hymns for weddings and funerals will know that the repertoire of many extends no further than 'Jerusalem', 'The Old Rugged Cross' and 'The Lord's My Shepherd'. Nevertheless, it is important to think about those who might be attending and to have a good mix of hymns, with there being at least a chance that some of the hymns will be recognised by your guests. If you decide to include some contemporary music then think about asking the music group and possibly a strong group of singers to play and sing one verse first. Read the words of the songs that you will be asking people to sing. There are some fine contemporary songs around but sometimes the words leave a great deal to be desired, while others are plain daft!

The priority of prayer

However busy the pre-launch period might be, that busyness should never be allowed to crowd out the place of prayer. Indeed, prayer will be more essential during this time than at any other. Various leaders, from Martin Luther to John Wesley, have been quoted as observing, 'I will be so busy today that I do not have time not to pray.' Although it is essential that prayer does not become a mechanistic law, it is nevertheless crucial to integrate prayer in all of the activity during this time so that it flows naturally from the life of the core group.

With this in mind, it can be very valuable to have specific days of prayer and fasting, each with particular prayer targets. Some in the group who feel a special call might choose a regular day of the week on which to pray and fast. Richard Foster's book, *Celebration of Discipline*, is a very helpful resource to assist in this matter.

Others in the group might be recruited as intercessors for particular people who have been invited to attend the launch occasion. It is very important that everyone who has been placed on the target list of those to be invited to attend the launch event be prayed for by name on a regular basis. It is astonishing how many genuine problems appear to prevent people from attending unless consistent prayer takes place for them. This critical point in the process is a time of spiritual warfare.

Even if you have not recruited any outside workers to help with the launch of the new work, I would strongly suggest that you at least enlist others from the body of Christ to stand with you in prayer. Place the welfare of the leaders high on the list of prayer priorities for others outside of the core group to pray for. This is a time when miracles will occur if, through prayer, we have pleaded with God to intervene. Planning will take care of a great deal, prayer will both accomplish that which we plan for and take care of the many things that we are not able to plan for. Our spiritual insight in terms of the battle that we are entering will inevitably be limited and so our planning will not be able to take account of all these unseen realities. Prayer is not a substitute for the things that we can do but helps us to deal with the things that we cannot even imagine are necessary.

You only launch once—unless you launch twice!

Clearly, the ideal is for the initial launch to go well and the church that is being planted to experience significant numerical and spiritual growth as a direct consequence of the launch. However, there will be occasions when, for a variety of reasons, the launch does not go according to plan. You may be a member of a church that has been planted recently, and which went into the launch a little too soon and so has missed out on the opportunities a strong launch programme can bring. Is everything lost in such a case?

Fortunately, it is possible to have a second attempt at a launch and so to put right the mistakes that were made first time round. The key to creating an opportunity for a second launch is to find a suitable and significant event in the development of your congregation around which to build what is effectively a re-launch. The two most obvious developments which can give rise to such an opportunity would be a move to another building or the calling of a minister.

Sometimes, the building that you choose just turns out to be a disaster. The caretaker doesn't turn up, the equipment is vandalised, no one in the community can find the place, the hirers shift you each week to a different room in the complex, there is a basketball game going on in the hall above and the noise drowns out all singing except for that one man who always sings off key, the accoustics are so bad that 'O for a Thousand Tongues' becomes a prayer instead of a hymn. You just have to find somewhere else. Why not turn a problem into an opportunity by using the move to plan a far better launch than the one you had first time?

It may be that the part-time Bible college student who was your leader when you first started has now moved on and it is possible for the church to employ someone else on a full or a part time basis. Such a development provides a significant enough landmark in the life of your church to go through all of the launch steps outlined earlier in the chapter. Without actually calling it a launch, it effectively amounts to the same thing.

There may be other developments in the life of your church that can also serve as a landmark event to enable you to gain a higher profile in the community than you have so far managed to obtain. Hopefully, a second or even a third launch will not be necessary. It is best to get it right first time round but nevertheless it is important to be aware that your church does not have to close down just because that first opportunity was lost. A redeeming God can help all of us to create fresh opportunities even when, because of our own failings, we did not make the best use of the opportunities we had first time round!

For discussion and further study

1. If you were to call on the homes in your community, what would the occupants have to say about your church?
2. What questions do you think should be included in a questionnaire for use in a target community in relation to church planting?
3. What other churches and/or individual Christians could you call on to pray with you in a church planting project?

Notes

1. Bob Hopkins also makes the point about the importance of the right time for a launch in the book that he has edited, *Planting New Churches* (Eagle, 1991), p 200.
2. Report 'Pub Home for Newest Baptist Church' in *The Baptist Times*, 19th April, 1988, p 10.
3. Roy Pointer, *How Do Churches Grow*? (MARC Europe), p 185.
4. *Ibid*.
5. Bob Hopkins points to the possibility of winning people to Christ by looking for the receptive during pre-launch activities; see *Planting New Churches*, p 200.
6. Martin Robinson, *Door to Door Calling* (Grove Booklets, 1991).

CHAPTER THIRTEEN

THE WEEK AFTER THE SUNDAY BEFORE

Martin Robinson

The launch had gone well. The original group of fifteen people had met in a weekly Bible study and had gradually grown to become thirty before they made the decision to launch. They had taken a year to plan the launch event. Altogether, close on 200 personal invitations had gone out, and on the day, 160 people had turned up in a hall that had an absolute maximum capacity of 200. It had felt very full. All those who were taking part had rehearsed long and hard. The special music pieces were excellent, the harmonies beautifully balanced.

Despite all the work, the group of thirty had not really dared to hope for an attendance of much over ninety—after all, that was three times the size of the whole group and it was rare for everyone in the group to be present at any one meeting. Ninety people would be four times as many as the number who normally came to the regular mid-week studies. What a feeling of euphoria there was as the hall filled up and more and more extra seats were put out. So many more had come at the last minute that the service was just a few minutes late starting, but apart from that, the timing had worked well. No one in the group could stop talking about it all when they met to review the event that Sunday evening. It was a tired but happy group that finally went home to bed late that Sunday night.

Next Sunday morning there was an attendance of just sixty-five, which was still a big improvement on the original thirty, but somehow the service didn't seem to go with the same swing as the week before. Who had chosen those hymns? No one seemed to know them, and as for the sermon, I'm sure that I had heard the preacher give those illustrations at least twice before and Billy Graham had used them before that. No, it wasn't the same event at all. The third Sunday the attendance was just forty-five and gave every indication of being smaller next week.

Fictional as the above account is, it is nevertheless illustrative of what can all too easily happen if a great deal of effort is put into the launch day without any thought being given to what might happen in the period immediately following the launch. The launch of any new work has the potential to attract a wide range of people, from Christians who have just moved into the area and are looking for a church, through to those who are thinking about spiritual matters but who have never had any contact with a church at all. The immediate post-launch period is critical in terms of reaping the greatest harvest possible from the opportunities provided by the launch.

Failure to think through the post-launch period will often result in a situation where the only extra growth to the original core group will come from those already committed Christians who were in any case looking for a place of worship. The group that will be the most difficult to reach will be those who have not yet become Christians. Therefore, what happens on the second, third and fourth weeks of a new church launch will be as critical as what happens on the actual launch day.

Attendance the week after the launch week is much more likely to give a realistic indication of the potential size of the church for the forseeable future, but even this potential will not be realised without a good deal of work in this immediate period.

Choosing the launch date

Church growth teaching has developed the concept of looking for receptivity and resistance factors in the community that we are seeking to evangelise. Research has concluded that the experience of change in people's lives is one of the most significant factors in creating an openness to the gospel message.[1] That change may be caused by such matters as unemployment, bereavement, marriage, divorce, the birth of a baby, or just moving home. Many of these changes relate to the natural life cycle of birth, marriage and death. It is no coincidence that the church has ceremonies to mark each of these significant changes in life. Many churches see these events of 'hatching, matching and dispatching' as primary opportunities for both pastoral care and evangelistic outreach. In view of the impact of change on people, it is perhaps not surprising that many churches find that young married couples display a real openness to the gospel. Such couples will have experienced a large number of changes in their lives. Marriage itself, the possibility if not the actuality of children, the probable move of house and possible change of employment, all of these changes, together with a host of other smaller changes, will have served to increase the potential receptivity of young couples.

In a similar way, those who have undergone a move to a totally new community will have experienced a large number of changes in their lives. Research indicates that those who have moved into a community from elsewhere are more open to the gospel in the first twelve months than at any other time.[2] One Anglican church that I know has grown significantly in the last ten years. Some 16 per cent of people in the parish attend a church somewhere, with the largest percentage attending the parish church. When the figures were further analysed, it was discovered that nearly all of the people who attended the church had moved into the community in the previous ten years. Those people who had lived in the area for twenty years or more represented the most resistant group in the whole neighbourhood.

As we noted in the previous chapter, the issue of change also impacts receptivity in an even more surprising way. Research has demonstrated that the move from one season to another brings an awareness of change in people's minds. The church has tradition- ally held major festivals which reflect to some extent the seasonal changes. Thus in the autumn time there is the harvest festival, in the winter we celebrate Christmas, at Easter the church remembers the crucifixion and resurrection of Jesus, while Whitsun or Pentecost Sunday falls in the summer. Even though these festivals, particularly Whitsun, do not have quite the same community impact that they once had, it is perhaps surprising to observe the extent to which festival occasions still raise issues of spirituality for many people who would not normally attend any church.

A good post-launch programme needs to take account of the issue of receptivity. Therefore, as we have already seen, launch dates for a church plant should be selected with the timing of the major Christian festivals in mind. For example, a launch date of the Sunday before Christmas, basing the programme on a community carol service, will almost certainly produce an astonishing launch attendance. However, can you imagine what you would have to do to produce a reasonable attendance on the Sunday following Christmas? It is not called 'low Sunday' in the church calendar for nothing! Even booking Cliff Richard for that Sunday might not produce a sell-out!

On the other hand, if you were to make your launch date four weeks before Christmas, you might still derive some benefit from the seasonal impact of the Christmas festival but you would also have time to produce an attractive programme for all four weeks before Christmas. For example, week two could be a Christingle with all of the appeal that such an event has for children and families. For Anglican church plants, week three would be an ideal time to prearrange a number of christenings. Those with a baptistic tradition would probably not have the same community impact with child dedications, but it would be a good opportunity to utilise some other community contacts that you have made for a special event on this Sunday. On such a schedule, the fourth Sunday would obviously be a community carol service, possibly with a performance of a nativity play.

The same kind of thinking would need to underlie whatever specific launch date was chosen. Thus, if the launch was to be in the spring time, the way in which the immediate post-launch period interacted with Easter would need to be thought through. In some communities, a large number of people are away over the Easter period and so the launch date needs to take account of this factor. Other communities are not so affected by absences at Easter time and so Easter Sunday or even Palm Sunday might actually be good times for the launch.

Some may ask, why go to all this trouble to put on a number

of special events? After all, the post-Christmas lull or other negative factors such as bad weather or holiday times have to be overcome sometime. You can't keep up a flow of special events for ever! Perfectly true, but the intention of such a sequence has two goals in mind. First, in terms of reaching those who have had little church connection in the past you are trying to build a churchgoing habit in the short term which will hopefully change people's orientation in the longer term. Second, and perhaps more importantly, you are in the process of building relationships. During this critical four-week period it will be possible to build sufficient relationships with unchurched people to be able to consider some kind of home study discovery groups to lead the contacts that you have made into a faith encounter with Christ. There is a much stronger possibility of drawing people into such groups after a number of visits to church rather than after a single visit to a one-off launch occasion.

Follow-up procedures

The sensitive follow-up of first-time visitors to your church is a critical issue in terms of obtaining the greatest benefit from the activity surrounding the launch period. There is some debate concerning the way in which the unchurched should be followed up. Essentially, there are two major schools of thought which, although they seem at first sight to disagree with each other, are not in fact quite so far apart.

The first school of thought emphasises anonymity. It can be argued that the last thing people want in coming to a church is to be jumped on as soon as they arrive. People need space and time in which to consider the claims of Christ. Those who have considerable experience in working with the unchurched have argued this case extremely well.[3] However, many growing churches give testimony to the need to do the reverse, namely to be very sure that you know who everyone is who come to your church and to follow them up effectively.[4]

I would suggest that both of these approaches have their place but that each of them is appropriate in different situations. There is a strong case for the approach of anonymity in situations where a specific approach to the completely un-churched, is being made, especially when the event itself has a high profile and attracts a large group of people. However, in the early days of a church plant, it is unlikely that the people who are being reached will fall into the category of those who would benefit from anonymity.[5] On the contrary, it is essential to be able to make a personal assessment of the needs and situation of every person with whom the church has contact precisely because their needs will almost certainly be somewhat diverse. Therefore, a personal visit at an early stage will enable the leadership to make an assessment of just how to help each individual who visits the church.

It is essential that the process for making such visits be as sensitive as possible. The first stage in such a process is to introduce a system for obtaining the name and address of everyone that comes. I have been present in churches in the United States where first-time visitors have been pressured to stand up at a certain point in the service and then to receive wild applause from the congregation. I have attended churches all my life but I can't say that I have ever enjoyed being the object of such high profile attention and I am certain that few others would enjoy it either! Fortunately, there are some other more low key approaches!

In an initial meeting, where many are attending because they have been invited by members, and others have been drawn through a variety of methods, it is almost impossible to speak to everyone or to remember accurately just who did come once the event is over. You might consider asking everyone present to fill in a simple welcome slip which could be inserted in the printed order of service. Be very open and simply tell people that you would like everyone present to have more information about the activities of the church and other community events and that it would therefore be helpful to have some simple information to make that possible. Ensure that pencils are provided and make it clear that the forms will be collected during the singing of the next hymn. As long as everyone is filling in the slips no one will feel specially singled out. You will need to be sure that your own people are aware before the event that this will be done so that they will not be taken by surprise. Ask people to do this while the welcome and notices are being given. If you are not embarrassed about making such an announcement and simply treat it as a matter of course, no one present will feel embarrassed either.

If you continue to have significant numbers of first-time visitors in succeeding services, you might want to make this a regular procedure, in which case such a system can also help you to provide pastoral care by giving you accurate information about who is present and who is missing. If you do make it a regular part of your services then you can add to your request the information that you are asking people to do this to help the church care more effectively for people's needs.

Another alternative is to arrange your exit area in such a way that there are enough people at the door to greet people as they leave and invite them to place their name and address in a visitors book. You can help this process by offering coffee at the end of the service and so slow down the speed at which people are leaving. However, even then, you might need more than one visitors book to avoid creating a traffic jam at the exits. The visitors book approach is usually easier to operate after a few weeks, when you find it easier to recognise those who are first-time visitors.

The next step is to ensure that all first-time visitors receive some follow-up as quickly as possible. It is important in deciding your follow-up strategy to attempt to strike a balance between an expression of care and interest on the one hand, and giving people some 'just looking' space. At the very least, it would be good to send a card to each new attender indicating how good it was to see them and extending them a warm invitation to attend on future occasions. However, there is no substitute for a sensitive personal visit. At this stage, your members are more likely to be effective in visitation than the clergy!

There are at least two reasons why it is vital to involve church members in this follow-up activity. First, in the initial stages there will hopefully be too many first-time visitors for any one person to follow up. Second, there is some evidence to suggest that a visit from a lay person rather than a clergyman is actually more effective at this stage. Why should this be? A visit from a lay person will usually be less threatening than the call of the professional clergy. Moreover, it conveys a powerful message about the nature of your church—after all, it is the job of clergy to visit people whereas lay people do it because they want to. The call of a lay person communicates that your church is a place where the members care and where there is a high degree of participation.

What should your lay members say when they call? One effective way of structuring a follow-up call is to create a welcome pack which the caller takes round and offers as his or her primary reason for calling. They might say something like 'My name is Doreen Smith and I'm from Heath Road Community Church. We're so glad that you were able to visit us on Sunday and we'd like you to have a welcome pack which gives further information on the church and the neighbourhood'. The pack should contain just that, information on the activities of the church, some details of who the leaders are, the reason why you are starting the church, the kind of church that you would like it to be and what you are hoping to achieve by bringing the church into being.

It is vital to include information on the community as well as the church. You might like to collect information on community services and place it on a sheet under the heading 'useful phone numbers'. Information could include the telephone numbers of the local doctors, hospitals, neighbourhood housing offices, library, schools, dentists, recreation centres, and so on. The possibilities are endless. Set some of your creative people to work on this project—the problem will then be how to limit the list! You might also invite local community organisations to place their publicity in the pack. Such an invitation will probably surprise them and might even lead to some of their leaders coming to church!

Ideally, the follow-up visit should lead to at least a ten minute conversation, which would give the caller enough time to assess the factors which have caused the person to attend. Clearly, simply thrusting a welcome pack into someone's hands on a doorstep will not necessarily lead to an invitation to come in and so you might want to consider asking the person to whom you give the pack if they could help you for a few minutes in filling out a simple questionnaire to help the church improve what it is offering to the community. The feedback that you receive from this form will probably give you enough information to allow some basic assessment to be made of how best to follow up this person as well as on ways of improving the pack. Whether or not a questionnaire is used, it is vital that there is proper feedback to one person who is coordinating the follow up so that a proper assessment can be made of how to progress every contact.

Clearly, if you do decide to adopt this strategy it will be necessary to train your callers and prepare the welcome pack well ahead of the launch date. *Door to Door Calling* by Martin Robinson (Grove Booklets) gives more detailed advice on how to prepare those who will go calling.

Caring for those who come

The launch of any new church has a way of disturbing the spiritual environment in a given area, with potentially unforseen consequences. All kinds of unusual people are likely to appear on your doorstep and you need to be ready to deal with them. Two major groups need to be mentioned.

The first of these will be a number of Christians who have been travelling around various local churches for some years already. They will often appear to be deeply spiritual people, often with a great concern for prayer, praise and evangelism. In the past they will have attended a number of smaller churches, most of which will have had a broadly evangelical or Pentecostal flavour. There is a strong possibility that they will be tithers, and it is almost a certainty that they will attend every meeting that is held, especially prayer meetings.

Now I do not mean to disparage such people. On the face of it they are just the people that a new church needs—good givers, highly committed and solid in their understanding of the Bible. However, we have to be realistic and recognise that those who have already done the rounds may very well not stay at your church either. This does not necessarily matter. Quite possibly it is God's intention that they should only stay for a while until the church has been strengthened. However, the issue is not the length of time that they stay but rather the manner of their going. All too often, not only do they go, but since their departure is very often accompanied by the raising of an issue of one kind or another, they may depart having unsettled a number of other people in your church that you really do need to keep. It is one thing for people to move on, it is quite another for them to take with them a group of others who will not benefit in the long term from their influence.

What do you do about such members? Clearly, there are no easy answers. I have seen some situations where a small group of wanderers finally have found their home and have stopped wandering. There are no hard and fast rules for dealing with this particular problem. However, it is important to be alert to the potential for problems so that you can exercise wisdom. The one area where advice can be given is that of leadership. Until it becomes very clear that a person's wandering has stopped you must not place that person in any position of leadership. Such advice is not always easy to follow because some of these people are natural leaders, and even if you do not extend any formal leadership position to them, you may well find that they become the de facto leader of their small group. Even more difficult, you may find that they are acting as informal counsellors to a number of people in the congregation simply through the development of natural friendships. Any moving on brings great pain to those who have developed warm friendships and who simply cannot understand how people can break relationships of trust apparently so easily. You can be sure that it will be the church leaders who will attract the blame for a situation like this. A newly planted church does not need this level of pain; there is enough to do without having to deal with this problem.

The second group of people that will almost certainly appear in your church are those who have profound problems. In some cases, they will have been in receipt of treatment from mental hospitals, nearly all will suffer from various nervous problems and many will have difficulty in forming personal relationships.

It is true that the church can provide some help to these casualties of our society and it is right that we should do so. These are part of those to whom God would have us be his representatives, extending his love and care.

Nevertheless, there are some practical problems which need to be addressed. The most obvious issue is that people with problems demand a great deal of our time. Unfortunately, new churches often attract a higher percentage of problem people than they can realistically cope with. This is not so much because the church is new, although that is a partial factor, it is much more the case that newly planted churches have a small core group and it is to the core group that people with problems are attracted. Not surprisingly, those who have significant problems are looking for the kind of care that a relatively small group of highly committed Christians can provide. Your core group of church planters will supply just that.

Those who have serious emotional problems are searching for a sense of family to replace the dysfunctional family that they have come from originally and which has played a large part in shaping the problems that they have. The consequence of this search is that as your church grows, those same people will either get better or they will leave in order to find another small church, but in the meantime, they will strongly resist the growth of your church.

It is therefore necessary to create some strategies for giving care to those with significant pastoral problems. At the very crudest level, you will only be able to keep the number of problem people that you can adequately care for. The most effective strategy is to operate on a gift basis. Two gifts are needed, that of pastor and that of counsellor. There are probably a number of people in your church who have some general pastoral gifts. It is good to employ these people for the kind of day-to-day pastoral concern and care that problem people need. You may only have one person who has specialist counselling gifts and, indeed, you may not have any. If you do not have such gifts you must be honest about the extent to which you can help people and ensure that they are referred elsewhere. Failure to be honest about the extent of the care that you can offer has the potential to halt your work and prevent you from accomplishing the many other aspects of the call of Christ upon the life of your church.

The perversity of people

Some years ago, I had a friend who was the minister of a church with about a thousand members. He was encouraged to leave that church to become the minister of a relatively new church with a much smaller membership. A large part of the reason for his acceptance of the new post was the vision of the leaders of the new church. They wanted to be radically committed to evangelism, and they believed that God was calling them to be a large church. There was one particular member of the new church who played a significant part in influencing my friend to move. He happened to be very wealthy, although it was not his wealth but his drive and vision that had impacted my friend.

After a time, the church to which my friend moved did grow, in fact it grew dramatically, so much so that even with the addition of extra services, it became clear that the building was too small. It would be necessary to put up a much larger building. Naturally, such an enterprise was expensive and the congregation was on the outer edges of what its faith and finance could sustain. Just at this time, the wealthy individual who had been such an influence decided to leave. My friend was devastated. He wanted to know what was wrong, and was told that the person concerned was leaving because he was no longer happy with the kind of church that had been created as a consequence of growth. He freely admitted that all that had happened was entirely consistent with the dream he had had of a larger church, but somehow the actual experience did not match the vision. The truth was that he was happier working with people in a smaller church. It was not a matter of influence or control, he genuinely did not want either; he just preferred the greater sense of family that he had known when the church had been smaller.

How frustrating people can be! Yet we have to face the fact that this is the kind of scenario that does take place in church life. The original group may be highly committed to a vision of growth and will work very hard to achieve it but there is no guarantee that they will like it once growth takes place. The worshipping community can look very different before and after the launch. Before you launch, you might have a group of fifty people, with perhaps a highly committed core of thirty people, all of whom know each other very well. The core of thirty is really a large house group and the core of fifty an extended family. A successful launch is very likely to result in an immediate growth to 100, and at the end of a year possibly 120 or even more. The group is now a sizable community and it may well be that not everyone in your original group will be able to face the change that has happened.

It is good to begin to face the issue of change before the launch and to maintain an open line of communication on how people are feeling after the launch. The creative use of house groups can help to maintain the sense of family for many people, but you will not win through in every case. Apart from the issue of group size and the way in which people relate to groups, there is also the issue of gifting. Frankly, some people have gifts which work well in a small group but which are not able to be stretched sufficiently to work in a larger group. For example, someone may be very adept at teaching a group of 30 but might struggle to find the very different communication skills needed to teach a group of 130. Others may have musical gifts which work well in the informality of the extended house group but they just don't have sufficient expertise to minister in the larger group. Some leaders are adept at working with groups of twenty and caring for that group until they are seventy strong, but just cannot take the group beyond that size. Other leaders might struggle with the spiritual stress that comes from the greater responsibility of the larger group. Whatever the reason, you need to be emotionally prepared that not everyone from the founding group will stay with you or play the same role in the new situation.

Nor will size be the only factor that determines whether or not your original group will be comfortable with the worshipping community that emerges from the new church launch. Just as important will be the underlying worship style or ethos. Although the launch sends out a powerful message about the kind of church that you intend this to be, your intentions may not always be fulfilled! At this point, your very success in attracting new people might undermine that which you are trying to create. It is almost impossible to determine ahead of time the exact spiritual culture that will be created as a consequence of a successful new church plant. I have known some churches launched by groups who were essentially from a Free Church/charismatic/evangelical background which have ended up with a much stronger Anglican/broad church feel simply because that was the underlying religious culture of the area and the church was successful in reaching the area. Conversely, I have known some fairly traditional groups who have launched out and have seen the church become much more charismatic and/or evangelical than they were comfortable with.

Now it is true that such changes in ethos do not always take place, but the essential point is that church planting is a somewhat uncertain birthing process. We cannot be sure that the original group will like the infant that it has produced! We can dream, plan and work but what comes cannot be determined entirely by our desires. Sometimes the very act of planting and evangelising among those in the community that we have not known well before produces a challenge to all that we have known and calls for extraordinary courage and spiritual insight. Such a process would not be new. That remarkable Jewish evangelist—the apostle Peter—faced such a crisis before he could be involved in church planting in Caesarea. He was asked in a dream to do something that he had never done before and which would have been entirely unacceptable to him:

'Get up, Peter. Kill and eat.' 'Surely not, Lord!' Peter replied. 'I have never eaten anything impure or unclean.' The voice spoke to him a second time, 'Do not call anything impure that God has made clean' (Acts 10:13, 14).

What might it be in our tradition and our expectations that God will need to challenge us over? 'Get up. Kill and eat', not so that tradition might be challenged for the sake of change but that the word of life might reach those who at this time are culturally, socially and spiritually distant from every existing expression of the gospel.

For discussion and further study

1. What festivals have the most impact on people in your community?
2. What receptive groups can you recognise in your target community?
3. What kind of church do you think would be the most effective in meeting the needs of those in your target community? Begin to describe what a worship service would look like in such a church.
4. What size of church do you have in mind when you are thinking of planting a new church? Do all the members of your core group agree on this issue?

Notes

1. Roy Pointer discusses the issue of receptivity in *How Do Churches Grow?*, pp 156ff. He also looks at the theory of change, although in this section he applies it to how churches can be helped to cope with change rather to evangelism (pp 46f).
2. Eddie Gibbs points to this factor in his book, *I Believe in Church Growth*, p 142.
3. Willow Creek Community Church in the suburbs of Chicago has pioneered a unique approach to the unchurched which depends heavily on the promise of anonymity.
4. Eddie Gibbs mentions the key issue of dealing with a welcome for first-time visitors in his book, *I Believe in Church Growth*, (MARC Europe, 1991), p 143.
5. Charlie Cleverly points out in his book, *Church Planting our Future Hope*, that the early growth of a church plant tends to come through those with some church connections, while completely new converts tend to take place once the church is large enough for them to feel more comfortable, (p 39).

Part Four
Shaping the Vision

CHAPTER FOURTEEN

FIRST CENTURY INSIGHTS FOR TWENTY-FIRST CENTURY STRATEGIES

Stuart Christine

... you will be my witnesses in Jerusalem, and in all Judea and Samaria, and to the ends of the earth (Acts 1:8).

I want you to know that God's salvation has been sent to the Gentiles, and they will listen! (Acts 28:27).

Acts begins and ends with clarion cries of confident commitment to comprehensive mission! From the lips of the Lord in Jerusalem, to the lips of Paul in Rome, the Book of Acts is as its name so accurately describes, the record of the activities of 'God's sent ones'—men with a mission.

Luke, is clearly a purposeful and skilful worker. The opening and closing of his work shows that his purpose is to set out how the church discovered what it meant in practice to become Jesus' team of international emissaries. Acts could well be described as an historical exposition of the eighth verse of the opening chapter. His work is of value to his readers because Luke believes that Jesus is not finished and the work of witnessing is not yet finished. It is the same Lord with whom the readers will need to co-operate as they are drawn into this ongoing mission.

So, like the first reader Theophilus, and countless committed believers throughout the world over the last 2,000 years, we allow the insights and records of Acts to challenge and inform our commitment to the witnessing task today. I'll be aiming to identify guiding principles that the early churches began to embrace as they reflected upon their experience of the Lord's work through them to extend the kingdom.

The wind of the Spirit blows and the church responds

As Luke records the churches' response to the work of the Holy Spirit among them, a shift begins to become apparent, from *reaction* to *reflection*.

Reaction (Acts 1–12)

In Chapters 1 to 12 we are given the picture of a church discovering its potential.

- God's ancient promises are fulfilled for them.
- God's miraculous power is at work through them.
- God's angels are active on their behalf.

They have become the lens through which the kingdom of God is to be projected into the world and they are presented as responding to each successive discovery with an almost breathless amazement:

> We cannot help speaking about what we have seen and heard. (4:20).

They react in almost crisis management mode to the unfolding drama in which they find themselves centre stage:

> When the apostles in Jerusalem heard that Samaria had accepted the word of God, they sent Peter and John to join them. (8:14).

We are given the picture of a church driven by the wind of the Spirit:

> The Spirit of the Lord suddenly took Philip away [and he] appeared at Azotus and travelled about, preaching . . . (8:39, 40).

The impression we get at times is that it must have been like playing a game of football and suddenly finding that not only have the goal posts been moved, or rather made a whole lot larger, but also that the rules of the game have been changed:

At Cornelius' house Peter says, 'God has shown me that I should not call any man impure or unclean . . .' and after the tremendous response to his preaching, he is confronted with the opportunity of baptising Gentiles.

When in Acts 11:1–17 we read Peter's defence of his

behaviour to a shaken and questioning church, his concluding words clearly convey the sense of almost bewildered compulsion:

> So if God gave them the same gift as he gave us, who believed in the Lord Jesus Christ, who was I to think that I could oppose God? (v 17).

God, the missionary God, God the Holy Spirit, was very much making the running and the church was having to run hard to keep up!

Reflection (Acts 13–28)

From the Antioch mission onwards, however, we find a somewhat more programmed and reflective attitude to mission being presented as Paul becomes the focus of Luke's record. It's not that there is a sudden move from *spontaneity* to *strategy* as the guiding principle, or that mission decisions change from being compulsions of the Holy Spirit to being conclusions of a holy huddle. There is, though, a clear impression that with increased experience of the activity of the Spirit, men like Paul were feeling increasingly confident in the role of committed team members working out a commonly agreed game plan, rather than that of unconscious pawns in the hands of the Master.

The wind of the Spirit is still driving the ship but there is a growing confidence to place a hand upon the tiller.

Then and now

This situation is being mirrored in the life of many of our UK churches at present. Two particularly significant points of correspondence exist between then and now in terms of our motivation for mission.

The first relates to the fresh *experience* of gift of the Spirit and the second relates to the *expectancy* of the return of the Lord. Both were absolutely crucial to the dynamics of mission in the early church. The Spirit was firing the boilers of the gospel train and its crew were anxious to keep up a good head of steam because there was a timetable to work to and a Lord to meet and give account to.

Not in living memory has the fire of the Spirit burned so

brightly in the churches of our land as it does today, and never has that fire spread so quickly across the globe. There is a projection of 562 million charismatic Christians by the year 2000.[1] After the first, sometimes painful, experience of renewal, new wineskins have now been created and some older ones have discovered unexpected flexibility to accomodate the vigour of new life. Many are now in the transition stage that faced the early church, moving from reaction to reflection in response to the Spirit's activity among them. The Spirit is putting his mission priorities back at the top of church agendas and strategic planning is very much the name of the game.

Not for a thousand years has the approach of a millennial milepost raised the national spiritual consciousness to question the course and the goal of history—a factor that is being taken perhaps more seriously outside the churches than within them! The powerful motif for challenge and motivation for reassessment represented by the year 2000 is increasingly driving the agendas of church and state alike. It conveys a sense of chapter closing in the affairs of men, of the significance of time. Tidal changes transforming the political map of the world, talk of a new world order, the growing popular awareness of global realities that threaten and influence national life as never before have served to heighten a growing sense of anticipation and unease in society at large. Within the UK church, the declaration of the 'Decade of Evangelism' and the proliferation of programmes, such as Challenge 2000, aiming to give impetus and strategic direction to our task of mission reflect the church's growing rediscovery of a sense of responsibility and accountability in the witnessing task today.

One further significant point of correspondence exists between the experience of the early church and that of today's church in the UK: the challenge of cross-cultural mission. The demands of a multicultural society compelled the leadership of churches then, as it does today, to radically rethink what 'gospel' means and what 'church' can look like among groups who do not share the cultural traditions of most Christian people.

The similarity of these important spiritual and social dynamics encourages the careful study of the experience of the early church as a helpful model for the rethinking of mission strategy in Britain at the present time.

Seven signposts for mission strategy development

As we study the record of the early church's reflections upon the work of the missionary Spirit among them, a number of principles that served to guide their missionary activity emerge to inform our own task of mission today. These can be helpfully gathered under seven headings:

1. A recognition of the *ekklesia*, the local worshipping community, as the prime agency of mission.
2. A recognition of association and co-operation as the appropriate relationship between local Christian communities in order to fulfil God's mission agenda.
3. A recognition of the importance of leadership development in the process of establishing new churches.
4. A recognition of the different needs of different cultural groups.
5. A recognition of the importance of strategic thinking in targeting evangelistic resources.
6. A recognition that extending the boundaries of the kingdom of God involves confrontation with the principalities and powers governing the kingdoms of men.
7. A recognition that the mission task demands that every place and people be served by a witnessing community.

We shall look in more detail at each of these insights and aim both to justify their adoption as guidelines for contemporary strategy development and also to explore some of the implications for programmes of mission that might arise from them.

1. A recognition of the ekklesia, the local worshipping community as the prime agency of mission

It is interesting to observe that in the reporting of the mission of the church in Acts an early focus on *evangelism* gives way to a concern to recount the *establishment of churches*. Records of the numbers of new believers give way to records of the numbers of new churches. So we read:

- 1:15–120 believers are congregating.
- 2:41–3,000 more are added.
- 4:4–5,000 men now belong to the movement.
- 5:14–'more and more men and women ... were added to their number.'
- 6:7–'the number of disciples ... increased rapidly.'

The conversion of 'a large number of priests' (6:7) must certainly have increased the sense of threat felt by the religious establishment at the runaway growth of the new movement, and capitalising upon the opportunity created by the Stephen incident (6:8–7:60), the authorities decide to prick the swelling balloon of church in Jerusalem and the church is scattered (8:1).

But even then, through chapters 8 and 9, the emphasis of the record continues to be upon the efficacy of the preaching and of signs and wonders; on people evangelism rather than church formation. Although the 'ekklesia throughout Judea, Galilee and Samaria' is mentioned in 9:31, the reference is in the singular and does not reflect the emergence of local communities with distinctive self-awareness.

However, in 11:19–26 we are told that the naming of Christians as a distinct group first occurred in Antioch. It is perhaps not without significance that precisely at this point we have the first explicit record of converts being gathered and ministered to as a local community, or ekklesia (v 26), as distinct from the ekklesia in Jerusalem (v 22). Barnabas may perhaps claim the honours as the first recorded ekklesia planter. This is not to suggest that new converts did not gather in groups as a result of previous evangelistic work, but rather to note that Luke's emphasis progressively shifts towards the reporting of church planting as the account of the missionary expansion continues. This becomes clear in the accounts of Paul's missionary endeavours.

In the story of Paul's first missionary journey steps are taken by the apostles to safeguard the faith of the new disciples by the appointment of elders for them in 'each church' (14:23). By Acts 16:5 the results of the second journey are described in terms of a multiplication of the number of churches in the areas covered. Some English translations can give the impression that it was the numbers of disciples in the existing churches that were increasing, but the Greek is clear in using the phrase 'the churches increased in number'. So attention fixes on to the establishment of churches.

The climax of the dramatic events at Philippi is expressed as the meeting of the new disciples at Lydia's house where they are encouraged before Paul moves on. A similar series of events is reported in Ephesus in Acts 20:1, where Paul farewells the Christian community which used to meet regularly in the debating hall of Tyranus (19:9).

Further study of the letters of Paul to the new churches confirms this guiding principle with which he worked; namely that the proper goal of evangelism was the establishing of witnessing communities.

It was heartening at the 1991 Anglican Church Planter's Conference to hear Archbishop George Carey affirm his recognition of this principle: 'I actually believe that church planting is taking us back to the proper theology of evangelism in the New Testament.' If that is indeed the case then it is proper for every denominational grouping and network of Christian communities to adopt the establishment of new congregations as a principle thrust of their evangelistic strategy.

2. A recognition of association and co-operation as the appropriate relationship between local Christian communities in order to fulfil God's mission agenda

The Antioch church was born through the mission support of the Jerusalem church (11:22), and an appreciation of the value of such networking in the support and multiplication of kingdom communities became a crucial characteristic of the church as it developed. Not only did the newborn congregation immediately show its concern for the material well-being of the believers in Jerusalem through the sending of a gift (11:30), but went on to become itself a centre for missionary expansion into Asia Minor, Cyprus and Europe by the activities it sponsored, through Paul, Barnabas, Silas, and others (Acts 13,16).

In chapter 15 the account of the Jerusalem Council meeting about the appropriate mission response to the Gentiles serves to trace the continuing development of interchurch co-operation in mission to which Paul so often alluded as enabling him to maintain the momentum of his missionary endeavours, for example, Philippians 4:15,16a where he commends the Philippians for their support of him and his team during the church planting activities in Thessalonica.

What was applauded by Paul was also being put into practice between other churches, as Acts 18:27–28 shows. The brothers in Ephesus are able to commend Apollos as an effective and trustworthy evangelist to the disciples in Corinth.

In an open and mobile world such as that within which Paul moved, association and co-operation in evangelism was a possibility and therefore a responsibility. What was true for a Roman citizen 1,900 years ago is even more true for the leadership of the church of Jesus in the United Kingdom today. Whether responding to the opportunities for planting into the virgin soil of new developments, replanting into the spiritual wastelands of some of our larger inner city areas or reclaiming the countryside for Christ, both the character of society and the enormity of the task demand a readiness to co-operate for growth, within and across denominational boundaries. Indeed, the ongoing process of internationalisation of British society, referred to earlier in this book, should encourage the churches to enlist the involvement of missionary personnel from right across the cultural-linguistic spectrum to enable us to design and implement strategies that can restore the matrix of Christian communities across the whole of our society.

The example of intercongregational co-operation among the units of the Ichthus and other new church networks, together with the models of mutual support and encouragement demonstrated, for example, by the emerging Asian Christian fellowships, are compelling evidence of the value of partnership in the planting of new witnessing groups. The older denominational groupings have already been helped on this journey by the processes of ecumenical dialogue and charismatic renewal. The Billy Graham missions and any number of local mission initiatives have provided a broadening field of experience upon which more comprehensive strategies might now be mapped out. The DAWN, 'Disciple A Whole Nation', movement is one very viable attempt to facilitate the development of such nationwide strategic thinking and could readily become a framework within which specifically denominational strategies for new church planting could be stimulated in such a way as to encourage a measure of mutual respect and national coherence.

3. A recognition of the importance of leadership development in the process of establishing new churches

It is spiritually gifted leadership which, more than any other single human factor, transmits the spark of divine life to a group or team seeded out to establish a new plant. Because this area has been extensively discussed in Chapter 9, particularly in relation to the experience of the early church, I shall confine myself here to addressing the question: Where have all the planters gone?

The experience of the church, as of industry, is that in the task of beginning new ventures, specifically gifted individuals are essential but hard to come by. In contrast to the commercial world, however, where those with entrepreneurial ability are sought after and highly compensated, the mainline denominations in particular often treat such individuals with suspicion and usually grant only the minimal levels of status and financial support. David Holloway identifies the problem when, after affirming that the prime requirement for church planting is church planters, he goes on to pose the question: 'Do we have, as yet, a sufficient number of people like that in our theological colleges?'[2]

The role of theological colleges is a key one, particularly for the denominations that tie in their leadership accreditation procedures to these training institutions. They stand aside the pathway into accredited ministry and in large measure determine the shape of leadership available to the churches.

The honest answer to Holloway's question is, of course, 'No. We do not', and this despite the protestations of most institutions that they are primarily concerned with producing 'church growers', the leader who is:

Clear sighted in his vision for the growth of the churches and is capable of working with others towards the fulfilment of his dreams.

He is the organizer who by dynamic leadership, evangelizes, expands and builds up the worshipping congregation ...[3]

The reason for the failure to attract the individuals who the Spirit does give to the church is quite simply that our colleges are not set up, either in terms of ethos or curriculum, to affirm and develop folk gifted in this way. Those possessed of a pioneering, creative, mission-oriented spirit recognise this and go elsewhere to pursue their vocational training and future ministry and the denominations are impoverished because of it.

Over the course of this century, almost without exception, the pastor-teacher has become the product of the training colleges, and the community of believers is the consumer. The curricula, educational method and ethos combine to produce this sort of leader—and do the job well. The problem is that the market is shrinking! With half a million less sheep in the fold over the past ten years, according to the English Churches Census, shepherds are finding it increasingly difficult to locate flocks that are willing to be pastored! The fact is that too much of what is on offer in our training colleges has long since passed its sell-by date. Some of it is in danger of posing a serious health hazard to the churches. The UK church is in a mission field environment but the colleges aren't producing mission leaders, rather administrators and overseers for a promised land that we no longer possess! The Christian community is being driven to the margins of society and is in desperate need of those who can help it to possess the land again.

In the light of the primacy of leadership in the task of replanting this corner of God's mission field, then, a serious question must be addressed by those who have responsibility or influence in the area of theological training: 'Is the response of our colleges adequate for the day in which God has called us to live and discharge the duty of preparing leadership for his church?'

It would be a grave mistake, however, to concentrate attention only upon the recognition and preparation of those who know the call of God into so-called full-time Christian leadership. Although such individuals are usually the strategists, permission givers and enablers of church planting it is a fact that in every denomination or area of the world where the church is growing most vigorously and most new churches are being established it can be seen that an emphasis upon *lay-leadership* is one of the key multiplication factors.

The Southern Baptist Convention has been referred to on several occasions as leading the field as far as Western church planting experience is concerned, and it is worthy of note that it has developed training programmes of various types to enable over 10,000 bi-vocational, or tent-making church planters to enjoy full freedom and support within the denominational set-up. Especially in the context of urban evangelisation, where the effectiveness of cell group networks as an expression of the church is proving so effective,[4] it is of the greatest importance that training and recognition programmes are embraced that can mobilise the entrepreneurial skills and Christian commitment of gifted individuals and multiply ground level leadership for new church planting.

A young man I heard on a television report recently gave a human voice to the grim message of the English Churches Census statistics: 'The church? I wouldn't touch it!' The fact is that a lot of ground has been lost that will not quickly be won back. New pathways into accredited and lay leadership need to be opened up that can attract those able to found the churches that must attempt to re-establish the credibility of the gospel among tomorrow's generation.

4. A recognition of the different needs of different cultural groups

Years of getting by with a largely monocultural outlook have left the British church a legacy of reluctance and uncertainty in regard to the possibility of different ways of living and presenting the faith. In many ways, the church today finds itself in a position not unlike that of the early disciples whose religious roots were so firmly grounded in the culture and traditions of their Jewish forebears. For the early Jewish church, one of the greatest challenges was that of how to deal with non-Jews—those who did not share their culture—turning to God. It's interesting to contrast the records of the response of the Jerusalem church to the reception of the word by the Samaritans

(Acts 8:14) with that of the Antiochene Greeks in Acts 11:1,2. On the one hand, there is the impression of ready affirmation, whilst on the other, at least by some, criticism.

The mission agenda of the Spirit of Jesus was evidently not limited to the renewal of traditional religion among the Jews but embraced all people and any people, here, there and everywhere. The experience of Paul and Barnabas served only to confirm the disturbing fact that, 'God ... had opened the door of faith to the Gentiles' (Acts 14:27). Suddenly, what had been a trickle of manageable exceptions became an overwhelming flood threatening to change the face of the kingdom. The church was being swamped by converts who didn't understand or share their Jewish cultural heritage, and God had to wrestle with his people to loosen their grip on their monocultural understanding of how he could be known and worshipped.

The work of the Spirit at the Council of Jerusalem (Acts 15:1–29) in freeing the early church from the potentially paralysing influence of cultural exclusivity is surely one of the most significant works of the Spirit in the history of the early church. It is a work that urgently needs to be repeated today.

Then, as now, the decision to go for a positive policy of mission across the boundaries of their historic cultural tradition was a strategic one. It was more than just a response to a particular local situation. The decision was to go for the Gentiles because it was acknowledged that God had gone for them. The mandate that Paul and Barnabas took back to the church at Antioch was not to conduct a holding operation aimed at preserving as much of the Jewishness of the church as possible, but rather a 'letting go' operation to allow God to lead them on into becoming the multicultural kingdom of his purpose. It was a mandate for mission rather than maintenance. The decision was strategic because it gave the Spirit freedom to renew the church's understanding of what it meant to be the community of the kingdom not only in a Jewish context but in a Greek one, a Roman one, and so on.

This new dynamic injected into the missions programme of the church had immediate results. Acts 16:4 and 5 tells how the decision stimulated the multiplication of new congregations in towns around the centres of Iconium, Derbe and Lystra in which churches had previously been established. In the freedom of this unshackled commitment to international mission, the Spirit was also able to rewrite Paul's planned itinerary in order to take them on into Europe (16:6–10). New churches and new frontiers and a new experience of the multicoloured richness of God's plan to draw people of every culture and class into his kingdom (Eph 3:6–10) are the themes of the new chapter that this strategic decision heralded for the life of the church.

No less an opportunity faces the UK churches at this close of the millennium. But a genuine recognition of the nature of the challenge and realignment of resources will be needed if the opportunity is to be grasped, for recent church history shows a poor record of mission across cultural barriers in Britain. A largely middle-class church has failed to expand the fragile bridgehead it has inherited among working class communities. Post World War II attempts at church planting on council housing estates are notable only for their lack of real success, a trend that has continued up to the present, leaving that group as the most significant underevangelised section of our society. Even among the new churches movement, where there is most experience of new energy and initiative in mission, it is acknowledged that the impact is mainly confined to the middle classes where 80 per cent of Christians are located. Tony Morton of the Community Church, Southampton, in a recent interview gave his assessment:

We reach a cross section of society, but our people are still middle class, literate, male and female more or less equally ... charismatic churches are middle class and will carry on reaching the middle class and will grow more and more middle class. They should do what they're best at.[5]

The inner cities have become population centres where fewer people worship Jesus as Lord than in most non-Muslim mission fields around the world, with only 1 white Christian in a 1,000 living there. Wherever the cultural fences are going up, the church has been and continues to lose ground.

Neither can it be argued that the emerging subcultures are

necessarily resistant to the gospel. In the period 1960–1990, when membership of Baptist Union churches in the metropolitan area of London fell from some 43,000 to around 25,000, at least 500 new congregations were formed in the inner city alone. The difference is that the large majority of these new groups are ethnic, culturally specific churches. The message is clear that where the distinctiveness of culture is taken seriously and allowed to colour the packaging of the gospel then the Holy Spirit is able to move with freedom and effectiveness.

If the Jerusalem church had an excuse for a monocultural outlook we certainly can no longer claim one. Many of our churches need to emerge from the blinkeredness that threatened the mission usefulness of the Jerusalem church and recognise the fact and the implications of the cultural diversity of today's mission field.

5. A recognition of the importance of strategic thinking in targeting evangelistic resources.

Charles Haddon Spurgeon once wrote: 'Every Christian denomination should be on the alert for London, for it is in some respects the very heart of the world.'[6] Spurgeon was a strategic thinker. He knew the importance of having the right men in the right places and developed programmes to find them, equip them and put them there. A century after his death, well over a hundred Baptist churches in London owe their origins to his work.

God gave the early church such a man in the person of Saul of Tarsus. Towards the end of his ministry, while giving testimony before King Agrippa in Caesarea, he declared: 'The king is familiar with these things ... because it was not done in a corner' (Acts 26:26). Paul aimed at high impact and a high profile in the presentation of the gospel. As we will see in a moment, he targeted both key people and key locations in his efforts to establish new churches.

Both Roland Allen in his book, Modern Missionary Methods— St Paul's or Ours, and also Michael Green in his Evangelism in the Early Church, emphasise the way in which Paul apparently selected his preaching centres. There is a marked difference in the descriptions Luke gives of the spreading of the gospel in Acts chapters 1–12 and in later chapters where Paul's approach to the missionary task is described.

In the early chapters of Acts typical phrases would be those found, for example in chapter 8:

Philip went down to a city in Samaria (v 5).
Peter and John returned . . . preaching in many Samaritan villages (v 25).
Philip travelled about, preaching the gospel in all the towns until he reached Caesarea (v 40).

From chapter 13 onwards, however, a much more purposeful itinerary is presented: places of Roman administration, Greek civilisation, of Jewish influence and of commercial importance— centres of life and influence out of which the warmth and light of the gospel would be naturally transmitted to surrounding areas whose community life was driven by the standards and agendas emanating from these strategic locations.

- He targets Paphos, the administrative centre of Cyprus (13:6).
- Philippi 'a Roman colony and the leading city of that district' (16:12).
- Corinth, again the administrative centre of the Roman Province of Achaia (18:1f).
- Ephesus the key commercial, communications and cultural centre of Asia Minor (19:1).
- And, of course, Rome as well (19:22).

Even the well-known passages about the Spirit's not allowing Paul to minister in certain areas (16:6–10) are indicative that he worked to a plan—and yet, very importantly, that he was open to the Spirit's guidance in the development of that plan. New church planting should aim to possess the high ground within every community, whether that community is defined by geographical or by cultural co-ordinates.

Paul worked not only to the premise that it made sense to target strategic locations, however, he also recognised the importance of focusing his evangelistic appeal on influential individuals. Once again, a contrast can be drawn between the initial and the later record that Luke has left us.

In the early Judean phase of church expansion, although the conversion of 'a large number of priests' is recorded in Acts 6:7, the picture is very much one of a church on the run from the authorities. With the advent of Paul we find that a more positive, even aggressive, strategy begins to emerge in relation to the authorities. Paul is presented as a man who felt at home with authority and knew how to work the authority structures for the benefit of the believers and the gospel. His use of his Roman citizenship to create space and opportunities for the gospel is equally well recorded for example, in Philippi (16:37ff), as well as in Jerusalem itself (22:25ff).

Before his conversion he recognised the value of gaining official sanction to pursue his crusade against the Christians (9:2). Once a Christian, he seems to have sought opportunities to persuade men and women of influence to embrace the gospel. Right from the outset, on his first missionary journey, he gains an audience with the Roman proconsul of Cyprus, Sergius Paulus (13:7). Publius, the chief official of Malta, the Roman procurators of Judea, Felix and Festus, King Agrippa and his Queen Bernice all become the objects of his evangelistic zeal despite his position as the object of their judicial authority! Certainly, the report of his defence before Agrippa shows that he used the judicial hearings as opportunities for evangelistic witness (26:28). Supremely, the emperor himself, together with those at the seat of imperial government, became the focus of his ambassadorial vocation. His letters confirm that he saw the strategic value of such high level contacts (eg, Phil 1:12,13). Paul himself is perhaps the prime New Testament example of the value of winning certain key figures for the gospel.

Parochialism and misplaced egalitarianism rob the Christian churches of the best possible return on their investment of the Lord's resources for mission. Too many churches are competing for space in their own back gardens when there are great tracts of good unplanted soil lying fallow in every corner of the British harvest field. Breadth of vision and clarity of purpose are needed to channel the efforts of God's people into replanting for a Christian Britain.

The importance of the task, its urgency, the resources at our disposal and the days of opportunity in which we live, cry out for serious strategic thinking and redeployment of resources into mission. Too much of the human and material resources of the kingdom are lying wrapped in bureaucratic restrictions or buried in repositories of worldly prudence. Strategic thinking and planning born out of apostolic vision is the need of every denomination and network if Christianity is to be re-established as the ground of our country's national life.

6. A recognition that extending the boundaries of the kingdom of God involves confrontation with the principalities and powers governing the kingdoms of men

In June 1990 a prayer letter I received from a missionary couple returning from their work in Zaire contained the following paragraph:

> Returning from a time abroad gives you an amazingly fresh view of Britain. Things that may have crept up on you, day by day, hit us between the eyes. It's more than culture shock and can be quite a painful experience. Where has this preoccupation with ghosts and demons come from? It seems as if every child's day-to-day contacts hinge around the occult.

When the light dims then the darkness can grow, and as the author of that letter observed, the darkness of godless powers and ideologies has been spreading across the landscape of British society at an alarming rate in recent years.

Increasingly, the work of the kingdom in our land is being characterised by conflict and confrontation with the powers of evil that was almost unheard of a century ago. Right across the social spectrum of national life, from the personal level to the political, the heritage of safeguards and standards founded upon Christian principles is being substituted by codes born of pragmatism and individualism. The process of immigration, while bringing cultural richness and missionary opportunity, inevitably adds the weight of non-Christian religious commitment to the pressures of secularism and post-secular superstition that are distancing society so rapidly from its socio-cultural reference points within the Christian faith. Nor is it for nothing that Europe is commonly referred to as today's dark continent, or that Johann Lukasse in his book on planting churches in post-Christian Europe refers to Europeans, no doubt Britains included, as 'cultivated pagans'.[7]

Closer ties with Europe will inevitably fuel the movement of Britain into a post-Christian era, as codes of practice that owe far less to an evangelical faith are imported along with the cheaper goods and greater opportunities for economic prosperity. Ralph Neighbour's recent assessment of the context of contemporary Christian mission is one that cannot be denied and dare not be ignored:

> We have entered an era of history when evangelism must be sharpened and honed to cut into the darkness of a burgeoning non-Christian world.[8]

Just as in the contemporary situation the churches are having to learn the skills and dangers of 'night fighting', so it was for the early Jewish-Christian missionaries. It was from out of the relative sanctuary of God-centred Jewish society that the early church was called to venture. And that calling meant conflict. Paul and all those who presumed to reach out to touch lives and communities previously dominated by godless and demonic powers were continually confronted by opposition expressed in every form of spiritual, social, and political antagonism.

Ill prepared, inadequately equipped or inexperienced leadership is most likely to be overcome by opposition, and once again there is in the portrait of Paul a pattern of preparedness that those responsible for putting troops into the field of spiritual warfare would do well to reflect upon.

Spiritual opposition is a reality to be faced

- In Cyprus Paul is compelled to confront Elymas, a sorcerer (13:6ff).
- In Philippi he feels constrained to confront a demon possessing a slave girl (16:16ff).
- In Ephesus, a renowned centre of the magical arts, Paul's exorcistic ministry was evidently also known, as the cautionary tale of the seven sons of Sceva shows (Acts 19:13).

It is interesting to compare the commercial consequences of

this direct confrontation with the demonic and idolatrous at Philippi and Ephesus with the experience of Jesus in his exorcism of the demonised man in Gadara (Mk 5:1–20). In all three instances the financial loss incurred by certain groups within the community resulted in a public outcry being fermented and the missionary being forced to leave. In each instance, however, this demonic strategem is overcome by the commissioning of local converts to remain and continue the missionary task (Mk 5:19,20; Acts 16:40; Acts 20:1).

In Asia Minor and in Greece Paul faces obstacles to his travel plans whose origin he correctly discerns as, in one case, being of the Holy Spirit (Acts 16:7–10), and in the other, being satanic (1 Thess 2:18–3:2). His responses, to acquiesce on the one hand and to circumvent on the other, are a reflection of his spiritual discernment, previously displayed in the case of the cripple in whom he perceived a faith given for healing (Acts 14:9).

Paul is conscious of being Spirit-led from beginning (Acts 13:2), to end (Acts 20:22). He is sensitive to perceive the guiding hand of the Spirit through visions and circumstances as well as in the counsel of the believers directing him to leave when the going got too dangerous. He displays that quality of streetwise spirituality that is an important feature of the spiritual profile of a planter constantly needing to give clear direction through the conflict and confusion of spiritual street fighting.

Disturbing the status quo brings opposition   The coming of the gospel, then as now, disturbs the status quo. It creates dislocations in the cultural landscape of a community's life as it shakes the religious, moral, social and political pillars upon which it is based. Jealous Thessalonian Jews hit the nail on the head when they called the Christian evangelists, literally 'men who unsettle the world' (Acts 17:6).

The intrusion of the kingdom causes disruption, and personalities both human and demonic, with vested interests are upset. It is not surprising to find that in every place that he worked to establish communities of the kingdom, it is recorded that Paul encountered opposition. Three distinctive consequences of that opposition should always be borne in mind.

First, the continuance of the work is threatened. Paul was:

- Expelled from Pisidian Antioch.
- Fled from Iconium.
- Stoned in Lystra.
- Requested to leave Philippi.
- Escaped by night from Thessalonica.
- Escorted away by brethren, under threat, from Berea.
- Left Ephesus after the riot.

Only in the larger centres of Corinth and Athens was Paul able to remain despite local pressure.

Second, the evangelistic group itself suffers.

- Paul was stoned at Lystra.
- Paul and Silas were flogged and imprisoned in Philippi.
- Aristarchus and Gaius were hauled before the mob in Ephesus.

Third, the new converts suffer.

- Jason and some other brothers were dragged before the authorities in Thessalonica.
- Sosthenes was publicly beaten in Corinth.

The realities of planting churches in the devil's backyard included frustration and suffering. Paul knew that. Anyone who has been involved in contemporary church planting knows that.[9] It is a factor that must be taken into account when strategies for church extension are being formulated. Support structures for planters and planting groups need to be in place to offer the spiritual, emotional and practical back-up that these frontline troops will need. Caring for 'the honourably wounded', as Marjorie Foyle so aptly describes the casualties of Christian service, should also be given specific consideration when envisaging such unambiguous invasion of enemy territory.

7. A recognition that the mission task demands that every place and people are served by a witnessing community.

> . . . a great persecution broke out . . . and all except the apostles were scattered throughout Judea and Samaria . . . (Acts 8:1).

The spread of the church in the early years was undoubtedly driven as much by persecution as it was by planning. Although the Spirit used the zeal of the refugees to establish new churches throughout the region (Acts 11:19–21), the terms of the Great Commission were being fulfilled more by accident than by design.

Paul, however, was not only possessed of a vision that in every place there should be an opportunity for people to hear the gospel, but was also committed to a programme to make it a reality. In Romans 15:19b–24 we are given a clear insight into both his mission goal and his own strategic role in achieving it. Three phrases are significant and, being mutually interpretive, best viewed together:

> I have fully proclaimed the gospel (v 19).
> ... preach the gospel where Christ was not known (v 20).
> ... there is no more place for me to work in these regions (v 23).

It is clearly not that every inhabitant of the regions Paul refers to had become a Christian, but rather that witnessing centres had been established from which the population could be reached. Now satisfied that a viable network had been laid down as far as Rome, he already had his sights set on extending the network of kingdom communities through to Spain (v 24). Paul was a driven man. He identified unreservedly with the Spirit's commitment to establish that there could be no 'no-go' areas for the gospel and no people that could remain outside the lordship of Christ.

There is a need for such a spirit among those leading our churches in Britain today. In the goal he embraced, the strategy he employed to achieve that goal and in his own unashamed and uncompromising commitment to the implementation of that strategy Paul stands as a model for men and women of mission in every age.

A Christian Britain can mean nothing less than a congregation of Christ's people in every community of our land. As we pray the kingdom into every corner, let us plant the kingdom into every corner. Let us church plant for a Christian Britain.

For discussion and further study

1. On what grounds can a study of the missionary expansion of the early church, as recorded in Acts, be taken as a helpful paradigm in the rethinking of mission strategy in Britain today?

2. Discuss which of the 'seven strategic signposts' might be most important for your own church group.

3. Identify difficulties that your own church group might have to overcome in the implementation of the seven strategy guidelines.

4. Consider how patterns for the training of 'lay' church planters might be introduced and what such courses might deal with.

Notes

1. Jimmy Maroney, senior consultant on evangelism and church growth for the Foreign Mission Board of the Southern Baptist Convention, 'Significant Christian Megatrends for the 90's and Beyond', *The Link*, vol 1, no 4 (1990).

2. David Holloway, *Ready, Steady, Grow* (Kingsway, 1989).

3. See Ian Bunting, *The Places to Train—A Survey of Theological Training in Britain*, (1990), pp 28–33. According to a study of 86 Christian Ministry training establishments, two-thirds of all Church of England colleges and courses, 92 per cent of other denominational colleges and 100 per cent of inter- and non-denominational colleges affirmed that this was a prime goal.

4. Footnote-reference in an excellent article by Ralph Neighbour, 'Planting Churches in non-Christian Contexts: a cell group perspective', *The Link*, Vol 1:1 (1990). See also Dale E. Galloway, *20/20 Vision—How to create a successful church with lay pastors and cell groups* (Scott Publishing: Oregon, 1986).

5. *Jesus Lifestyle*, no 17 (1991): p 13.

6. *The Sword and Trowel* (1875): p 147; cited by Mike Nicholls, 'C. H. Spurgeon: Church Planter', *Mission to the World* (Baptist Quarterly Historical Society, 1991): p 22.

7. Johann Lukasse, *Churches with Roots* (Monarch, 1990), p 85.
8. Ralph Neighbour, 'Church Planting in non-Christian contexts', *The Link*, vol 1:1 (1990): p 2.
9. Four of the most recently published books on the subject of church planting devote space to this issue; Peter Wagner, *Church Planting for a Greater Harvest* (Regal Books, 1991), pp 50, 51; Lukasse, *op cit*, ch 5; Charlie Cleverly, *Church Planting our Future Hope*, ch 13; David Schenk and Ervin Stutzman, *Creating Communities of the Kingdom* (Herald Press, 1988) ch 5.

ASSESSING THE RELATIVE NEED FOR CHURCH PLANTING

The procedure that follows offers a straightforward and manageable way of getting a feel for the level of Christian/non-Christian contact there is within a given community as a measure of the opportunity that unchurched people have of encountering the gospel in a form that facilitates a positive response to it.

Step 1.—Find the number of residents and households in the target community

This can be most conveniently done if the extent of the area in which the community is resident is defined in terms of 'census enumeration areas'—these are the smallest units about which specific information is available from the ten-yearly national census. A visit to the Council Planning Department will put you in touch with those who can supply this information.

For example:
Population: 6,000   Households: 3,000

Step 2.—List the churches that regard the community as in their 'patch'

This is necessary since the point has already been made that evangelisation is the responsibility of all who own the name of Christ. The survey will enable you to judge how effective each of the responsible groups is in fact being—including, perhaps, your own!

For each group you will want to obtain information about their level of contact in the target community. This will also provide the natural first chance to share with them your interest in a possible planting project and will do so in a way that should be relatively non-threatening. An offer to share the results of your survey with each group will probably be gratefully accepted and encourage openness and co-operation. It's worth spending time in making these initial contacts personally and sensitively since attitudes formed as a result of the first encounter can colour reactions to everything that follows.

The following data could be sought (examples given):

Name of Church/Denomination:	United Reformed
Churchmanship:	Liberal
Location:	Argyle Street
Time on foot and by car from target area:	20 mins/5 mins
Approx size of main weekly congregation:	85
Is the church growing, static or declining:	Static
What is the church's most effective ministry:	Counselling
How many church members live in target area:	15
How many of these hold leadership positions:	0
How many households are represented:	6
Church activities that reach the target area:	Scouts—5
(No of unchurched folk from target community going)	Play group—4
	Services—6
What is the church's mission attitude to area:	Passive
What is the initial reaction to plant proposal:	Guarded

Once the results for all the churches have been assembled you will have very simply obtained a most helpful overview of Christian presence and activity in the area of the target community.

Step 3.—Express the totals of churchgoers and households as % of whole community

For example:

Churchgoers: 150   Total population: 6,000

Unchurched people in target community = 6,000 − 150 = 5,850
ie (150/6,000)*100 = 2.5% of community attend church;
or (5,850/6,000)*100 = 97.5% of community *do not* attend church.

For example:
Households: 50   Total no of households: 3,000

Households with no Christian presence = 3,000 − 50 = 2,950
ie (50/3,000)*100 = 1.6% of households have a churchgoer;
or 98.4% of households have no churchgoer.

Step 4.—Estimate the likely mission contact of the resident Christians

To get some idea of the number of people likely to have meaningful contact with the gospel in any given time, estimate that each Christian has 10 friendship or service contacts that serve as opportunities to communicate the challenge of faith with unchurched people. If you feel this is unrealistically low, (or high!), then replace 10 with a number you feel is more accurate. If in doubt, ask some of your members to make their own lists—the results might surprise you! Remember that the aim is only to get a general feel for the level of Christian penetration of the community, not a figure that will stand up in court! Provided that you stick with a reasonable figure for all the communities that you compare then it won't make a lot of difference whether you choose 10 or 5.

For example, 100 resident churchgoers each with 10 contacts = 1,000 contacts at any one time as a result of Christian friendship or service. (A total as high as this might well make you question whether 10 represented a rather generous average figure!)

Step 5—Estimate how many people from the target community are reached by the activities run by the churches in the area

Simply add up all the contacts registered in the local churches survey and express as a proportion of the total population.

For example, total number of activity contacts between churches = 200 (ie, of the 5,850 unchurched community members, 200 are being reached at any one time through church activities).

It should be noted that unless an individual actually comes into contact with Christians, there is little reason to consider that he or she is being reached in any significant way. Many churches register a large 'fringe' by counting all the families of individuals who are involved in church activities. Although it is true that such people are potentially more accessible in terms of invitations to church functions, etc, they are not themselves being reached unless the link that they have with the church is actually being exploited and personal contact with Christians achieved.

Step 6—Calculate the Christian contact count for the target community

CCC = Resident Christian contacts + activity contacts

For example, 1,000 + 200 gives a Christian Contact Count of 1,200; ie, 1,200 or a little less than 20 per cent of the unchurched population of 5,850 have the possibility of meaningful contact with active Christians at any one time, or 4,650 or some 80 per cent of the unchurched people living in the target community have no realistic opportunity of having meaningful contact with an active Christian at any one time.

Some general observations

Some might very well complain that the procedure outlined above does not take into account a whole range of potentially significant factors, such as the quality of spiritual life of the active churchgoers, the mission value of the contacts that exist through church activities, the impact of other Christian influences, perhaps from Christian relatives or colleagues at work, or indeed any number of other experiences that God's Spirit might be able to use to point people to Christ. Such objections are quite valid if the intention was to produce some absolutely accurate survey. That is not and could never be the case.

The results have most value for comparison purposes. For

example, a CCC of 20 per cent compared to one of 5 per cent would strongly suggest that the latter area was more in need of a new church plant than the former. Or, if the former figure represented the estimated impact in the area around the existing church then the lower figure would show just how much more needy the projected area was.

It cannot be stressed too strongly that there is great value in conducting a survey of this nature since it brings a measure of objectivity both to the estimate of need and to the evaluation of the effectiveness of existing mission programmes.

A more detailed community survey would undoubtedly offer more accurate results but would also be a lot more time- and energy-consuming. The purpose of the survey suggested is only to give an indication as to the appropriateness or not of proceeding with a plant in a particular location. Its merit is that it can be achieved basically through in-house research, ie, among the Christian community itself, and that the very process of surveying can serve as an introduction of the possibility of planting to the other groups with whom you share the mission responsibility for the area in view.

APPENDIX B

A SUGGESTED PROCEDURE FOR CONDUCTING A COMMUNITY SURVEY

Information gathered in a community survey can be helpful in deciding the 'shape' of the proposed church plant.

People and places to visit

1. Members of the local community, especially those closely in touch with the social life of the community, eg, shopkeepers, managers of recreational facilities and so on.
2. The Local Authority Planning Department.
3. The Town Hall.
4. The Electoral Registry Office.
5. The Local Authority Housing Department/local estate agents.
6. Local schools.
7. Local police stations.

To this list should be added other agencies that have a stake in the life and well-being of the target community. If there is a local library this can often be a good source of local history and information. Visits to council offices should not be foregone, however, even if most of the actual data can be obtained elsewhere.

Collecting the information

Information-gathering activities and visits should be properly arranged and carefully prepared for. The manner in which they are conducted will make a lasting impression about the quality of the congregation and the seriousness of their interest in serving the community.

Appointments with community leaders and council officers

343

are best arranged by phone or letter and carried out by responsible representatives of the new congregation.

In every instance interviews should be carried out in a courteous and pleasant manner with a clear idea of what information is being sought and why.

The lists that follow will serve as a guide in this process of data collection.

Interviews with local residents

A hundred such interviews would be a reasonable target. Aim to get a reasonable cross-section of the community by interviewing at different times and places.

> Excuse me, we are from . . . and are trying to find the answers to ten questions about what it's like to live here and what people who live here think about the church. We will be most grateful if you could help us for a couple of minutes.
>
> Have you lived in the area long? (Length of time.)
>
> Do you think that it has changed much since you've been here? (How?)
>
> Do you find it a friendly place to live? (Why?)
>
> What do you think are the best and worst things about living here? (Best . . . worst.)
>
> Is it easy to find out about what's going on in the community? (How?)
>
> Could you tell me where there is a church in the area? (Which/where.)
>
> Have you ever been there? (Why/why not?)
>
> Do you know anyone who attends there regularly? (How many folk?)
>
> If you were in charge of a new church here what would you get it to do and where and when would you have it meet? (What? . . . Where? . . . When?)
>
> Finally, do you plan to stay in the area long? (How long?)

After the interview has been completed, a note should be made by the interviewer of the time and place of the interview, together with the sex, ethnic origin and approximate age of the interviewee.

Local Authority Planning Department
Obtain:

- The local plan or draft plan. (This document should include detailed maps of the area.)
- Any community 'Profiles' or studies conducted by the department.

- The latest area census figures (Small Area Statistics Sheets). You might need to define your area in terms of 'enumeration' numbers. A helpful department will assist you.

The Town Hall

Obtain:

- Information on local amenities, organisations, etc.
- Details of public transport routes and timetables.
- Current and back copies of local papers.

Electoral Registry Office

Obtain:

- Purchase the electoral roles for the streets in the target area.

Housing Department and estate agents

The following questions might be asked:

- How easy is it to get accommodation in the area?
- What is the typical occupancy period for housing there?
- What sort of people are moving into, or out of, the area?
- What would be a typical price/rent for a two-bedroomed unit?
- How would you describe the general quality of housing in the area?

Local schools

The following questions could be asked of the head teacher:

- What ages are catered for in the school?
- What is the catchment area of the school?
- Are there any other schools serving the target area?
- In what ways is the pupil population changing?
- Are there any community issues that are of particular concern to the school in regard to children's welfare?
- What would be the most pressing problem currently facing the school?
- Does the school already have links with any local church group?
- Are there any ways in which the school could work in partnership with a local church in addressing these or other issues?

Police

The following questions could be asked of the PR man or community policeman responsible for the target area:

- How would you describe the law and order situation in the area?
- What would be the biggest problem from a police point of view?
- What is reckoned to be the cause of this?
- Are there any specific consequences of this situation for the different groups of residents in the area?
- Are there any particular contributions that a new church could make in the community?
- When and where might a new church meet, to be as available as possible to the community?

Sorting out what information will be most useful

1. Mark all housing areas, amenities, public transport routes, and natural 'obstacles', such as main roads, steep hills, etc, on a large scale map of the community area.
2. Summarise the replies obtained to the questions asked in the various interviews with community residents and officials.
3. Ask those involved in the visits to the community to give their general impressions of what they experienced.
4. Prepare posters or overhead projector transparencies showing the headlines of local papers over the last six months or so, to indicate the issues that the local community has been facing.
5. Draw up a brief outline of the history of the community, giving particular attention to the periods during which significant change has taken place and noting the consequences of those changes for life in the community.
6. Extract the following information from the census documents about the current make-up of the community:

   - Total population of the community.
   - Population breakdown by age groups: 0–4/5–14/15–24/25–44/45–64/65+.
   - Ethnic groups with more than 100 members.
   - Significant social groups: working women/unemployed/students 16+/singles/institutionalised people, etc.

- Total number of housing units.
- Housing types: private, public rent, private rent, hostels, etc.

7. Review any plans for the development of the area that emerge from official documents or contact with community leaders.
8. List names and addresses of significant community leaders.
9. List names and addresses of any individuals who have expressed a particular interest in the church planting project.

Presenting the information

This is a vital part of the process and a good deal of thought should go into each presentation. Basics to remember are:

- Be clear about what you want to achieve through the presentation.
- Think about your audience and what information it is that they need.
- Only present material that is relevant to your goal and their needs.
- Make the presentation clear, using a variety of different ways of getting the material across.

A guided tour of the community by videotape might be a good way of setting the scene, followed by a brief review of the history, presented by a pair of 'newscasters'.

Statistics are best displayed using an overhead projector with simple and easy-to-understand transparencies. Get someone who is used to producing these to help here.

Results of interviews can be put across in role play and personal impressions can be shared by some of those involved.

Be sure that there is time for discussion of the presentation, perhaps after a break for refreshments.

Prayer will usually be the most appropriate way of drawing all of the facts and feelings together.

SELECT BIBLIOGRAPHY ON CHURCH PLANTING

1. General overview

Church Planting—Our Future Hope, Charlie Cleverley, (Scripture Union, 1991). A good general introduction to local church planting. UK written from an Anglican perspective.
Church Planting for a Greater Harvest, C. P. Wagner, (Regal, 1990). Much of his 'How to Plant a Church' tapes are contained in this book. A good apologetic for church planting but rather weak on the biblical basis for church planting.

2. Biblical and theological background

Creating Communities of the Kingdom, New Testament Models of Church Planting, D. Schenk and E. Stutzman, (Herald Press, 1988). An excellent book. The best general book on church planting from the perspective of biblical content and its practical devotional nature.

3. Planting out, procedures and supervision

A Supervisor's Manual for New Church Development, R. Logan and J. Rast, (Fuller Institute, 1986). Written from an American perspective. Useful in the UK for Missioners and their equivalents involved in plant oversight and goal setting.
Church Planting, Models for Mission in the Church of England, B. Hopkins, (Grove Evangelism Booklets 4 and 8, 1988–1989). Two short thirty-page booklets, good on models and clearly most relevant to the Anglican community.
Planting New Churches, J. Redford, (Broadman, 1978). A full and helpful approach, especially strong on the practical aspects of church planting, particularly from a Baptist perspective.
The Church Planter's Checklist, R. Logan, (Fuller Institute, 1978). This comes with two tapes, it has an American perspective and can be commended for its very clear approach.

348

Where Do We Go From Here? A Guide Book for the Cell Group Church, Ralph W. Neighbour Jnr., (Touch Publications, 1990). Strong on the urban church.

4. The Development of ministry, philosophy and programmes

Focus the Power of People Group Thinking, J. Robb, (Marc, 1989).
Marketing the Church, G. Barna, (Nav Press, 1990).

5. Cross Cultural

American Evangelical Missionaries in France 1945–1975, Allen J. Koop, (University Press of America, 1986). A very instructive study of the successes and failures of one aspect of cross-cultural mission. We all ought to be able to learn from this. *Indigenous Church Planting*, C. Brock, (Broadman, 1981). A basic and clear approach intended mainly for overseas missions.
Planting Churches Cross Culturally. A Guide for Home and Foreign Missions, David Hesselgrave, (Baker, 1978). A comprehensive study which is biblically and theologically based.

6. Church planters, selection and training

Church Planting Through Obedience Oriented Teaching, George Patterson, (William Carey Library, 1989). Particularly helpful on the preparation of lay church planters.
How to Select Church Planters, C. R. Ridley, (Fuller Institute, 1987). A very helpful book if you are involved in the selection of church planters.
The Indigenous Church, M. Hodgers, (Gospel Publishing, 1976). Chapter Five on training planters is particularly stimulating.

7. The formulation of denominational strategies

Associational Church Extension Guide, J. L. Hill, (Home Mission Board SBC, 1989). The title is a good guide to its usefulness.
Church Planting at the End of the Twentieth Century, C. C. Chaney, (Tyndale, 1982). Strong on the biblical basis for church planting and on strategy, preparation and contextualisation.
Dawn 2,000, J. Montgomery, (Highland Books, 1990). Explains the Dawn strategy, (Discipling a Whole Nation), very thorough.

8. Collections of articles

How to Plant Churches, Ed. Monica Hill, (Marc Europe, 1984). A collection of essays which tends towards the theoretical but which is useful for background study.

Planting New Churches, Ed. Bob Hopkins, (Eagle, 1991). Papers from the 1991 Anglican Church Planters' Conference. Chapter 13 by George Lings on statistics is particularly helpful. Other chapters represent the actual experiences of Anglican churches in the field of church planting.

9. Church growth thinking

How Do Churches Grow?, Roy Pointer, (Marc Europe, 1984). Probably the most concise and helpful book on church growth yet published.

I Believe in Church Growth, Eddie Gibbs, (Hodder and Stoughton, Revised 1990). A very comprehensive guide to church growth.

Leading Your Church to Growth, C. P. Wagner, (Marc Europe, 1986). Strong on the application of church growth to leadership issues.

Strategies for Church Growth, C. P. Wagner, (Marc Europe, 1988). Strong on the strategic principles of church growth.

10. Evangelistic Strategies

Door to Door Calling, Martin Robinson, (Grove Booklets on Evangelism No 14 1991). A very practical guide to door to door visitation.

Entering the Kingdom, Ed. Monica Hill, (Marc Europe, 1986). More theoretical but with a very strong practical chapter on the role of the local church by Michael Wooderson.

Evangelism Through the Local Church, Michael Green, (Hodder and Stoughton, 1990). Not new thinking for many people but very comprehensive and well worth reading.

The Church Down Your Street, Michael Wooderson (Monarch, 1989). A guide to everyday evangelism, practical and with a UK background.

INDEX

Afro-Caribbean churches 71,
111–12, 195, 198
Anglican Church: church
planters' conferences 117,
(1989) 79–80, (1991) 49, 76–7,
82, 148, 321; cross-cultural
work 203; cultural ethos 28;
and ecumenism 131, 134;
history 63–4, 65–6; plantings
67, 68, 74, 75–7, 96–7, 107–9,
147, 232, 261, 272, 301;
structure 101, 110, 131, 132,
134, 152, 272; *see also
individual churches*
Anglo-Catholic churches 66, 112
Apostolic Church 69
Argyle, Adrian 208, 234
Assemblies of God 42, 44, 69–70,
134–5

Baptist Church: Bacup (Baptist
Network of Church Planters)
78, 167–8; Baptist Missionary
Society 203, 230; Baptist Union
77–8, 79, 203, 227, 328; in
Brazil 44, 150, 208, 237–8;
cross-cultural work 203–4; in
Ethiopia 228; in London 38, 53,
128, 129, 175, 203–4, 230–2,
328; Mexborough church 271,
280, 283; New Zealand Union
57; in Peterborough 145;
planting strategy 77–8, 129,
131–2, 148–9, 227, 228, 230; in

USA 42–4, 189, 204, 325; *see
also individual churches and
organisations*
Bible Society, British and Foreign
81, 87, 94–5, 98, 99, 101
Blair, Patrick 108
Bonke, Reinhard 119
Bracknell Family Church 94
Bristol Christian Fellowship 74
Brompton; Holy Trinity Church
76, 79, 104–5, 121
Bryant, Philip 179, 180, 208, 261
Bunting, Ian 75, 108, 336

Campus Crusade 135
Carey, George 76–7, 130, 132–3,
134, 148, 321
Celtic Church 27, 60–3, 266
Chalke, Steve 77
Challenge 2000 81, 318
Chester le Street; St Mary's
Church 75, 107–8, 109, 280
Chorleywood; St Andrew's
Church 76
Church of God of Prophecy 71
Church Growth Movement 83–7,
98
Churches of Christ 78–9
Coates, Gerald 23, 34, 73, 74
Coffey, David 78
Collins, John 82, 105
Creech St Michael, Taunton;
Zion Baptist Church 109–10,
273, 280

British Church Growth Association

The British Church Growth Association was formed in September 1981 by a widely representative group of Christians committed to church growth either as researchers, teachers, practitioners or consultants.

The BCGA aims to help and encourage the church in Britain to move into growth in every dimension. The facilities and resources of the BCGA are available to researchers, consultants, teachers, practitioners and those just setting out in church growth thinking. The Association endeavours to offer practical help as well as encouraging and initiating church growth thinking and research.

Membership of the BCGA is open to both individuals and organisations interested in or involved in the theory or practice of church growth. On payment of an annual subscription members are entitled to receive the *Church Growth Digest* (the journal of the Association) four times a year, information about activities through the Newsletters, special discounts on conferences and books, membership of the Church Growth Book Service, voting rights to elect members to the Council every two years, links with other researchers, teachers, practitioners, and consultants on a regional or national level as well as help or advice on allied matters.

Further information about the Association and membership is available from the Secretary, British Church Growth Association, 3a Newnham Street, Bedford, MK4 2JR, Tel: 0234 327905.